CW00765967

Drools JBoss Rules 5.0 Developer's Guide

Develop rules-based business logic using the Drools platform

Michal Bali

PUBLISHING

BIRMINGHAM - MUMBAI

Drools JBoss Rules 5.0 Developer's Guide

Copyright © 2009 Packt Publishing

All rights reserved. No part of this book may be reproduced, stored in a retrieval system, or transmitted in any form or by any means, without the prior written permission of the publisher, except in the case of brief quotations embedded in critical articles or reviews.

Every effort has been made in the preparation of this book to ensure the accuracy of the information presented. However, the information contained in this book is sold without warranty, either express or implied. Neither the author, Packt Publishing, nor its dealers or distributors will be held liable for any damages caused or alleged to be caused directly or indirectly by this book.

Packt Publishing has endeavored to provide trademark information about all the companies and products mentioned in this book by the appropriate use of capitals. However, Packt Publishing cannot guarantee the accuracy of this information.

First published: July 2009

Production Reference: 1060709

Published by Packt Publishing Ltd.
32 Lincoln Road
Olton
Birmingham, B27 6PA, UK.

ISBN 978-1-847195-64-7

www.packtpub.com

Cover Image by Vinayak Chittar (vinayak.chittar@gmail.com)

Credits

Author

Michal Bali

Reviewers

James Taylor

Sammy Larbi

Acquisition Editor

Sarah Cullington

Development Editor

Siddharth Mangarole

Technical Editors

Aanchal Kumar

Conrad Sardinha

Indexer

Rekha Nair

Editorial Team Leader

Gagandeep Singh

Project Team Leader

Priya Mukherji

Project Coordinator

Zainab Bagasrawala

Proofreader

Claire Lane

Production Coordinator

Shantanu Zagade

Cover Work

Shantanu Zagade

Foreword

Open Source Decision Management

Companies of every size are realizing that smart, simple, agile processes require that operational decisions should be managed, automated, and improved. These high volume transactional decisions must be made to keep data flowing through processes, to empower customers to self-serve, to make systems act more intelligently. As Neil Raden and I discussed in Smart (Enough) Systems, these decisions commonly have distinct characteristics. These decisions are high volume, low latency, and necessary for both straight through processing and unattended operation so they must be automated. Yet they must also change in response to external variability, demonstrate compliance, manage risk, and be personalized so traditional approaches to automation are problematic. Coding decisions in Java makes it hard to show those decisions to a regulator to prove compliance and hard to change the decision making approach quickly and cheaply. It makes it hard for business users to truly collaborate on how these decisions should be made, limiting the ability to bring risk management and personalization to these decisions.

Fortunately, there exists a technology and an approach to deal with these challenges. Instead of using traditional approaches companies attacking the decisions as a separate problem and managing those decisions explicitly. Decision management externalizes these decisions as decision services so they can reused and systematically improved. Decision management replaces traditional procedural code with business rules—declarative, atomic, manageable fragments of business logic. Business rules allow business users to participate in writing business logic.

With Drools 5, JBoss and the open source community have delivered a true business rules management system for the first time. Using Drools, organizations can take control of the logic that drives their operational decisions. They can build simpler, smarter, and more agile business processes and systems.

Michal introduces business rules and JBoss Drools to programmers in this book, walking them through all the major features of the product. Extensive code extracts and worked examples illustrate all the major, and many of the minor, features in the new release. Whether you are new to Drools or used to a previous version, Michal's book will help you navigate the new release. With Drools 5 you can take control of the logic in your systems and manage your decisions for better business results and greater agility, and this book will show you how.

It's time to change the way you build system, time to manage operational decisions, time to put business rules to work.

James Taylor
CEO, Decision Management Solutions
Author, with Neil Raden, of Smart (Enough) Systems (Prentice Hall, 2007)
blog: jtonedm.com, twitter: jamet123

About the Author

Michal Bali is a senior software developer at DeCare Systems, Ireland. He has four years experience working with Drools and has extensive knowledge of Java, JEE. Michal designed and implemented several systems for a major dental insurance company. Michal is an active member of the Drools community and can be contacted at michalbali@gmail.com.

I thank Drools lead Mark Proctor and his team that consists of Edson Tirelli, Michael Neale, Kris Verlaenen, Toni Rikkola, and other contributors for giving me something to write about. They were of great help while I was writing the book. Edson and Mark reviewed the book and helped me to correct various inaccuracies.

I'd like to thank all reviewers and the whole editorial team for their patience and help while I was writing this book. In particular, Sarah Cullington, Siddharth Mangarole, Aanchal Kumar, Conrad Sardinha, James Taylor, Sammy Larbi, Zainab Bagasrawala, Shilpa Dube, Lata Basantani, and other anonymous reviewers.

I thank James Taylor for writing the foreword and reviewing the book. I am honored that he chose to participate in this project.

Finally, I thank my fiancée Michala for supporting me and putting up with me while I wrote.

About the Reviewers

James Taylor is CEO of Decision Management Solutions and one of the leading experts in decision management. James works with clients to develop effective technology solutions to improve business performance. He has over 20 years experience in developing software and is the foremost thinker and writer on decision management. James was previously a Vice President at Fair Isaac Corporation where he developed and refined the concept of enterprise decision management. The best known proponent of the approach, James is a passionate advocate of decision management.

James has experience in all aspects of the design, development, marketing, and use of advanced technologies including CASE tools, project planning, and methodology tools as well as platform development in PeopleSoft's R&D team and management consulting with Ernst and Young. He develops approaches, tools, and platforms that others can use to build more effective information systems.

James is the lead author of *Smart (Enough) Systems: How to Deliver Competitive Advantage by Automating Hidden Decisions* (Prentice Hall, 2007) and he has contributed chapters to *The Decision Model* (forthcoming), *The Business Rules Revolution: Doing Business The Right Way*, and *Business Intelligence Implementation: Issues and Perspectives*. James writes several blogs and his articles appear in industry magazines and on leading industry and technical web sites.

Sammy Larbi works as a programmer for desktop, web, console, and service applications using a diverse range of technologies, including Ruby, .NET, ColdFusion, Java, C/C++, and Perl. In addition to typical and atypical business domains, he also works in the field of bioinformatics and has a keen interest in artificial intelligence.

After many long years and sleepless nights since learning to program in his youth, he graduated with degrees in Computer Science and Political Science in 2004, and finished a master's degree in Computer Science in 2008.

Sam shares his thoughts about programming and software development online at his weblog, www.codeodor.com.

Table of Contents

Preface

Business rules and processes can help your business by providing a level of agility and flexibility. As a developer, you will be largely responsible for implementing these business rules and processes effectively, but implementing them systematically can often be difficult due to their complexity. Drools, or JBoss Rules, makes the process of implementing these rules and processes quicker and handles the complexity, making your life a lot easier!

This book guides you through various features of Drools, such as rules, ruleflows, decision tables, complex event processing, Drools Rete implementation with various optimizations, and others. It will help you to set up the Drools platform and start creating your own business. It's easy to start developing with Drools if you follow our real-world examples that are intended to make your life easier.

Starting with an introduction to the basic syntax that is essential for writing rules, the book will guide you through validation and human-readable rules that define, maintain, and support your business agility. As a developer, you will be expected to represent policies, procedures, and constraints regarding how an enterprise conducts its business; this book makes it easier by showing you the ways in which it can be done.

A real-life example of a banking domain allows you to see how the internal workings of the rules engine operate. A loan approval process example shows the use of the Drools Flow module. Parts of a banking fraud detection system are implemented with Drools Fusion module, which is the Complex Event Processing part of Drools. This in turn, will help developers to work on preventing fraudulent users from accessing systems in an illegal way.

Finally, more technical details are shown on the inner workings of Drools, the implementation of the ReteOO algorithm, indexing, node sharing, and partitioning.

What this book covers

Chapter 1: This chapter introduces the reader to the domain of business rules and business processes. It talks about why the standard solutions fail at implementing complex business logic. It shows a possible solution in the form of a declarative programming model. The chapter talks about advantages and disadvantages of Drools. A brief history of Drools is also mentioned.

Chapter 2: This chapter shows us the basics of working with the Drools rule engine—Drools Expert. It starts with a simple example that is explained step-by-step. It begins with the development environment setup, writing a simple rule, and then executing it. The chapter goes through some necessary keywords and concepts that are needed for more complex examples.

Chapter 3: This chapter introduces the reader to a banking domain that will be the basis for examples later in this book. The chapter then goes through an implementation of a decision service for validating this banking domain. A reporting model is designed that holds reports generated by this service.

Chapter 4: This chapter shows how Drools can be used for carrying out complex data transformation tasks. It starts with writing some rules to load the data, continues with the implementation of various transformation rules, and finally puts together the results of this transformation. The chapter shows how we can work with a generic data structure such as a map in Drools.

Chapter 5: The focus of this chapter is on rules that are easy to read and change. Starting with domain specific languages, the chapter shows how to create a data transformation specific language. Next, it focuses on decision tables as another more user-friendly way of representing business rules. An interest rate calculation example is shown. Finally, the chapter introduces the reader to Drools Flow module as a way of managing the rule execution order.

Chapter 6: This chapter talks about executing the validation decision service in a stateful manner. The validation results are accumulated between service calls. This shows another way of interacting with a rule engine. Logical assertions are used to keep the report up-to-date. Various ways of serializing a stateful session are discussed.

Chapter 7: This chapter talks about Drools Fusion—another cornerstone of the Drools platform is about writing rules that react to various events. The power of Drools Fusion is shown through a banking fraud detection system. The chapter goes through various features such as events, type declarations, temporal operators, sliding windows, and others.

Chapter 8: This chapter goes into more detail about the workflow aspect of the Drools platform. It is showed through a loan approval service that demonstrates the use of various nodes in a flow. Among other things, the chapter talks about implementing a custom work item, human task, or a sub-flow.

Chapter 9: The purpose of this chapter is to show you how to integrate Drools in a real web application. We'll go through design and implementation of persistence, business logic, and presentation layers. All of the examples written so far will be integrated into this application.

Chapter 10: The focus of this chapter is to give you an idea about the various ways of testing your business logic. Starting with unit testing, integration testing through acceptance testing that will be shown with the help of the Business Rules Management Server—Guvnor, this chapter provides useful advice on various troubleshooting techniques.

Chapter 11: This chapter shows integration with the Spring Framework. It describes how we can make changes to rules and processes while the application runs. It shows how to use an external build tool such as Ant to compile rules and processes. It talks about the rule execution server that allows us to execute rules remotely. It briefly mentions support of various standards.

Chapter 12: This chapter goes under the hood of the Drools rule engine. By understanding how the technology works, you'll be able to write more efficient rules and processes. It talks about the ReteOO algorithm, node sharing, node indexing, and rule partitioning for parallel execution.

Appendix A: It lists various steps required to get you up and running with Drools.

Appendix B: It shows an implementation of a custom operator that can be used to simplify our rules.

Appendix C: It lists various dependencies used by the sample web application.

What you need for this book

In order to learn Drools and run the examples in this book, you'll need a computer with any Operating System (Windows, Mac, or Linux), Java Development Kit (JDK) version 1.5 or later, Drools binary distribution, some IDE—preferably Eclipse IDE for Java EE developers, Drools plugin for Eclipse, and some third-party libraries that will be specified per chapter. All of the mentioned software is freely available on the Internet under a business friendly license.

You can download some additional support material from
`http://code.google.com/p/droolsbook/`.

Who this book is for

The book is for Java developers who want to create rules-based business logic using the Drools platform. Basic knowledge of Java is essential.

 Readers are requested to note that they should follow the text carefully. Some additions to the code are required in order to run the examples successfully.

Conventions

In this book, you will find a number of styles of text that distinguish between different kinds of information. Here are some examples of these styles, and an explanation of their meaning.

Code words in text are shown as follows: "Drools keywords are rule, when, then, and end."

A block of code will be set as follows:

```
package droolsbook;

rule "basic rule"
  when
   Account( balance < 100 ) // condition
  then
   System.out.println("Account balance is " +
     "less than 100"); // consequence
end
```

New terms and **important words** are shown in bold. Words that you see on the screen, in menus or dialog boxes for example, appear in our text like this: "After it finishes execution, **Action** is executed, the flow continues to another ruleflow group called **Group 2**, and finally it finishes at an **End** node".

 Warnings or important notes appear in a box like this.

 Tips and tricks appear like this.

Reader feedback

Feedback from our readers is always welcome. Let us know what you think about this book—what you liked or may have disliked. Reader feedback is important for us to develop titles that you really get the most out of.

To send us general feedback, simply drop an email to feedback@packtpub.com, and mention the book title in the subject of your message.

If there is a book that you need and would like to see us publish, please send us a note in the **SUGGEST A TITLE** form on www.packtpub.com or email suggest@packtpub.com.

If there is a topic that you have expertise in and you are interested in either writing or contributing to a book, see our author guide on www.packtpub.com/authors.

Customer support

Now that you are the proud owner of a Packt book, we have a number of things to help you to get the most from your purchase.

Downloading the example code for the book

Visit http://www.packtpub.com/files/code/5647_Code.zip to directly download the example code.

The downloadable files contain instructions on how to use them.

Errata

Although we have taken every care to ensure the accuracy of our contents, mistakes do happen. If you find a mistake in one of our books—maybe a mistake in text or code—we would be grateful if you would report this to us. By doing so, you can save other readers from frustration, and help us to improve subsequent versions of this book. If you find any errata, please report them by visiting http://www.packtpub.com/support, selecting your book, clicking on the **let us know** link, and entering the details of your errata. Once your errata are verified, your submission will be accepted and the errata added to any list of existing errata. Any existing errata can be viewed by selecting your title from http://www.packtpub.com/support.

Piracy

Piracy of copyright material on the Internet is an ongoing problem across all media. At Packt, we take the protection of our copyright and licenses very seriously. If you come across any illegal copies of our works in any form on the Internet, please provide us with the location address or web site name immediately so that we can pursue a remedy.

Please contact us at copyright@packtpub.com with a link to the suspected pirated material.

We appreciate your help in protecting our authors, and our ability to bring you valuable content.

Questions

You can contact us at questions@packtpub.com if you are having a problem with any aspect of the book, and we will do our best to address it.

1
Introduction

The need to build more and more complex systems is increasing. We're trying to automate all kinds of business processes and implement complex business decisions. However, these processes and decisions are not very well represented using traditional programming languages such as Java or C#. Instead, we should use specialized technology such as the Drools platform.

In this chapter, we'll look at why there is a need for the Drools platform, what advantages and disadvantages it brings, and when (not) to use it. We'll briefly look at its history and what modules it consists of. We'll also see some commercial and open source alternatives.

Problems with traditional approaches

Enterprise systems usually have multiple layers. From top to bottom they are: presentation layer, business logic layer, and persistence layer. The middle layer—business logic represents the core of the application where all of the business processes and decisions take place.

The requirements for the business logic layer tend to change more often than the requirements for the rest of the application. We might be lucky when we get a complete specification, but that happens rarely. Even then, the requirements usually evolve over time and are often re-worked. As this happens, a standard solution using imperative style language (imperative programs are a sequence of commands for the computer to perform; for example, languages such as Java and C#) would quickly end up with so-called *spaghetti code*—lots of nested if-else statements.

It is often a good idea to document the following separately:

- **Business processes**: Represent what the business does
- **Business rules**: Represent decisions that the business does
- **Requirements**: Represent how the system supports the business, defines goals

These areas change at different schedules, have a different degree of business user involvement, and none the less they are implemented differently.

I am referring to these three areas simply as requirements.

There is no well defined way of representing the business logic in Java or C#. What usually happens is that every application represents business logic differently.

For example, consider the following code that does some checking on customer level, customer accounts, and account balance:

```java
if (customer.getLevel() == Level.Gold) {
    //do something for Gold customer
} else if (customer.getLevel() == Level.Silver) {
    if (customer.getAccounts() == null) {
        //do something else for Silver customer with no accounts
    } else {
        for (Account account : customer.getAccounts()) {
            if (account.getBalance < 0) {
                //do something for Silver Customer that has
                //account with negative balance
            }
        }
    }
}
```

Code listing 1: Code written in standard Java (or any imperative style language).

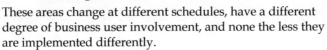

Readers are requested to note that they should follow the text carefully. Some additions to the code are required in order to run the examples successfully.

First, the code checks if the customer is a Gold level customer and does something, then it checks if the customer is a Silver level customer, and if so, it checks if this customer has no accounts and does something in this case. If the customer has accounts, the code performs some logic for each account that has negative balance.

The point of this Java 'spaghetti code' is to give you an idea what we are trying to prevent. You may think that it doesn't look that bad. However, after a couple of changes in requirements and developers that are maintaining the code, it can get much worse. It is usually the case that if you fix one bug, you are more likely to introduce five new bugs. A lot of requirements are literally packed into a few lines of code. This code is hard to maintain or change in order to accommodate new requirements.

As more conditions are added, the performance of this system will degrade. Moreover, when we want to change the behavior of the application, we'll have to re-compile and re-deploy the whole application.

It is not only difficult to represent business logic in a imperative programming style language, but also hard to differentiate between code that represents the business logic and the infrastructure code that supports it.

For developers, it is hard to change the business logic. For domain experts, it is impossible to verify the business logic and even harder to change it.

There is a need for a different paradigm for representing the business logic.

The solution

The problem is that with an imperative style language, we are implementing both, **what** needs to be done (business requirements) and **how** it needs to be done (algorithm). Let's look at declarative style programming, such as SQL, in relational databases (other declarative style languages include, for example, Prolog or XSLT). SQL describes what we want to search, it doesn't say anything about how the database should find the data. This is exactly what we need for our business requirements.

A rule engine provides an alternative computational model. We declare rules in pretty much the same way as the business analyst does the requirements—as a group of if-then statements. The rule engine can then take these rules and execute them over our data in the most efficient way. Rules, which have all of their conditions true, have their then part evaluated. This is different from imperative style programming languages where the developer has to specify how it needs to be done explicitly (with a sequence of conditionals and loops).

If we rewrite the code from code listing 1 in a declarative manner, it might look like the following:

```
if Customer( level == Level.Gold )
then do something else for Gold customer
if Customer( level == Level.Silver )
and no Account( )
```

```
then do something for Silver customer who has no accounts
if Customer( level == Level.Silver)
and Account( balance < 0, customer.accounts contains account )
then do something for Silver Customer that has account with negative
balance
```

Code listing 2: Rules from code listing 1 written using declarative style.

Each rule represents one requirement. This is more readable and maps to business requirements more naturally.

Advantages

The following is a summary of various advantages of a declarative style solution that Drools brings:

- **Easier to understand**: Rules are easier to understand for a business analyst or a new developer than a program written in Java or other imperative style languages. It is more likely for a technically skilled business analyst to verify or change rules than a Java program.
- **Improved maintainability**: As rules are easier to understand, a developer can spend more time solving the actual problem. We don't care about **how** to implement a solution. We only care about **what** needs to be done to solve a problem.
- **Deals with evolving complexity**: It is much easier to add new rules, modify or remove existing rules than to change, for example, a Java program. The impact this has on other rules is minimal in comparison with an imperative style implementation.
- **Flexibility**: It deals with changes to the requirements or changes to the data model in a much better way. Changing or rewriting an application is never an easy task. However, thanks to formalism that rules bring, it is much easier to change rules than to change a Java program.
- **Reasonable performance**: Thanks to the Rete algorithm that is behind Drools, in theory, the performance of the system doesn't depend on the number of rules. Because a rule engine is essentially a generic if-then statement executor, there are numerous performance optimizations that can be applied independently of the rules. With every release of Drools, the performance of the engine is getting better, by adding various optimizations such as Rete node sharing, node indexing, parallel execution.

- **Requirements can be naturally translated into rules**: The representation of business rules is consistent. For example, let's take some business rule and implement it in Java. Developers, depending on their experience, tend to use different ways to solve a problem. We'll find out that the possible solutions will wary greatly. Whereas with rules, this diversification becomes less apparent. It is simply because we are expressing 'what' instead of 'how'. As a result, the code is much easier to read even by new developers.

- **Ability to apply enterprise management to our rules**: This builds on the previous advantage of consistent representation. If we have consistent representation, it is much easier to introduce new features that apply across all of our rules (for example, auditing, logging, reporting, or performance optimizations).

- **Reusability**: Rules are kept in one place (separation of business logic from the rest of the system), which means easier reusability (for example, imagine you've written some validation rules for your application and later on there is a need to do some batch imports of data; you could simply reuse the validation rules in you batch import application)

- **Rules model the application invariants more closely**: Imperative style solutions tend to impose arbitrary and often unnecessary ordering on operations depending on the algorithm chosen. This then hides the original invariants of the application.

- **The Drools platform brings unification of rules and processes**: It is easy to call rules from a process or vice-versa.

- **Independent Lifecycle**: Rules and processes tend to change far more often than anything else in the application. With Drools, the rules and processes can be authored, deployed, versioned, managed, and so on, independently from the rest of the application.

- **Embedability**: Drools can be easily embedded into existing applications in order to implement just a section of a system.

Disadvantages

On the other hand, don't think of Drools as the silver bullet. Writing systems that make complex decisions is never an easy task. Drools just helps to make it a bit easier. You'll have to invest in training developers. Failing to do so can result in inefficient rules and seemingly unpredictable results. The developers need to adopt a different way of thinking in order to write business rules declaratively. It may look difficult at first but once we master this, the rules will be much easier and faster to write. If we look again at the SQL/Database analogy—SQL queries require developer training in order to be efficiently written, in the same way as rules do. Also, the quality of the data model is directly proportional to the easiness of writing SQL queries and their efficiency, in the exact same way that the quality of the domain model is directly proportional to the easiness of writing rules and their efficiency

We don't specify how the business rules should be implemented, and instead we just specify what needs to happen. Therefore, we don't know how it happened, and hence it may be difficult to troubleshoot. This is a valid point and to resolve this Drools comes with a variety of tools that greatly help you with troubleshooting. Thanks to these tools, troubleshooting becomes a piece of cake.

When you are debugging a program written in Java, you can easily step through the program flow and find out what is going on. Debugging of rules can be more difficult without an understanding of how the underlying system works. Rule engines have many advantages, but on the other side they can be dangerous if you don't know exactly what's going on. In this book, you'll learn just that.

Another disadvantage of a rule engine is its memory consumption. This is the price rule engines have to pay for being efficient. A lot of calculations are being cached to avoid processing them again. However, this is no longer a problem as memory is so cheap nowadays.

Interaction of rules can be quite complex, especially, when some rules modify data that other rules depend on—it can easily cause recursion. The Drools platform provides many ways to prevent this from happening. This is where Drools Flow module comes in action. It can provide a well defined flow of program execution and can separate rules into groups that can be sequentially executed. Integration testing can also help here.

However, it should be stated that the requirements are to blame for this recursion most of the time. A well written rule does only what the business requirements specify. If the requirements are ambiguous, then the resulting rules will be ambiguous as well, potentially causing painful debugging.

When not to use a rule engine

You probably don't need a rule engine:

- If your project is small, possibly with less than 20 rules, then a rule engine would probably be an overkill. However, think twice before making a decision because many systems start small but as more requirements are implemented, they suddenly become unmanageable.

- If your business logic is well defined/static and doesn't change often, you don't need to change rules at run-time.

- If your rules are simple, self-contained, and usually spanning only a single object (for example, a check that user's age is less than 21). If in pseudo-code you don't have more than two nested `if-then` statements. Again, consider this carefully because every system grows in complexity over time.

- If performance is your primary concern. Are you implementing some algorithm where you want to have precise control over its execution? For example, it is not a good idea to write video code in a rule engine. Do you have a memory constrained environment?

- If your project is a one-shot effort and it will never be used again or maintained over time.

- If you don't have the time and money to train your developers to use a rule engine. If developers have no prior experience with logical programming, you need to include it in your time planning. It can take a few weeks to get used to the syntax and start writing rules. It is always good if a more experienced Drools developer reviews the code. The use of a rule engine requires investment at the start; however, in the long term, it brings all of the benefits that we've discussed.

If you answered yes to any of these questions, you probably shouldn't use a rule engine.

Drools

Drools is a **Business Logic integration Platform (BLiP)**. It is written in Java. It is an open source project that is backed by JBoss and Red Hat, Inc. It is licensed under the Apache License, Version 2.0 (`http://www.apache.org/licenses/LICENSE-2.0.html`). This book will focus on version 5.0 of this platform that was released in May 2009.

Work on Drools (the rule engine) began in 2001. From its beginning, Drools underwent many changes. Drools 1.0 started with a brute force linear search. It was then rewritten in version 2.0, which was based on the Rete algorithm. The Rete algorithm boosted Drools performance. Rules were written mainly in XML. The next version (3.0) introduced a new `.drl` format. This is a specific language specially crafted for writing rules. It proved to be a great success and it became the main format for writing rules. Version 4.0 of the rule engine had some major performance improvements together with the first release of a **Business Rules Management System (BRMS)**. This formed the base for the next big release (5.0) where Drools became a Business Logic integration Platform. The platform consists of four main modules:

1. Drools Expert: The rule engine itself.
2. Drools Fusion: Complex Event Processing (CEP) module. It will be covered in Chapter 7, *Complex Event Processing*.
3. Drools Flow: Workflow—combines rules and processes together. It will be introduced at the end of Chapter 6, *Stateful Session* and then fully covered by chapter 8, *Drools Flow*.
4. Drools Guvnor: A Business Rules Management System (BRMS). It won't be covered in this book except for testing and rule analysis in Chapter 10, *Testing*.
5. Drools Solver: This is an optional module. It's a search algorithm built on top of the Drools rule engine to solve planning problems (for example, creating timetables). It won't be covered in this book.

Another very important part of Drools is its Eclipse plugin. It greatly helps with writing and debugging rules and processes. It checks for syntax errors, offers auto completion, and has lots of other useful features.

Drools has a very active and friendly community. It is growing every year. You can get in touch with this community by visiting the Drools blog, wiki, or the mailing lists. For more information, please visit Drools web site at `http://www.jboss.org/drools/`.

Alternatives to Drools

For completeness, we'll also mention alternative rule engines/expert systems. These include commercial products such as ILOG (now IBM)—JRules, Fair Isaac—Blaze Advisor, Corticon's BRMS, Haley (now Oracle) Business Rules Engine, Pegasystems—PegaRules, Production Systems Technologies—OPSJ, Innovations Software. Some products for the .NET platform are: Microsoft BizTalk Server, InRule for Windows Workflow Foundation, ILOG, and Fair Isaac. Alternative open source products include CLIPS and products with dual licenses such as OpenRules or Jess.

Alternatively, you can build a rule engine yourself. It may be appropriate in some specific scenario, but most of the time you'll only be re-inventing the wheel. More importantly, your solution probably won't be as efficient as an existing mature product such as Drools.

Summary

We've learned why there is a need for a BLiP such as Drools, what problems it is trying to solve, and in what way it is trying to solve them. We've seen the advantages and disadvantages of this solution.

Drools provides a different computational model for business process and rule execution. It is a generic algorithm with generic optimizations to provide 'good enough' performance while giving us lots of benefits such as flexibility and declarative programming.

We know that this platform consists of multiple modules and in the following chapters we're going to look at them in more detail, starting with the core rule engine itself—Drools Expert.

2
Basic Rules

In this chapter, we'll start writing our first set of rules in Drools. We'll go through some basics needed to write and execute rules. We'll learn the necessary keywords of the Drools rule language.

But before all this, we'll have to set up our development environment. If you haven't already done so, please refer to *Appendix A* on development environment setup.

Rule basics

We'll now write our first Drools rule. Let's say that we have an `Account` bean that has one property called `balance`. For every `Account` bean, in which the balance is less than `100`, we'll write a message to the standard output as follows:

```
package droolsbook;
rule "basic rule"
 when
  Account( balance < 100 ) // condition
 then
  System.out.println("Account balance is " +
    "less than 100"); // consequence
end
```

Code listing 1: Basic rule file—`basic.drl`.

The basic rule file (`basic.drl`) shown in the preceding code starts with a package name. Package acts as a name space for rules. Rule names within a package must be unique. This concept is similar to Java's packages (classes within a Java package must have different names). After the package definition comes the rule definition. It starts with the rule name; the condition and consequence sections follow. Drools keywords are `rule`, `when`, `then`, and `end`. This rule is triggered for every bean instance of type `Account`, whose balance is less than `100`. The rule prints a message to `System.out`. As we're used to in Java, `//` denotes a comment.

Very simply said, the condition section defines the patterns that the rule matches with. Consequence is a block of code that is executed when all of the patterns within the condition are matched. Note that the condition is sometimes referred to as **LHS (Left Hand Side)**, and consequence as **RHS (Right Hand Side)**.

> Most of the time, the code listings in this book won't contain Java import statements. Use the auto import feature of your favorite editor to import the correct Java type. We'll be using classes from the standard Java library. In case of a third party library, the correct package will be explicitly mentioned. Drools has some classes with same names in different packages. Luckily, they are located in separate modules. Always prefer classes from the `drools-api` module.

`Account` bean/**POJO (Plain Old Java Object)** is straightforward. It has one field with a `get` and a `set` method as shown in the following code:

```java
package droolsbook;

import org.apache.commons.lang.builder.EqualsBuilder;
import org.apache.commons.lang.builder.HashCodeBuilder;
import org.apache.commons.lang.builder.ToStringBuilder;

public class Account {
  private long balance;

  public long getBalance() {
    return balance;
  }
  public void setBalance(long balance) {
    this.balance = balance;
  }
  @Override
  public boolean equals(final Object other) {
    if (this == other)
      return true;
    if (!(other instanceof Account))
      return false;
    Account castOther = (Account) other;
    return new EqualsBuilder().append(balance,
        castOther.balance).isEquals();
  }
  @Override
  public int hashCode() {
    return new HashCodeBuilder(1450207409, -1692382659)
```

```
        .append(balance).toHashCode();
    }
    @Override
    public String toString() {
      return new ToStringBuilder(this)
          .append("balance", balance).toString();
    }
}
```

Code listing 2: `Account` bean/POJO.

Drools accesses the `balance` property through the `get` method, `getBalance()`. Please note that the rule and the `Account` bean are in the same package. This means that we don't have to import anything in our rule file.

The `Account` bean overrides `equals`, `hashCode`, and `toString` methods. They must be implemented correctly. Drools needs to know when two different objects are logically equal (whether they represent the same thing). Apache Commons Lang library is used to simplify the implementation of these methods. It follows the rules laid out in *Effective Java* by Joshua Bloch. This library can be downloaded from `http://commons.apache.org/downloads/download_lang.cgi`. If we didn't override these methods, they would inherit the default implementation from `Object` class. The `equals` method by default returns `true` if the input parameter is the same object instance/reference. By default, the `hashCode` method returns different values for different object instances. This is not the logical equality check that we're after.

Executing rules

We have written a rule and a POJO. Now, we'll write an application to execute our rule. The application will create a session and will insert one instance of the `Account` POJO into the session and execute the rule. The `session` represents our interaction with the Drools engine.

```
public class BasicRulesApp {
  public static final void main(String[] args) {
    KnowledgeBase knowledgeBase = createKnowledgeBase();
    StatefulKnowledgeSession session = knowledgeBase
        .newStatefulKnowledgeSession();

    try {
      Account account = new Account();
      account.setBalance(50);
      session.insert(account);
      session.fireAllRules();
```

```
        }
        finally {
        session.dispose();
        }
    }
}
```

Code listing 3: The first part of a simple application for executing Drools.

The first part of this code shows the creation of a `KnowledgeBase`. It is created by calling `createKnowledgeBase` method.

org.drools.KnowledgeBase

It is an interface that manages a collection of rules, processes, and internal types. In Drools, these are commonly referred to as knowledge definitions or knowledge. Knowledge definitions are grouped into knowledge packages. Knowledge definitions can be added or removed. The main purpose of `KnowledgeBase` is to store and reuse them because their creation is expensive. `KnowledgeBase` provides methods for creating knowledge sessions. Their creation is very lightweight. By default, `KnowledgeBase` maintains a reference to all of the created knowledge sessions. This is to accommodate updates to `KnowledgeBase` at runtime. Drools has one implementation of this interface. This implementation is serializable. We can reuse the serialized `KnowledgeBase` instead of creating a new one every time. This implementation is based on the Rete (usually pronounced as *reet*, *ree-tee*, or *re-tay*) algorithm.

`KnowledgeBase` is then in turn used to create a stateful knowledge session. For now, we won't mind that it is stateful.

org.drools.runtime.StatefulKnowledgeSession

It is the main interface for interacting with the Drools engine. It has methods for inserting, updating, and retracting facts. `StatefulKnowledgeSession` is also used to set the session's global variables. It also has a transient reference to parent `KnowledgeBase`. Probably, the most interesting part of its API is the `fireAllRules` method, which is used to execute all rules. Event handlers can be registered on `KnowledgeBase` for auditing, debugging, or other purposes. When you finish working with `StatefulKnowledgeSession`, do not forget to call the `dispose` method, otherwise this object can't be garbage collected.

A new `Account` instance is then created and its balance is set to 50. This instance is inserted into the session.

 If we want to reason over an object, we'll have to insert it into the session. The object is sometimes referred to as a **fact**.

Finally, we call `fireAllRules` method to execute our basic rule and `dispose` method to release resources. At this point, we're done with the `main` method.

We'll continue with the implementation of the `createKnowledgeBase` method.

```
private static KnowledgeBase createKnowledgeBase() {
    KnowledgeBuilder builder = KnowledgeBuilderFactory
        .newKnowledgeBuilder();
    builder.add(ResourceFactory
        .newClassPathResource("basicRule.drl"),
        ResourceType.DRL);

    if (builder.hasErrors()) {
      throw new RuntimeException(builder.getErrors()
          .toString());
    }

    KnowledgeBase knowledgeBase = KnowledgeBaseFactory
        .newKnowledgeBase();
    knowledgeBase.addKnowledgePackages(builder
        .getKnowledgePackages());
    return knowledgeBase;
  }
}
```

Code listing 4: The second part of an application for executing Drools with a method for creating a `KnowledgeBase`.

A new `KnowledgeBuilder` is created and our rule file is passed into its `add` method. The rule file is read from the classpath and translated to a Resource—`ResourceFactory.newClassPathResource("basicRule.drl")`. Alternatively, the rule file can be loaded from an ordinary URL, a byte array, `java.io.InputStream`, `java.io.Reader` (allows to specify encoding), or from the file system as `java.io.File`.

org.drools.builder.KnowledgeBuilder

This interface is responsible for building `KnowledgePackage` from knowledge definitions (rules, processes, types). The knowledge definitions can be in various formats. If there are any problems with building, `KnowledgeBuilder` will report errors through these two methods: `hasErrors` and `getError`. As we've learned already, one or many `KnowledgePackage` instances forms `KnowledgeBase`.

After the package is built, it is added to a newly created `KnowledgeBase`. It can then be used to create knowledge sessions. This whole process of creating a knowledge session is shown in the following figure:

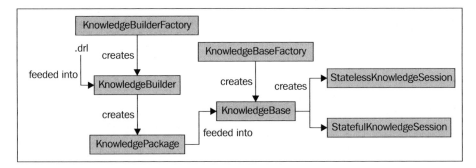

When we run the application the following message should be displayed in the console:

```
Account balance is less than 100
```

This means that the rule was successfully executed. Now, we change the rule's condition to `Account ( balance > 100 )` so that it matches an `Account` in which the balance is greater than `100`. If we run the application again, we won't see the message. This means that the rule's consequence hasn't been executed this time, which is expected.

You may be wondering what's actually happening? In a nutshell, Drools tries to match every fact in the knowledge session with every rule condition to see if all of the rule's conditions can be satisfied. This is sometimes called "pattern matching". The condition represents the pattern that the facts are matched against. If all of the conditions within a rule are satisfied, the rule's consequence may be executed. In our case it is and we can see it from the console output. If we have multiple rules and multiple facts, it would be a bit more complicated — we'll get to that shortly.

Rule syntax

The following section will provide more details on rule (`.drl`) syntax. It will form the basis for later examples.

Rule concepts

A rule can contain many conditions/patterns. For example:

```
Account( balance == 200 )
Customer( name == "John" )
```

Code listing 5: Two rule conditions, one for type `Account` and one for type `Customer`.

Drools will then try to match every `Account` in the session in which the balance is equal to `200` with every `Customer` whose `name` is `John`. If we have three `Account` objects that meet this criteria and two that don't, and five `Customer` objects that meet this criteria and three that don't, it would create (3+2)*(5+3)=40 possible matches. However, only 3*5=15 of them would be valid. This means that a rule with these two conditions will be executed exactly 15 times.

Variables in rules

Rules can declare variables as follows:

```
$account : Account( $type : type )
```

Code listing 6: A simple condition. It matches every `Account` and creates a rule variable with name `$type`, which is bound to a field `type`.

In this example, we declared `$account` variable of type `Account`. The variable name starts with a `$` symbol. It's a common naming practice. `$type` is another variable that is mapped to a field of the `Account` bean. Variables can be declared up front for later use. For example:

```
$account : Account( )
Customer( account == $account )
```

Code listing 7: Conditions with a join. It matches every `Customer` with his/her `Account`.

Please note that the order of fields in a condition is important. It will be incorrect to write `Customer( $account == account )`. Drools would try to find the `Customer.get$account()` method, which probably doesn't exist.

Types

Drools can work with all native Java types and more. Examples of various types that can be used in rule condition are as follows:

- String:

```
Customer( name == "John")
```

Code listing 8: `String` — Matches every `Customer` with `name`.

- Regular expression:

```
Customer( name matches "[A-Z][a-z]+" )
```

Code listing 9: Regular expression — Matches every `Customer` with a `name` that starts with an uppercase letter followed by one or more lowercase letters.

The `matches` operator supports any valid Java Regular Expression as defined by `java.util.regexp` API. It simply delegates to `String.matches` method. (Regular expressions are also supported in the `mvel` dialect, which will be covered later).

- Date:

```
Account( dateCreated > "01-Jan-2008" )
```

Code listing 10: `Date` — Matches every `Account` that was created after a specified date.

The default date format is "dd-mmm-yyyy". This can be customized by changing the `java.lang.System` property — `drools.dateformat`.

- Boolean:

```
Transaction( isApproved == true )
```

Code listing 11: `Boolean` — Matches every approved `Account`.

- Enum:

```
Account( type == Account.Type.SAVINGS )
```

Code listing 12: `Enum` — Matches every savings `Account`.

Comments

Comments are very useful in any programming language — this goes for rules as well. Ideally, every complex rule should be commented. It can greatly reduce the time needed to understand a rule. The declarative nature of rules helps a great deal in readability, but a comment is always helpful. Comments are of the following two types:

- Single line:

```
#single line comment, that can be placed anywhere in the file
//another single line comment
```

- Multi line:

```
/* multi-line comment,
another line */
```

Package

As we already know, package is a group of related rules. We'll now go through the configuration that can be applied at the package level.

Imports

Rule imports have the same purpose as standard Java imports. They allow us to use types from different Java packages by using just their simple name, which consists of a single identifier (for example, ArrayList). Otherwise, a fully qualified name would be required (for example, java.util.ArrayList). An example of using import within a rule file is as follows:

```
import com.mycompany.mypackage.MyClass;
import com.mycompany.anotherPackage.*;
```

Code listing 13: An example of using import within a rule file.

For every rule package, Drools automatically imports all types from the Java package with the same name. java.lang package is included automatically.

Global variables

Global variables are variables assigned to a session. They can be used for various reasons as follows:

- For input parameters (for example, constant values that can be customized from session to session)
- For output parameters (for example, reporting—a rule could write some message to a global report variable)
- Entry points for services such as logging, which can be used within rules

Steps needed to use global variables are as follows:

1. Declare the global variable (with name `accountService`) in the rule file as follows:

    ```
    import com.mycompany.services.AccountService;
    global AccountService accountService;
    ```

    Code listing 14: Global variable declaration in which the name is `accountService`.

    Firstly, the `AccountService` class is imported into the package, and then the global variable is declared. It takes the type and an identifier. In this case, it is a global variable of type `AccountService`, accessible under the name `accountService`.

2. Set the global variable into the rule session. A good practice is to do it before inserting any objects/facts.

    ```
    AccountService accountService = //..
    StatefulKnowledgeSession session =
        knowledgeBase.newStatefulKnowledgeSession();
    session.setGlobal( "accountService", accountService );
    ```

    Code listing 15: Setting of global variable `accountService` into the knowledge session.

3. Use the global variable in a rule condition or a consequence. If used in a condition, they must return a time-constant value while the rule session is active. Otherwise, the results will be unpredictable. An important point to remember is that the rule engine doesn't track changes to global objects.

    ```
    accountService.saveAccount($account);
    ```

    Code listing 16: Use of global variable in a rule consequence.

The use of global variables is generally discouraged in most of the programming languages. However, global variables in Drools are different because they are scoped to a session. Hence, in this sense they are not truly global. Care should also be taken not to overuse them. Generally speaking, if you need to reason over an object (use it in a condition) then you must insert it into the session rather than have it as a global variable.

Functions

Functions are a convenience feature. They can be used in conditions and consequences. Functions represent an alternative to the `utility/helper` classes. Their most common use is to remove duplicated code.

```
function double calculateSquare(double value) {
    return value * value;
}
```

Code listing 17: An example of a function definition in a rule file.

```
long square = calculateSquare(123);
```

Code listing 18: Calling a function from a rule consequence.

Dialect

Dialect specifies the syntax used in any code expression that is in a condition or a consequence. This includes `return values`, `evals`, `inline evals`, `predicates`, `salience expressions`, `consequences`, and so on. The default value is `Java`. Drools currently supports one more dialect called `mvel`. The default dialect can be specified at the package level as follows:

```
package org.mycompany.somePackage
dialect "mvel"
```

Code listing 19: Specifying a default `mvel` dialect for every rule in a package.

mvel

`mvel` is an expression language for Java-based applications. `mvel` supports field and method/getter access. It is based on Java syntax. More information about this language can be found at `http://mvel.codehaus.org/`. Some of its features include:

- **Simple property expressions**:
  `($customer.name == "John") && (balance > 100)`
- **Property navigation**:
  - **Bean properties**: `$customer.address.postalCode`. For example, in a rule consequence instead of writing `$customer.getAddress().setPostalCode("12345")`, one can just write `$customer.address.postalCode = "12345"`.
  - **List access**: `$customer.accounts[3]`
  - **Map access**: `$customer.mapOfAccountNoToAccounts["000123456"]`

- **Inline list, maps,** and **arrays**:
  - ○ **Maps**: For example, to create map of string to account beans, use:
    ```
    [
    "0001" : new Account("0001"),
    "0002" : new Account("0002")
    ].
    ```
  - ○ **Lists**: For example, list of strings— ["0001", "0002", "0003"]
  - ○ **Arrays**: For example, array of strings— { "0001", "0002", "0003" }
- **Projections**: It allows us to inspect complex object models inside collections. For example, if we want to get a list of post codes across all customer's addresses (a customer has only one address)—listOfPostCodes = (address.postCode in $customers);

  Projections can be nested. For example, if the customer had many addresses:
  ```
  listOfPostCodes = (postCode in (addresses in $customers));
  ```
- **Coercion**: Let's say we have the following array—array = { 1, 2, 3 }; and a Java method that takes int []. If we call this method using mvel, it will correctly coerce our array to the needed type. Internally, mvel uses untyped arrays such as Object [].
- **Return values**: mvel expressions use the "last value out" principle. For example, the value of the expression a = 10; b = 20; a; will be 10. For better clarity, the return keyword is supported as well.

  Further, mvel supports method invocations, control flows, assignments, dynamic typing, and so on. Please use mvel with caution. It has very good performance, but it is still interpreted (as opposed to standard Java code that is compiled), and hence, it has performance costs.

  Some core features in Drools are implemented using mvel (for example, nested accessors).

Rule condition

We'll look at the additional Drools keywords used in conditions. Each of these will be demonstrated with an example.

And

and can be implicitly used within conditions (here it is called **Constraint Connective**).

```
Customer( name == "John", age < 26 )
```

Code listing 20: Condition with multiple field constraints joined by implicit and.

Another use of and is between conditions, as we've seen in code listing 5 (here it is called **Conditional Element**). Both of these uses are implicit.

Or

or can also be used within conditions (here it is called Constraint Connective).

```
Customer( name == "John" || age < 26 )
```

Code listing 21: Condition with multiple field constraints joined by or.

A more concise form can be used if matching is performed on a single field:

```
Customer( age < 26 || > 70 )
```

Code listing 22: Condition with multiple field constraints joined by or in more concise form.

More advanced conditions are as follows:

```
$customer :
Customer( ( name == "John" && age < 26 ) ||
          ( name == "Peter" && age < 30 ) )
```

Code listing 23: Condition with more complex constraints.

```
$customer : (
    Customer( name == "John", age < 26 ) or
    Customer( name == "Peter", age < 30 )
)
```

Code listing 24: Another condition with more complex constraints.

Each condition matches a Customer with name John and age less than 26 or a Customer with name Peter and age less than 30.

As you can see, and and or are used between patterns as they are conditional elements, while && and || are used inside patterns between constraints as they are constraint connectives.

Not

not matches the non existence of a fact in the session. For example, the following condition will be true only if there is no SAVINGS account in the session:

```
not Account( type == Account.Type.SAVINGS )
```

Code listing 25: Condition with negation.

Exists

Exists is the inverse to not. It evaluates to true only if the rule session contains at least one instance of the given type.

```
exists Account( type == Account.Type.SAVINGS )
```

Code listing 26: Condition that tests the existence of savings account in rule session.

Eval

eval is a catch-all solution. It allows execution of any Java/MVEL code (according to the selected dialect) that returns true or false. It should be used only as a last resort when all other options have failed. This is because the rule engine cannot optimize eval. The expression is evaluated every time there is a change in the current rule's condition (a fact is added, modified, or removed). They don't have to return time-constant values. Writing eval as the last condition in a rule is a good practice.

```
$account : Account( )
eval( accountService.isUniqueAccountNumber($account) )
```

Code listing 27: An example with eval that calls custom service method.

Return value restriction

An example of a return value restriction is as follows:

```
$customer1 : Customer( )
Customer( age == ($customer1.getAge() + 10) )
```

Code listing 28: Condition with a return value restriction.

Age is being compared to the return value of the expression, $customer1.getAge() + 10. Please note that a return value restriction requires brackets around the expression. The expression must return time-constant results while the session is active, otherwise the outcome will be unpredictable. Also note that the getAge() method is being called explicitly in this case.

Inline eval

The previous example can be rewritten using inline eval as follows:

```
$customer1 : Customer( )
Customer( eval( age == $customer1.getAge() + 10) )
```

Code listing 29: Condition with an inline eval.

When comparing inline `eval` with standard `eval`, we can see that they both must return `true` or `false`. However, inline `eval` must be a time-constant expression. It is evaluated only once and then it is cached by Drools.

Testing object identities/equalities

```
$customer1 : Customer(  )
$customer2 : Customer( this != $customer1 )
```

Code listing 30: Comparing two `Customer` instances using `Customer.equals` method.

```
$customer1 : Customer(  )
$customer2 : Customer( eval( customer$2 != $customer1 ) )
```

Code listing 31: Comparing two `Customer` instances using their object identity (object references).

In the second example, the variable `$customer2` was used instead of `this` because `this` cannot be used within an `eval` code block.

Nested accessors

Nested accessors are internally rewritten by the rule engine as `mvel` dialect inline `eval`. This allows us to use the `mvel` property navigation.

```
$customer : Customer( )
Account( this == $customer.accounts[0] )
```

Code listing 32: An example of nested accessors. Matches `customer` and first account from his/her account list.

Nested accessors must be a time-constant expression (as we already know it is a requirement of all inline `eval`).

If we change a value of a nested property (for example, changing the `balance` of a customer's first account), we should use a `modify` block (will be explained later) to notify Drools about this change (`modify` (`$customer`) { ... }). Drools will then automatically update itself. Nested accessors can be used on either side of the operation symbol. For example, `Account(this.uuid == $cusotmer.accounts[0].uuid)`.

This

Sometimes, we need to refer to the current fact inside a pattern. The `this` keyword is exactly for that purpose:

```
$customer1 : Customer( )
$customer2 : Customer( this != $customer1 )
```

Code listing 33: Conditions that match two different customers.

We have to include the constraint `this != $customer1`; otherwise, the same `Customer` fact could match both conditions and that is probably not what we want.

Working with collections

Drools provides various ways to work with collections of objects. We'll now go through some of them.

(Not) contains

The `contains` operator tests whether a collection has an element. Let's imagine that a customer can have multiple bank accounts. We have multiple customers with their accounts in the rule session.

```
$account : Account( )
Customer( accounts contains $account )
```

Code listing 34: Condition that matches `Customer` with his/her `Account`.

```
$account : Account( )
Customer( accounts not contains $account )
```

Code listing 35: Condition that matches `Customer` and an `Account` that does not belong to him/her.

(Not) memberOf

The `memberOf` operator tests whether an element is in a collection. It is complementary to `contains`. Conditions in code listing 33 can be rewritten as:

```
$customer : Customer( $accounts : account )
Account( this memberOf $accounts )
```

Code listing 36: Condition that matches `Customer` and his/her `Account`.

Or more concisely as:

```
$customer : Customer( )
Account( this memberOf $customer.accounts )
```

Code listing 37: Condition that matches `Customer` and his/her `Account`.

Similar to `contains`, `memberOf` can also be used with `not`.

From

Another very useful keyword is `from`. We can simplify our rules, especially if we use complex hierarchical models. `from` can reason over objects from nested collections. For example:

```
$customer : Customer( )
Account( ) from $customer.accounts
```

Code listing 38: Condition that matches `Customer` and his/her `Account`.

The advantage is that we don't have to insert the `Account` objects into the rule session. `from` accepts any `mvel` expression that returns a single object or a collection of objects. It can reason over facts and global objects. Any service method can be called.

Rule consequence

When all of the conditions in a rule are met, the rule gets activated. After all of the rules are evaluated, some of them are activated. The rule engine will then pick one activated rule and execute its consequence. Then we say that a rule has *fired*. The activated rule is chosen based on a conflict resolution strategy. The conflict resolution strategy uses multiple criteria to decide which rule to fire. After the rule has fired, the engine re-evaluates any changes that have been made by the previous rule's consequence execution. This may activate or deactivate other rules. This process repeats again until there is no activated rule.

Rule consequence represents the actions that will be executed once the rule fires. It can contain any valid Java code. We should try to minimize the amount of code.

 It is considered very bad practice to have conditional logic (`if` statements) within rule consequence. Most of the time, a new rule should be created.

Rule condition should contain simple actions. The facts can be modified, which may cause other rules to fire. Drools comes with these convenience methods for working with current `KnowledgeSession`, which are as follows:

- `modify`: For updating existing facts in the session. For example, a rule that adds interest for deposited money:

```
rule "interest calculation"
no-loop
    when
        $account : Account( )
    then
        modify($account) {
          setBalance((long)($account.getBalance() * 1.03) )
        };
end
```

Code listing 39: Rule that adds interest for an `account`.

The `modify` block can contain many expressions. These expressions must be separated by a comma (,). Note that Drools also supports an `update` method; however, its use is discouraged and the `modify` block should be used instead.

- `insert`: For inserting new facts into the session (for example, `insert(new Account());`).

- `retract`: For removing existing facts from the session.

When a fact is inserted/modified/retracted the rule engine works with a new set of facts; rules may be activated/deactivated.

Rule attributes

Rule attributes are used to modify/enhance the standard rule behavior. All attributes are defined between the `rule` and `when` keywords. For example:

```
rule "rule attributes"
salience 100
dialect "mvel"
no-loop
    when
        //conditions
    then
        //consequence
end
```

Code listing 40: An example of a rule structure with three attributes.

Rule attributes shown in the preceding code are described in the following sections.

salience (priority)

salience is used by the conflict resolution strategy to decide which rule to fire first. By default, it is the main criterion. We can use salience to define the order of firing rules. salience has one attribute, which takes any expression that returns a number of type int (positive as well as negative numbers are valid). The higher the value, the more likely a rule will be picked up by the conflict resolution strategy to fire.

```
salience ($account.balance * 5)
```

Code listing 41: An example of a dynamic salience expression. It can reference any bound or global variables.

The default salience value is 0. We should keep this in mind when assigning salience values to some rules only.

No-loop

This attribute informs the rule engine that a rule should be activated only once per matched facts. For example, the rule in code listing 39 will be activated only once per Account instance. If it doesn't have the no-loop attribute, it will cause an infinite loop because the consequence is updating the $account fact.

Dialect

We've already seen that dialect can be specified on package level in code listing 19. This can be overridden by specifying it on rule level (as seen in code listing 40).

Summary

In this chapter, we've learned some basics about the Drools rule engine. We've also learned to write and execute simple rules. We've covered some package and rule components. We've touched upon what happens when Drools executes. For more information, please look into the Drools documentation, which can be found at http://www.jboss.org/drools/documentation.html.

3
Validation

In this chapter, we'll look at building a decision service for validating a domain model. By writing a set of rules, we'll be separating the validation logic from the rest of the system. This set of rules can be then reused in other systems. For example, it may not only be used as part of the service layer in a web application, but also as a part of high performance batch application for processing large volumes of data.

Before we start with validation, we'll define a simple banking domain model that will be used in examples throughout this book.

Banking domain model

The following figure shows the UML diagram of a simple banking system. It defines four entities: `Customer`, `Address`, `Account`, and `Transaction`.

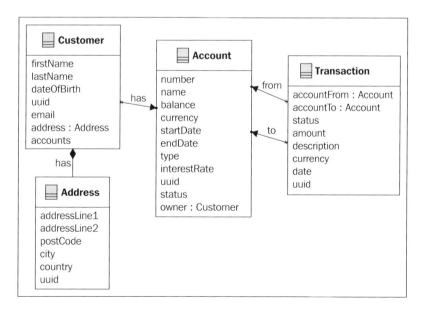

Every bank needs a customer. The customer information that is stored is the name, date of birth, and address. For every address, the model stores two address lines, postal code, city, and country. The customer can have zero or many accounts. Each account has a number, name, actual balance, and currency. Account can be of specific type; the following types are considered:

- **Transactional**—for day-to-day banking, usually with very little rate of interest.

- **Savings**—account for saving money. Start date represents the date when the money was lodged into this account and end date represents the date when it was withdrawn.

- **Student**—designed specifically for younger customers who are price sensitive; however, they don't need more advanced services.

A bank would be useless without the ability to make transactions. Every transaction has an `accountFrom` property, which represents the source account where a sum is subtracted and an `accountTo` property, which represents the destination account where the sum is added. Status of a transaction can have the following values: `pending`, `completed`, `canceled`, or `refused`. Transaction takes place on a certain date; it has a description, amount of money that is involved, and the currency used.

Every object in this model has a **Universally Unique Identifier (UUID)** property. It helps us to easily identify an instance of an object.

This model will be enhanced as we get into more complex Drools features.

The implementation of this model won't be shown in this book. All objects are simple POJOs as described in Chapter 2, *Basic Rules*, where we've implemented an `Account` POJO.

Problem definition

Imagine that we have the following subset of requirements for validating a banking domain from a business analyst:

- Customer's phone number is required
- If customer doesn't provide an address, a warning message should be displayed
- Account number must be unique
- Account balance should be at least 100, otherwise a warning message should be displayed
- Only customers below 27 years of age can open a student account

We'll be validating our banking domain model and the result of this process should be a report informing us of all the problems with the input data.

Analysis

After reading the above problem definition, it seems that each line from the list represents a single rule. The rules are simple—few conditions and a consequence. The consequence will report a customer that failed a validation rule. Two types of messages will be used—**error** and **warning**.

We'll now define a report model that will store this information. The model might look like the following figure:

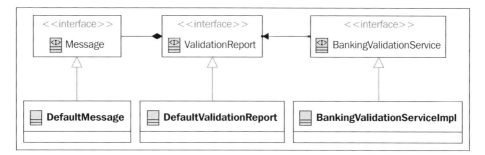

As it can be seen in the above figure, we have a `Message` interface and a `ValidationReport` interface. This validation report is then used by a `BankingValidationService`, which represents some service that will run the validation rules and will act upon the validation report. The diagram also shows the default implementation of these interfaces.

Design

We'll now define each interface. Their implementations will be presented at the end of this chapter. Let's start with `Message` that encapsulates one report message. Every `Message` will have a `type` that can be `ERROR` or `WARNING`, a `key` and a `context` as shown in the following code:

```
/**
 * represents one error/warning validation message
 */
public interface Message {
  public enum Type {
    ERROR, WARNING
```

```
    }
    /**
     * @return type of this message
     */
    Type getType();
    /**
     * @return key of this message
     */
    String getMessageKey();
    /**
     * objects in the context must be ordered from the least
     * specific to most specific
     * @return list of objects in this message's context
     */
    List<Object> getContextOrdered();
}
```

Code listing 1: `Message` interface.

The `key` is used for localized message lookups. `Message` also defines a `context`, which is of type `List` and can contain various objects. Objects should be ordered from least specific (to the `Message`) to most specific. This may be useful for localized messages that have parameters. For example, instead of just saying "Account has negative balance" we can be more specific and say which account has the negative balance by having the account part of the context.

Next is the `ValidationReport` interface (shown in the following code) that holds all of the messages generated during validation. It will allow us to get all of the messages or to get messages by type—only warnings or errors. `Message` can be added into the `ValidationReport`. It will have a convenient method for checking if a message exists for a particular key.

```
    /**
     * represents the result of the validation process
     */
    public interface ValidationReport {
      /**
       * @return all messages in this report
       */
      Set<Message> getMessages();
      /**
       * @return all messages of specified type in this report
```

```
    */
    Set<Message> getMessagesByType(Message.Type type);
    /**
     * @return true if this report contains message with
     *  specified key, false otherwise
     */
    boolean contains(String messageKey);
    /**
     * adds specified message to this report
     */
    boolean addMessage(Message message);
}
```

Code listing 2: `ValidationReport` interface.

As best practice, we'll create a factory that will manage object creation for `Message` and `ValidationReport` classes:

```
public interface ReportFactory {
    ValidationReport createValidationReport();

    Message createMessage(Message.Type type, String messageKey,
        Object... context);
}
```

Code listing 3: `ReportFactory` interface.

Note that the `createMessage` accepts an array of objects as the context—`Object... context`.

Validation package

Before writing our first validation rule, the domain model must be imported. The following three global objects will be used:

1. Report for storing messages.

2. Factory for creating messages.

3. Banking inquiry service for information lookup. It contains one method for testing if an account number is unique—`boolean isAccountNumberUnique (Account account)` (We won't define and implement this service in this book).

This information goes into `validation.drl` (rules will be gradually added into this file as we'll be implementing them).

```
package droolsbook.validation;

import org.drools.runtime.rule.RuleContext;

import droolsbook.bank.model.*;
import droolsbook.bank.service.*;

global ValidationReport validationReport;
global ReportFactory reportFactory;
global BankingInquiryService inquiryService;

import function droolsbook.bank.service.ValidationHelper.error;
import function droolsbook.bank.service.ValidationHelper.warning;
```

Code listing 4: Rule declarations in `validation.drl` file.

As it can be seen in the code above, we're defining a `droolsbook.validation` package, importing some classes and functions, and defining already mentioned global variables.

We've decided to use `validationReport` as a global variable. Individual rules will use this global variable in their consequences and they'll add error/warning messages into this validation report.

Alternatively, instead of using `validationReport` as a global variable, it could be inserted into the rule session like any other fact. We could be writing rules reasoning over this report. For example, checking if the number of error messages in the report has crossed some threshold value, and in that case stopping the validation process. The same could be applied for individual report messages. If we need to reason over them, they can be added into the knowledge session as well.

The last two methods in code listing 4 are used for actual reporting (they create a message object and add it to the global report). They are imported from a `ValidationHelper` utility class. Please note that the method must be declared as `public static`. (Internally, Drools uses a feature in Java 5 called `static import` to import these methods). Both the methods can be imported in one go by using the following form:

```
import function droolsbook.bank.service.ValidationHelper.*;
```

Code listing 5: Importing multiple functions at once.

The actual implementation of the `error` method is shown in the following code:

```
public class ValidationHelper {
  /**
    * adds an error message to the global validation report
    * @param kcontext RuleContext that is accessible from
    * rule condition
    * @param context for the message
    */
  public static void error(RuleContext kcontext,
      Object... context) {
    KnowledgeRuntime knowledgeRuntime = kcontext
        .getKnowledgeRuntime();
    ValidationReport validationReport = (ValidationReport)
        knowledgeRuntime.getGlobal("validationReport");
    ReportFactory reportFactory = (ReportFactory)
        knowledgeRuntime.getGlobal("reportFactory");
    validationReport.addMessage(reportFactory.createMessage(
        Message.Type.ERROR, kcontext.getRule().getName(),
        context));
  }
  ...
```

Code listing 6: Error reporting function that comes from a utility class—`ValidationHelper`.

Normally, you would expect the `error` method to take the message key and the context as parameters. However, instead of a message key, the method takes `RuleContext`. We'll use the current rule name as the message key and `RuleContext` can be used to retrieve the current rule name.

org.drools.runtime.rule.RuleContext

An instance of this class is accessible from each rule consequence. It is injected into rule consequence at runtime and can be accessed under the identifier **kcontext**. It has various convenience methods for interaction with the knowledge session, that is, for inserting/updating/retracting objects, retrieval of various objects (such as current rule, propagation context, activation, knowledge runtime, and others).

In the methods in the preceding code, `RuleContext` is also used to retrieve two global variables. Because global variables are normally not accessible inside functions, this is a simple workaround. Alternatively we could simply pass the global variables into the function. By passing in the RuleContext we're minimizing the amount of duplicated code as we'll see later on.

`reportFactory` is used to create a new `Message` and then this message is added into the validation report. The code `kcontext.getRule().getName()` will return the current rule name, which is used as a *message key*. This is why we don't need the message key as an argument for the function. Most, if not all validation rules, will create only one message. However, this is a shortcut that we should be aware of. It saves us time to think about a unique message key and also time to maintain this key. If the rule name gets changed, the message key will have to be changed too.

Object required type rules

Now that all infrastructure is in place, let's write some validation rules—starting with the simple ones that check an object for missing fields:

```
rule "addressRequired"
    when
        Customer( address == null )
    then
        warning(kcontext);
end
rule "phoneNumberRequired"
    when
        Customer( phoneNumber == null || == "" )
    then
        error(kcontext);
end
rule "accountOwnerRequired"
    when
        $account : Account( owner == null )
    then
        error(kcontext, $account);
end
```

Code listing 7: Simple object/property required type validation rules in the `validation.drl` file.

The `addressRequired` rule will be activated for each customer with no address. Similarly, the `phoneNumberRequired` rule will be activated for each customer with null or blank phone number. In each case, the rule consequence simply calls the appropriate error/warning function and passes `RuleContext` object with optional context. The first two rules have passed no context to the error/warning function. However, the last rule passes the `$account` fact as the context.

For execution of these validation rules, we'll use a stateless knowledge session. It is enough to evaluate each rule only once and there is no need to keep the state between session invocations.

org.drools.runtime.StatelessKnowledgeSession

This is a type of knowledge session that doesn't keep any state between invocations (an **invocation** is a call of the `execute` method). From the rules perspective, a stateless session is no different than a stateful session — the rules look exactly the same. The benefit that statelessness brings is that the rule engine can do more optimizations. `StatelessKnowledgeSession` as well as stateful session support a command interface (command design pattern). There is no need to dispose a stateless session after it has been used.

Testing

Every rule that will be written needs to be unit tested. Ideally we should test all possible cases or at least the most important ones. Use your common sense as to how high code/rule coverage you need. JUnit version 4 will be used for this purpose. More information about JUnit can be found at the project's homepage, `http://junit.sourceforge.net/`. Make sure that you have this library on the classpath. Eclipse provides an environment for running these tests.

The following code sets up a JUnit test class for testing validation rules. Each rule will be tested by at least one test method. The validation test class will define one setup method — `setupClass` that will run only once (we'll use the `@BeforeClass` JUnit4 annotation) per test class. It will create `KnowledgeBase` that will be in turn used to create `StatelessKnowledgeSession`. This session will then be reused for each test method. By doing this, we'll avoid creating `KnowledgeBase` for every test method execution because it is an expensive object to create. We can push this even further by caching the session because it is stateless. We can also cache some global variables needed by our rules — `BankingInquiryService` and `ReportFactory`. These objects are stateless as well. The only thing we cannot reuse is the validation report that will be generated. We'll worry about it, shortly. The `ValidationTest` class is as follows:

```
public class ValidationTest {
  static StatelessKnowledgeSession session;
  static ReportFactory reportFactory;

  @BeforeClass
  public static void setUpClass() throws Exception {
    KnowledgeBuilder builder = KnowledgeBuilderFactory
```

```
        .newKnowledgeBuilder();
    builder.add(ResourceFactory.newClassPathResource(
        "validation.drl"), ResourceType.DRL);
    if (builder.hasErrors()) {
      throw new RuntimeException(builder.getErrors()
          .toString());
    }

    KnowledgeBaseConfiguration configuration =
      KnowledgeBaseFactory.newKnowledgeBaseConfiguration();
    configuration.setOption(SequentialOption.YES);

    KnowledgeBase knowledgeBase = KnowledgeBaseFactory
        .newKnowledgeBase(configuration);
    knowledgeBase.addKnowledgePackages(builder
        .getKnowledgePackages());

    BankingInquiryService inquiryService =
        new BankingInquiryServiceImpl();
    reportFactory = new DefaultReportFactory();

    session = knowledgeBase.newStatelessKnowledgeSession();
    session.setGlobal("reportFactory", reportFactory);
    session.setGlobal("inquiryService", inquiryService);
  }
...
```

Code listing 8: JUnit4 `ValidationTest` set up method.

Please note that `KnowledgeBase` creation process is little bit different than we've seen in Chapter 2, *Basic Rules*. We're using `KnowledgeBaseConfiguration` to create a **sequential** `KnowledgeBase`.

In a sequential `KnowledgeBase`, all of the rules are matched and executed sequentially one by one (the ones that have satisfied all of the conditions). It is a fast, optimized single pass process. From a rules perspective, it is more or less the same. However, as we'll be writing those rules, we should remember this. Every rule will be fired at most, once.

A KnowledgeBase factory takes `KnowledgeBaseConfiguration` that can contain various configuration options for the knowledge base. In this case, we're setting `SequentialOption.YES`.

As it can be seen at the bottom of the preceding code, two global objects are inserted into the session with a `setGlobal` method. These global variables are *scoped to the session*, which means that they will be shared by all of the test methods as well. We can do this because they are immutable. The only global object that is not immutable is the validation report itself. We'll need to scope it to the *session execution call*, which will be done soon.

Also note that the `setupClass` method is static as needed by JUnit4.

Now that the test class has been set up, let's write a test for the `addressRequired` rule. We'll validate a customer that has no address and another customer that has an address. In the first case, we're expecting to see a warning message in the report and in the second case, the report should be empty:

```
@Test
public void addressRequired() throws Exception {
   Customer customer = createCustomerBasic();
   assertNull(customer.getAddress());
   assertReportContains(Message.Type.WARNING,
      "addressRequired", customer);

   customer.setAddress(new Address());
   assertNotReportContains(Message.Type.WARNING,
      "addressRequired", customer);
}
```

Code listing 9: Test for the `addressRequired` rule.

 We've used some static Junit4 methods such as `assertNull` that have to be imported by using: `import static org.junit.Assert.*;`. Simply add it to the import statements section of this file.

The `addressRequired` test method creates a basic customer by using the `createCustomerBasic` method, which creates an empty customer object with one empty account. The test then assumes that the customer's address is null, calls the `assertReportContains` method, which runs the validation, and asserts that the report contains `addressRequired` warning message.

We'll use a different way of executing the validation rules. As we already know, the knowledge session supports a command interface. Two commands will be created. One will insert a new validation report. (Remember? It needs to be *scoped to the execution call* by setting the global object this way—we'll achieve just that). The second command will insert all of our facts into the session. Both the commands will then be run and the report will be populated with messages. This `assertReportContains` method is implemented in the following code:

```
void assertReportContains(Message.Type type,
    String messageKey,Customer customer,Object... context) {
  ValidationReport report =
      reportFactory.createValidationReport();
  List<Command> commands = new ArrayList<Command>();
  commands.add(CommandFactory.newSetGlobal(
      "validationReport", report));
  commands.add(CommandFactory
      .newInsertElements(getFacts(customer)));
  session.execute(CommandFactory
      .newBatchExecution(commands));

  assertTrue("Report doesn't contain message [" + messageKey
      + "]", report.contains(messageKey));
  Message message = getMessage(report, messageKey);
  assertEquals(Arrays.asList(context),
      message.getContextOrdered());
}

private Collection<Object> getFacts(Customer customer) {
  ArrayList<Object> facts = new ArrayList<Object>();
  facts.add(customer);
  facts.add(customer.getAddress());
  facts.addAll(customer.getAccounts());
  return facts;
}
```

Code listing 10: Re-usable method for running validation, and asserting that the report contains specified objects.

The command for inserting facts, `CommandFactory.newInsertElements` `(getFacts(customer))`, gets passed in all of the facts as returned by a `getFacts` method. We're inserting all of the objects that we want to reason with into the session. It's the customer, customer's address, and all the accounts.

Next, the `assertReportContains` method verifies that the message is in the report, `assertTrue(...)`. The message is then retrieved from the report by the `getMessage` method. It takes `messageKey` as an argument and simply iterates over all of the messages inside the report, and if it finds a message with such `messageKey`, it returns it. Finally, the `assertReportContains` method verifies that the message has the expected context.

If we run the `addressRequired` test, it should pass successfully.

Minimal account balance rule

The next rule that will be implemented checks the account balance. According to our original requirements, the account balance should be at least 100. As a good practice from **Test Driven Development (TDD)**, this time we'll start with a test first. More information about TDD can be found at `http://en.wikipedia.org/wiki/Test-driven_development`.

```
@Test
public void accountBalanceAtLeast() throws Exception {
    Customer customer = createCustomerBasic();
    Account account =customer.getAccounts().iterator().next();
    assertEquals(BigDecimal.ZERO, account.getBalance());
    assertReportContains(Message.Type.WARNING,
        "accountBalanceAtLeast", customer, account);

    account.setBalance(new BigDecimal("54.00"));
    assertReportContains(Message.Type.WARNING,
        "accountBalanceAtLeast", customer, account);

    account.setBalance(new BigDecimal("122.34"));
    assertNotReportContains(Message.Type.WARNING,
        "accountBalanceAtLeast", customer);
}
```

Code listing 11: Test that checks the account balance.

The test verifies that for account balance of `zero` and `54`, a warning is generated (the first two paragraphs of the code above). The account balance is then increased to `122.34` (the last/third paragraph of the code above), which doesn't generate the warning. We can now run this test and see that it fails—like in true TDD. Let's fix it by implementing the rule. The rule is as follows:

```
rule "accountBalanceAtLeast"
    when
        $account : Account( balance < 100 )
    then
        warning(kcontext, $account);
end
```

Code listing 12: Rule that operates over the `java.math.BigDecimal` object in the `validation.drl` file.

The rule is straightforward. Please note that the balance is of type `java.math.BigDecimal`. When Drools evaluates this rule, it takes our hard-coded value `100` and correctly creates a `BigDecimal` instance. Then the `compareTo` method of `BigDecimal` is used to make the actual comparison.

Student account rule

The next business rule will add an error message to the report if a customer (who is 27 years old or more) has a student account. Let's write the test first:

```java
@Test
public void studentAccountCustomerAgeLessThan()
      throws Exception {
  DateMidnight NOW = new DateMidnight();
  Customer customer = createCustomerBasic();
  Account account =customer.getAccounts().iterator().next();
  customer.setDateOfBirth(NOW.minusYears(40).toDate());
  assertEquals(Account.Type.TRANSACTIONAL,
      account.getType());
  assertNotReportContains(Message.Type.ERROR,
      "studentAccountCustomerAgeLessThan", customer);

  account.setType(Account.Type.STUDENT);
  assertReportContains(Message.Type.ERROR,
      "studentAccountCustomerAgeLessThan",customer,account);

  customer.setDateOfBirth(NOW.minusYears(20).toDate());
  assertNotReportContains(Message.Type.ERROR,
      "studentAccountCustomerAgeLessThan", customer);
}
```

Code listing 13: Test for the `studentAccountCustomerAgeLessThan` rule.

The test creates a customer, sets his age to `40` years (that is, his date of birth is set to current time minus 40 years), and verifies that he has a CURRENT account and that there is no validation error. It is similar for the rest of the cases.

The `org.joda.time.DateMidnight` type comes from the **Joda-Time** library (this library can be found at `http://joda-time.sourceforge.net/`). It is a very useful library for working with dates, times, periods, and so on. This library is also recommended by the Drools team when working with dates. After downloading the library from the project homepage, add the `joda-time-1.6.jar` file to the classpath (just like we've added the Drools libraries in Appendix A—the development environment setup). Please note that the version number may be different.

Depending on your circumstances, you may need to explicitly specify the time zone as well. By default, most of the date manipulation libraries use local time zone when working with dates. For example, if your system will be deployed in multiple time zones and there is a potential of sharing some data between them, you should specify the time zone as well.

Implementation of the `studentAccountCustomerAgeLessThan` rule might look like the following code:

```
rule "studentAccountCustomerAgeLessThan"
    when
        Customer( eval (yearsPassedSince(dateOfBirth) >= 27) )
        $account : Account( type == Account.Type.STUDENT )
    then
        error(kcontext, $account);
end
```

Code listing 14: Rule for testing a student's age in the `validation.drl` file.

The rule in code listing 14 matches any `Customer` and `Account` objects in the rule session that satisfy the specified constraints.

Care should be taken when doing this. It will only work if we have one customer in the rule session at a time. In case of multiple customers, an additional check should be added that ties the `Customer` to the `Account` that is, `Account( owner == $customer )` or `Customer (accounts contains $account)`.

Let's have a closer look at the customer's age condition. `yearsPassedSince` is a function that is defined as follows:

```
/**
 * @return number of years between today and specified date
 */
public static int yearsPassedSince(Date date) {
  return Years.yearsBetween(new DateMidnight(date),
      new DateMidnight()).getYears();
}
```

Code listing 15: Imported function that calculates number of years that have passed since a date.

The main work is done by the Joda-Time library (the `Years` class is from this library as well). This static function can be added to the `ValidationHelper` class that was shown in the code listing 6. It can then be imported as was shown in the code listing 4.

Unique account number rule

The last requirement states that "Account number must be unique". To check the uniqueness of an account number, we'll use `BankingInquiryService`. For testing purposes, we'll write a mock implementation, or you can use any mocking library for this purpose as well. The test is as follows:

```
@Test
public void accountNumberUnique() throws Exception {
    Customer customer = createCustomerBasic();
    Account account = customer.getAccounts().iterator()
        .next();
    session.setGlobal("inquiryService",
        new BankingInquiryServiceImpl() {
            @Override
            public boolean isAccountNumberUnique(
                Account account) {
              return false;
            }
        });
    assertReportContains(Message.Type.ERROR,
        "accountNumberUnique", customer, account);
}
```

Code listing 16: Test for `accountNumberUnique` rule.

The test creates a customer and a new mock implementation of `BankingInquiryService` with `isAccountNumberUnique` method that always returns `false`. The `inquiryService` global variable is set. Rules are executed and the test verifies that there is an error in the report. The real test should also include an option where the account number is unique (the service method returns `true`).

The following is the implementation of the rule that checks the uniqueness of an account number:

```
rule "accountNumberUnique"
    when
        $account : Account(eval(
            !inquiryService.isAccountNumberUnique($account)))
    then
        error(kcontext, $account);
end
```

Code listing 17: Rule for checking account number uniqueness in the `validation.drl` file.

The `accountNumberUnique` rule demonstrates the usage of a service method in a rule. The method is being called through an inline `eval`. An inline `eval` can evaluate any code block that returns `true` or `false`. The results must be constant during the session execution (if we evaluate the code block multiple times, we must get the same result). The code also shows that we can use any bound variable inside the code block (in this case, it is the `$account` variable).

Implementation

In this section, we'll define the implementation for various interfaces that we've defined in this chapter. You can skip this section if you like. It is here for completeness.

First, let's look at an implementation of the `Message` interface, which is shown in the following code. The message is essentially another POJO, so it will basically have `get` and `set` methods, and it will also override the `equals`, `hashCode`, and `toString` methods.

```
import org.apache.commons.lang.builder.EqualsBuilder;
import org.apache.commons.lang.builder.HashCodeBuilder;
import org.apache.commons.lang.builder.ToStringBuilder;
//... other imports
public class DefaultMessage implements Message, Serializable {
  private Message.Type type;
  private String messageKey;
  private List<Object> context;

  public DefaultMessage(Message.Type type, String messageKey,
      List<Object> context) {
    if (type == null || messageKey == null) {
      throw new IllegalArgumentException(
          "Type and messageKey cannot be null");
    }
    this.type = type;
    this.messageKey = messageKey;
    this.context = context;
  }

  public String getMessageKey() {
    return messageKey;
  }
```

```
    public Message.Type getType() {
      return type;
    }
    public List<Object> getContextOrdered() {
      return context;
    }
    @Override
    public boolean equals(final Object other) {
      if (this == other)
        return true;
      if (!(other instanceof DefaultMessage))
        return false;
      DefaultMessage castOther = (DefaultMessage) other;
      return new EqualsBuilder().append(type, castOther.type)
          .append(messageKey, castOther.messageKey).append(
              context, castOther.context).isEquals();
    }
    @Override
    public int hashCode() {
      return new HashCodeBuilder(98587969, 810426655).append(
          type).append(messageKey).append(context).toHashCode();
    }
    @Override
    public String toString() {
      return new ToStringBuilder(this).append("type", type)
          .append("messageKey", messageKey).append("context",
              context).toString();
    }
  }
```

Code listing 18: Implementation of the `Message` interface.

`DefaultMessage` has a constructor that takes the `Message.Type` and key. It guarantees that these two properties will be always set (not `null`); the `context` is optional.

Next, we'll look at the implementation of the `ValidationReport` interface. It will store all of the messages in a map. The key of this map will be the message type and the value will be a set of messages. A "set" because we're not interested in the order of messages. We're interested only in unique messages (in the `DefaultMessage.equals` method sense). The declaration will look like this: `Map<Message.Type, Set<Message>> messagesMap`. Then, we only need a bunch of methods that will work on this map. The implementation of this interface, `DefaultValidationReport`, is as follows:

```java
public class DefaultValidationReport implements
    ValidationReport, Serializable {
  protected Map<Message.Type, Set<Message>> messagesMap =
    new HashMap<Message.Type, Set<Message>>();

  public Set<Message> getMessages() {
    Set<Message> messagesAll = new HashSet<Message>();
    for (Collection<Message> messages : messagesMap.values()){
      messagesAll.addAll(messages);
    }
    return messagesAll;
  }

  public Set<Message> getMessagesByType(Message.Type type) {
    if (type == null)
      return Collections.emptySet();
    Set<Message> messages = messagesMap.get(type);
    if (messages == null)
      return Collections.emptySet();
    else
      return messages;
  }

  public boolean contains(String messageKey) {
    for (Message message : getMessages()) {
      if (messageKey.equals(message.getMessageKey())) {
        return true;
      }
    }
    return false;
  }

  public boolean addMessage(Message message) {
    if (message == null)
      return false;
    Set<Message> messages =messagesMap.get(message.getType());
    if (messages == null) {
      messages = new HashSet<Message>();
      messagesMap.put(message.getType(), messages);
    }
    return messages.add(message);
  }
}
```

Code listing 19: Implementation of `ValidationReport` interface.

Please note that the code above doesn't show the implementation of `equals`, `hashCode`, and `toString` methods. All of them operate only on the message map.

Next, we'll look at the implementation of the `ReportFactory` interface. It simply creates a new instance of a `DefaultMessage` or a `DefaultValidationReport` object.

```
public class DefaultReportFactory implements ReportFactory {
   public Message createMessage(Message.Type type,
       String messageKey, Object... context) {
      return new DefaultMessage(type, messageKey, Arrays
         .asList(context));
   }
   public ValidationReport createValidationReport() {
      return new DefaultValidationReport();
   }
}
```

Code listing 20: Implementation of `ReportFactory`.

Validation service

All of the rules are implemented as unit tests, and we can write a validation service that our clients can access. It will define one method for validating a customer. The following code shows the `BankingValidationService` interface:

```
/**
 * service for validating the banking domain
 */
public interface BankingValidationService {
   /**
    * validates given customer and returns validation report
    */
   ValidationReport validate(Customer customer);
}
```

Code listing 21: `BankingValidationService` interface.

The interface defines one method that validates a `Customer` object and returns `ValidationReport`. As all of the objects in our domain model are accessible (traversable) from the `Customer` object, it is sufficient to just pass this class as the method parameter. The implementation is more interesting:

```
public class BankingValidationServiceImpl implements
    BankingValidationService {
   private KnowledgeBase knowledgeBase;
   private ReportFactory reportFactory;
   private BankingInquiryService bankingInquiryService;
```

```
/**
 * validates provided customer and returns validation report
 */
public ValidationReport validate(Customer customer) {
  ValidationReport report = reportFactory
      .createValidationReport();
  StatelessKnowledgeSession session = knowledgeBase
      .newStatelessKnowledgeSession();
  session.setGlobal("validationReport", report);
  session.setGlobal("reportFactory", reportFactory);
  session
      .setGlobal("inquiryService", bankingInquiryService);
  session.execute(getFacts(customer));
  return report;
}

/**
 * @return facts that the rules will reason upon
 */
private Collection<Object> getFacts(Customer customer) {
  ArrayList<Object> facts = new ArrayList<Object>();
  facts.add(customer);
  facts.add(customer.getAddress());
  facts.addAll(customer.getAccounts());
  return facts;
}
...
```

Code listing 22: Section of banking validation service implementation.

This implementation needs to have set `ruleBase`, `reportFactory`, and `bankingInquiryService`. The setters for these properties are not shown; they are straightforward. The `validation` method creates a report that will be returned and a stateless rule session, sets three global objects, and finally calls the `execute` method with all of the facts grouped into one collection. As a stateless session is used, all of the facts need to be passed in one go.

Note the different style of using a stateless session. In this case, we set all three global variables through the `setGlobal` method. By setting them this way, the global objects are scoped to the session. Hence, we cannot reuse this session across multiple validate method invocations (across multiple threads). This is why the session variable is scoped to the `validate` method and not the class as was the case with our unit tests. This is just to show you a different way of working with the session without using commands.

Summary

Let's look at what we've achieved in this chapter. By separating the validation rules from the rest of the application, we've made it easier for the others to identify and understand them. Because of the declarative nature of rules, they can be maintained and re-factored more easily. We can easily change rules or add new ones without increasing the overall complexity.

A simple extensible reporting model has been defined and later used in the customer validation rules. Throughout this chapter, a stateless session has been used, which is ideal for these types of *decision* rules. Remember that it is stateless only because it doesn't hold a state between invocations. A special feature of the stateless session is that it can be executed in a sequential mode, which has big performance benefits. We've learned about `RuleContext`, which is present in every rule consequence. We've discussed the use of validation report as a global variable versus being inserted into the session as an ordinary fact. We've also discussed use of `BigDecimal` as a type for floating point numbers, and Joda-Time as the date-time manipulation library.

4
Data Transformation

Almost any rewrite of an existing legacy system needs to do some kind of data transformation with the old legacy data before they can be used in the new system. It needs to load the data, transform it so that it meets the requirements of the new system, and finally store it. This is just one example of where data transformation is needed.

Drools can help us with this data transformation task as well. Depending on our requirements, it might be a good idea to isolate this transformation process in the form of rules. The rules can be reused later, maybe when our business will expand and we'll be converting data from a different third-party system. Of course other advantages of using rules apply.

If performance is the most important requirement (for example, if all of the data has to be converted within a specified time-frame), rules may not be the ideal approach. Probably the biggest disadvantage of using rules is that they need the legacy data in memory, so they are best suited to *more complex data transformation* tasks. However, consider it carefully if you think your data transformation will grow in complexity as more requirements are added.

When writing these transformation rules, care should be taken not to confuse them with validation rules. In a nutshell, if a rule can be written working just with the domain model, it is most likely a validation rule. If it uses concepts that cannot be represented with our domain model, it is probably a transformation rule.

Process overview

Let's demonstrate this data transformation through an example. Imagine that we need to convert some legacy customer data into our new system.

As not all of the legacy data is perfect, we'll need a way to report the data that, for some reason, we've failed to transfer. For example, our system allows only one address per customer. Legacy customers with more than one address will be reported. We'll reuse the reporting component from the validation chapter.

In this section we'll:

1. Load the customer data from the legacy system. The data will include address and account information.

2. Run the transformation rules over this data and build an execution report.

3. Populate the domain model with transformed data, run the validation rules (from previous section), and save it into our system.

Getting the data

As a good practice, we'll define an interface for interacting with the other system. We'll introduce a LegacyBankService interface for this purpose. It will make it easier to change the way we communicate with the legacy system. Another nice side effect is that the tests will be easier to write.

```
package droolsbook.transform.service;

import java.util.List;
import java.util.Map;

public interface LegacyBankService {

    /**
     * @return all customers
     */
    List<Map<String, Object>> findAllCustomers();

    /**
     * @return addresses for specified customer id
     */
    List<Map<String, Object>> findAddressByCustomerId(
        Long customerId);

    /**
     * @return accounts for specified customer id
     */
    List<Map<String, Object>> findAccountByCustomerId(
        Long customerId);
}
```

Code listing 1: Interface that abstracts the legacy system interactions.

The interface defines three methods. The first one can retrieve a list of all customers, the second and third retrieve a list of addresses and accounts for a specific customer. Each list contains zero or many maps. One map represents one object in the legacy system. The keys of this map are object property names (for example, addressLine1) and the values are the actual properties.

We've chosen a map because it is a generic data type that can store almost any data which is ideal for a data transformation task. However, it has a big disadvantage—the rules will be a bit harder to write in it.

The implementation of this interface will be defined at the end of this chapter.

Loading facts into the knowledge session

Before writing some transformation rules, the data needs to be loaded into the knowledge session. This can be done by writing a specialized rule just for this purpose:

```
package droolsbook.transform;

import java.util.*;

import droolsbook.transform.service.LegacyBankService;
import droolsbook.bank.model.Address;
import droolsbook.bank.model.Address.Country;

global LegacyBankService legacyService;

rule findAllCustomers
dialect "mvel"
    when
        $customerMap : Map( )
            from legacyService.findAllCustomers()
    then
        $customerMap["_type_"] = "Customer"
        insert( $customerMap )
end
```

Code listing 2: Rule that loads all Customer facts into the knowledge session (dataTransformation.drl file).

The findAllCustomers rule, shown in the code above, matches on a Map instance that is obtained from our legacyService. It adds the type in the consequence part (so that we can recognize that this map represents a customer) and inserts this map into the session. There are few things to be noted here:

- A mvel dialect is used which helps readability of the consequence part (otherwise, we'd have to write $customerMap.put("_type_", "Customer");).

- A rule is being used to insert objects into the knowledge session; this just shows a different way of loading objects into the knowledge session.

- Every customer returned from the findAllCustomers method is being inserted into the session. This is reasonable only if there is a small amount of customers. If it is not the case, we can paginate, that is, process only N customers at once, then start over with next N customers, and so on. Alternatively, the findAllCustomers rule can be removed and customers can be inserted into the knowledge session at session creation time. We'll now focus on this latter approach (for example, only one Customer instance is in the knowledge session at any given time); it will make the reporting easier.

- A type of the map is being added to the map. This is a disadvantage of using HashMap for every type (Customer, Address, and so on)—the type information is lost. It can be seen in the following rule that finds addresses for a customer:

```
rule findAddress
dialect "mvel"
    when
        $customerMap : Map( this["_type_"] == "Customer" )
        $addressMap : Map( )
            from legacyService.findAddressByCustomerId(
                $customerMap["customer_id"] )
    then
        $addressMap["_type_"] = "Address"
        insert( $addressMap )
end
```

Code listing 3: Rule that loads all Address instances for a Customer into the rule session (dataTransformation.drl file).

Let's focus on the first condition line. It matches customerMap. It has to test if this Map contains customer's data by executing this["_type_"] == "Customer". To avoid carrying out these type checks in every condition, a new custom map type can be created for example, LegacyCustomerHashMap. The rule might look like as follows:

```
$customerMap : LegacyCustomerHashMap( )
```

Code listing 4: Matching on customer map without doing the type check.

We'll continue with the second part of the condition. It matches an addressMap that comes from our legacyService as well. The from keyword supports parameterized service calls. customer_id is passed into the findAddressByCustomerId method. Another nice thing about this is that we don't have to cast the parameter to java.lang.Long—it is done automatically.

The consequence part of this rule just sets the type and inserts `addressMap` into the knowledge session. Please note that only addresses for loaded customers are loaded into the session. This saves memory but it could also cause lot of "chattiness" with the `LegacyBankService` interface if there are many child objects. It can be fixed by pre-loading those objects. The implementation of this interface is the right place for this.

Similar data loading rules can be written for other types for example, `Account`.

Writing transformation rules

Now that all of the objects are in the knowledge session, we can start writing some transformation rules. Let's imagine that in the legacy system, there are many duplicate addresses. We can write a rule that removes such duplication:

```
rule twoEqualAddressesDifferentInstance
    when
        $addressMap1 : Map( this["_type_"] == "Address" )
        $addressMap2 : Map( this["_type_"] == "Address",
            eval( $addressMap1 != $addressMap2 ),
            this == $addressMap1 )
    then
        retract( $addressMap2 );
        validationReport.addMessage(
            reportFactory.createMessage(Message.Type.WARNING,
            kcontext.getRule().getName(), $addressMap2));
end
```

Code listing 5: Rule that removes redundant address (`dataTransformation.drl` file).

The rule matches two addresses. It checks that they don't have the same object identities by calling `eval( $addressMap1 != $addressMap2 )`. Otherwise, the rule could match single address instance. The next part, `this == $addressMap1`, translates to `$addressMap1.equal($addressMap2)` behind the scenes. If this equal check is true, it means that one of the addresses is redundant and can be removed from the session. The address map that is removed is added to the report as a warning message.

Testing

Before we continue with the rest of the rules, we'll set up unit tests. The test initialization method is similar to the one from the validation chapter. We'll still use a stateless session:

```
session = knowledgeBase.newStatelessKnowledgeSession();
session.setGlobal("legacyService",
    new MockLegacyBankService());
```

Code listing 6: Section of the test `setUpClass` method (`DataTransformationTest` file).

The `legacyService` global variable is set to new instance of `MockLegacyBankService`. It is a dummy implementation that simply returns `null` from all of the methods. In most of the tests, we'll insert objects directly into the knowledge session (and not through the `legacyService`).

We'll now write a helper method for inserting objects into the knowledge session and running the rules. The helper method will create a list of commands, it will execute these commands and the resulting object — `ExecutionResults` — will be returned back to the caller. The following commands will be created:

- One for setting the global variable, `validationReport`; a new validation report will be created.

- One for inserting all of the objects into the session.

- One for firing only rules with specified name. This will be done through an `AgendaFilter` interface. It will help us to isolate the rule that we'll be testing.

- One for getting back all of the objects in a knowledge session that are of certain type. These objects will be returned from the helper method as part of the `results` object.

org.drools.runtime.rule.AgendaFilter

When a rule is activated, `AgendaFilter` determines if this rule can be fired or not. The `AgendaFilter` interface has one `accept` method that returns `true` or `false`. We'll create our own `RuleNameEqualsAgendaFilter` that fires only rules with specific name.

The helper method is as follows:

```java
/**
 * creates multiple commands, calls session.execute and
 * returns results back
 */
protected ExecutionResults execute(Iterable objects,
    String ruleName, final String filterType,
    String filterOut) {
  ValidationReport validationReport = reportFactory
      .createValidationReport();
  List<Command<?>> commands = new ArrayList<Command<?>>();
  commands.add(CommandFactory.newSetGlobal(
      "validationReport", validationReport, true));
  commands.add(CommandFactory.newInsertElements(objects));
  commands.add(new FireAllRulesCommand(
      new RuleNameEqualsAgendaFilter(ruleName)));
  if (filterType != null && filterOut != null) {
    GetObjectsCommand getObjectsCommand =
      new GetObjectsCommand( new ObjectFilter() {
          public boolean accept(Object object) {
            return object instanceof Map
                && ((Map) object).get("_type_").equals(
                    filterType);
          }
        });
    getObjectsCommand.setOutIdentifier(filterOut);
    commands.add(getObjectsCommand);
  }
  ExecutionResults results = session
      .execute(CommandFactory.newBatchExecution(commands));
  return results;
}
```

Code listing 7: Test helper method for executing the transformation rules
(`DataTransformationTest` file).

To write a test for the redundant address rule, two address maps will be created. Both will have their street set to `Barrack Street`. After we execute rules, only one address map should be in the knowledge session. The test looks like the following code:

```java
@Test
public void twoEqualAddressesDifferentInstance()
    throws Exception {
  Map addressMap1 = new HashMap();
```

```
addressMap1.put("_type_", "Address");
addressMap1.put("street", "Barrack Street");

Map addressMap2 = new HashMap();
addressMap2.put("_type_", "Address");
addressMap2.put("street", "Barrack Street");
assertEquals(addressMap1, addressMap2);

ExecutionResults results = execute(Arrays.asList(
    addressMap1, addressMap2),
    "twoEqualAddressesDifferentInstance", "Address",
    "addresses");

Iterator<?> addressIterator = ((List<?>) results
    .getValue("addresses")).iterator();
Map addressMapWinner = (Map) addressIterator.next();
assertEquals(addressMap1, addressMapWinner);
assertFalse(addressIterator.hasNext());
reportContextContains(results,
    "twoEqualAddressesDifferentInstance",
    addressMapWinner == addressMap1 ? addressMap2
        : addressMap1);
}
```

Code listing 8: Test for the redundant address rule.

The `execute` method is called with the two address maps, the agenda filter rule name is set to `twoEqualAddressesDifferentInstance` (only this rule will be allowed to fire), and after the rules are executed, all of the maps of the type `Address` are returned as a part of the result. We can access them by `results.getValue("addresses")`. The test verifies that there is only one such map.

Another test helper method — `reportContextContains` — verifies that `validationReport` contains expected data. The implementation of the `reportContextContains` method is as follows:

```
/**
 * asserts that the report contains one message with
 * expected context (input parameter)
 */
void reportContextContains(ExecutionResults results,
    String messgeKey, Object object) {
  ValidationReport validationReport = (ValidationReport)
      results.getValue("validationReport");
  assertEquals(1, validationReport.getMessages().size());
  Message message = validationReport.getMessages()
      .iterator().next();
```

```
        List<Object> messageContext = message.getContextOrdered();
        assertEquals(1, messageContext.size());
        assertSame(object, messageContext.iterator().next());
    }
```

Code listing 9: Helper method, which verifies that report contains supplied object.

Address normalization

Our next rule will be a type conversion rule. It will take a `String` representation
of country and convert it into `Address.Country` enum. We'll start with the
following test:

```
@Test
public void addressNormalizationUSA() throws Exception {
    Map addressMap = new HashMap();
    addressMap.put("_type_", "Address");
    addressMap.put("country", "U.S.A");

    execute(Arrays.asList(addressMap),
        "addressNormalizationUSA", null, null);

    assertEquals(Address.Country.USA, addressMap
        .get("country"));
}
```

Code listing 10: Test for the country type conversion rule.

The test creates an address map with the country set to `U.S.A`. It then calls
the `execute` method passing in the `addressMap` and allowing only the rule
`addressNormalizationUSA` to fire (no filter is used in this case). Finally, the test
verifies that address map has the correct country value. Next, we'll write the rule:

```
rule addressNormalizationUSA
dialect "mvel"
    when
        $addressMap : Map( this["_type_"] == "Address",
            this["country"] in ("US", "U.S.", "USA", "U.S.A"))
    then
        modify( $addressMap ) {
            put("country", Country.USA)
        }
end
```

Code listing 11: Rule that converts `String` representation of country into `enum`
representation (`dataTransformation.drl` file).

The rule matches an address map. The `in` operator is used to capture various country representations. Let's look at rule's consequence in more detail. By calling `$addressMap.put("country", Country.USA)`, we change the address map identity (if we look at the implementation of `HashMap` equals or `hashCode` methods, they take into account every element in the map). The code that updates `addressMap` needs to be executed inside a modify block as we've done code listing 11.

As we already know, the modify construct takes an argument and — a block of code. Before executing the block of code, it retracts the argument from the knowledge session, then it executes the block of code, and finally the object is inserted back into the knowledge session. This way even though the object's identity is changed, the rule engine remains consistent.

Fact's identity

As a general rule, do not change the object's identity while it is in the knowledge session. Otherwise, the rule engine behavior will be undefined. (Same as changing an object while it is in `java.util.HashMap`)

Testing the findAddress rule

Before continuing, let's write a test for the `findAddress` rule from code listing 3. The test will use special `LegacyBankService` mock implementation that will return the provided `addressMap`:

```
public class StaticMockLegacyBankService extends
    MockLegacyBankService {
  private Map addressMap;
  public StaticMockLegacyBankService(Map addressMap) {
    this.addressMap = addressMap;
  }
  public List findAddressByCustomerId(Long customerId) {
    return Arrays.asList(addressMap);
  }
}
```

Code listing 12: `StaticMockLegacyBankService` which returns the provided `addressMap`.

`StaticMockLegacyBankService` extends `MockLegacyBankService` and overrides the `findAddressByCustomerId` method. The `findAddress` test looks as follows:

```
@Test
public void findAddress() throws Exception {
  final Map customerMap = new HashMap();
  customerMap.put("_type_", "Customer");
```

```
        customerMap.put("customer_id", new Long(111));

        final Map addressMap = new HashMap();
        LegacyBankService service =
            new StaticMockLegacyBankService(addressMap);
        session.setGlobal("legacyService", service);

        ExecutionResults results = execute(Arrays
            .asList(customerMap), "findAddress", "Address",
            "objects");

        assertEquals("Address", addressMap.get("_type_"));
        Iterator<?> addressIterator = ((List<?>) results
            .getValue("objects")).iterator();
        assertEquals(addressMap, addressIterator.next());
        assertFalse(addressIterator.hasNext());

        // clean-up
        session.setGlobal("legacyService",
            new MockLegacyBankService());
    }
```

Code listing 13: Test for the `findAddress` rule.

The test then verifies that address map is really in the knowledge session, that it has the _type_ key set, and that there is no other address map.

Unknown country

The next rule will create an error message if the country isn't recognizable by our domain model. The test creates address map with some unknown country, executes rules, and verifies that the report contains an error.

```
    @Test
    public void unknownCountry() throws Exception {
        Map addressMap = new HashMap();
        addressMap.put("_type_", "Address");
        addressMap.put("country", "no country");

        ExecutionResults results = execute(Arrays
            .asList(addressMap), "unknownCountry", null, null);

        ValidationReport report = (ValidationReport) results
            .getValue("validationReport");
        reportContextContains(results, "unknownCountry",
            addressMap);
    }
```

Code listing 14: Test for the `unknownCountry` rule.

The rule implementation will test if the country value from the `addressMap` is of the type `Address.Country`. If it isn't, an error is added to the report. This rule should be executed after all address normalization rules:

```
rule unknownCountry
salience -10 //should fire after address normalizations
    when
        $addressMap : Map( this["_type_"] == "Address",
            eval(!($addressMap.get("country") instanceof
            Address.Country)))
    then
        validationReport.addMessage(
            reportFactory.createMessage(Message.Type.ERROR,
            kcontext.getRule().getName(), $addressMap));
end
```

Code listing 15: Rule that reports unknown countries (`dataTransformation.drl` file).

The type checking is done with `instanceof` operator of `mvel`.

Currency conversion

As a given requirement, the data transformation process should convert all of the accounts to EUR currency. The test for this rule might look like this:

```
@Test
public void currencyConversionToEUR() throws Exception {
    Map accountMap = new HashMap();
    accountMap.put("_type_", "Account");
    accountMap.put("currency", "USD");
    accountMap.put("balance", "1000");

    execute(Arrays.asList(accountMap),
        "currencyConversionToEUR", null, null);

    assertEquals("EUR", accountMap.get("currency"));
    assertEquals(new BigDecimal("670.000"), accountMap
        .get("balance"));
}
```

Code listing 16: Test for the EUR conversion rule.

At the end of the code snippet above, the test verified that currency and balance were correct. Exchange rate of 0.670 was used. The rule implementation is as follows:

```
rule currencyConversionToEUR
    when
        $accountMap : Map( this["_type_"] == "Account",
            this["currency"] != null && != "EUR" )
        $conversionAmount : String() from
            getConversionToEurFrom($accountMap["currency"])
    then
        modify($accountMap) {
            put("currency", "EUR"),
            put("balance", new BigDecimal(
                $conversionAmount).multiply(new BigDecimal(
                (String)$accountMap.get("balance")))))
        }
    end
```

Code listing 17: Rule that converts account balance and currency to EUR (dataTransformation.drl file).

The rule uses the default Java dialect. It matches on an account map and retrieves conversion amount using the from conditional element. In this case, it is a simple function that returns hard coded values. However, it can be easily replaced with a service method that could, for example, call some web service in a real bank.

```
function String getConversionToEurFrom(String currencyFrom) {
    String conversion = null;
    if ("USD".equals(currencyFrom)) {
        conversion = "0.670";
    } else if ("SKK".equals(currencyFrom)) {
        conversion = "0.033";
    }
    return conversion;
}
```

Code listing 18: Dummy function for calculating the exchange rate (dataTransformation.drl file).

Note the way in which we're calling the function. Instead of calling it directly in the consequence, it is called from a condition. This way, our rule will fire only if the function returns some non-null result.

The rule then sets the currency to EUR and multiplies the balance with the exchange rate. This rule doesn't cover the currencies for which the `getConversionToEurFrom` function returns null. We have to write another rule that will report unknown currencies:

```
rule unknownCurrency
    when
        $accountMap : Map( this["_type_"] == "Account",
            this["currency"] != null && != "EUR" )
        not( String() from
            getConversionToEurFrom($accountMap["currency"]) )
    then
        validationReport.addMessage(
            reportFactory.createMessage(Message.Type.ERROR,
            kcontext.getRule().getName(), $accountMap));
    end
```

Code listing 19: Rule that adds an error message to the report if there is no conversion for a currency (`dataTransformation.drl` file).

Note that in this case, the `getConversionToEurFrom` function is called from within the `not` construct.

One account allowed

Imagine that we have a business requirement where only one account from the legacy system can be imported into the new system. Our next rule will remove redundant accounts while aggregating their balances.

The test inserts two accounts of the same customer into the knowledge session and verifies that one of them was removed and the balance was transferred:

```
@Test
public void reduceLegacyAccounts() throws Exception {
    Map accountMap1 = new HashMap();
    accountMap1.put("_type_", "Account");
    accountMap1.put("customer_id", "00123");
    accountMap1.put("balance", new BigDecimal("100.00"));

    Map accountMap2 = new HashMap();
    accountMap2.put("_type_", "Account");
    accountMap2.put("customer_id", "00123");
    accountMap2.put("balance", new BigDecimal("300.00"));

    ExecutionResults results = execute(Arrays.asList(
        accountMap1, accountMap2), "reduceLegacyAccounts",
```

```
        "Account", "accounts");
    Iterator<?> accountIterator = ((List<?>) results
        .getValue("accounts")).iterator();
    Map accountMap = (Map) accountIterator.next();
    assertEquals(new BigDecimal("400.00"), accountMap
        .get("balance"));
    assertFalse(accountIterator.hasNext());
}
```

Code listing 20: Test for the `reduceLegacyAccounts` rule.

The rule should fire after all currency conversion rules. The account `balance` must be of the type `BigDecimal`. This is partially (non EUR accounts) done by the currency conversion rules. For the EUR accounts, a new rule can be written that simply converts the type to `BigDecimal` (we can even update the `unknownCurrency` rule to handle this situation).

```
    rule reduceLegacyAccounts
       when
           $accountMap1 : Map( this["_type_"] == "Account" )
           $accountMap2 : Map( this["_type_"] == "Account",
              eval( $accountMap1 != $accountMap2 ),
              this["customer_id"] ==$accountMap1["customer_id"],
              this["currency"] == $accountMap1["currency"])
       then
          modify($accountMap1) {
             put("balance", (
                (BigDecimal)$accountMap1.get("balance")).add(
                (BigDecimal)$accountMap2.get("balance")))
          }
          retract( $accountMap2 );
    end
```

Code listing 21: Rule that removes redundant accounts and accumulates their balances (`dataTransformation.drl` file).

The rule above matches two `accountMap` facts. It ensures that they represent two different instances (`eval( $accountMap1 != $accountMap2 )`), they both belong to the same customer (`this["customer_id"] ==$accountMap1["customer_id"]`), and have the same currency (`this["currency"] == $accountMap1["currency"]`). The consequence sums up the two balances and retracts the second `accountMap`.

We are creating dependencies between rules (because this rule should fire after all currency conversion rules). In this case it is tolerable as only a few rules are involved. However, with more complex dependencies, we'll have to introduce a **ruleflow**.

Transformation results

Now, that we've written all transformation rules, the data from the legacy system is in good shape for our model—we can start with populating it. To extract data from the knowledge session, we'll use Drools **queries**.

Query

Drools query looks like a normal rule without the then part. It can be executed directly from a stateful knowledge session for example, session.getQueryResults ("getAllCustomers") or by using QueryCommand. It returns a QueryResults object that can contain multiple QueryResultsRow objects. Every QueryResultsRow instance represents one match of the query. Individual objects/facts can be retrieved from QueryResultsRow. Drools queries are a convenient way of retrieving objects/facts from the knowledge session that match conditions specified by the query. Queries can be parameterized. In a KnowledgeBase, all of the queries share the *same namespace*.

Lets implement queries for retrieving transformed data.

```
query getCustomer
    $customerMap : Map( this["_type_"] == "Customer" )
end

query getAccountByCustomerId (Map customerMap)
    $accountMap : Map( this["_type_"] == "Account",
        this["customer_id"] == customerMap["customer_id"] )
end
```

Code listing 22: Queries for retrieving customer and accounts (dataTransformation.drl file).

The getCustomer query matches any customer map. The second query, getAccountByCustomerId, takes one parameter: customerMap. The customer map parameter is then used to match only accounts that belong to this customer.

We have the ability to extract data from the knowledge session. Let's write the transformation service. It will have only one method for starting the transformation process. This method calls a processCustomer method for every customer map that comes from legacyService.findAllCustomers. Body of the processCustomer method is as follows:

```
/**
 * transforms customerMap, creates and stores new customer
 */
protected void processCustomer(Map customerMap) {
```

```
ValidationReport validationReport = reportFactory
    .createValidationReport();

List<Command<?>> commands = new ArrayList<Command<?>>();
commands.add(CommandFactory.newSetGlobal(
    "validationReport", validationReport));
commands.add(CommandFactory.newInsert(customerMap));
commands.add(new FireAllRulesCommand(
    new RuleNameEqualsAgendaFilter("findAllCustomers")));
commands.add(CommandFactory.newQuery(
    "address", "getAddressByCustomerId",
    new Object[] { customerMap }));
commands.add(CommandFactory.newQuery(
    "accounts", "getAccountByCustomerId",
    new Object[] { customerMap }));
ExecutionResults results = session.execute(
    CommandFactory.newBatchExecution(commands));

if (!validationReport.getMessagesByType(Type.ERROR)
    .isEmpty()) {
  logError(validationReport
      .getMessagesByType(Type.ERROR));
  logWarning(validationReport
      .getMessagesByType(Type.WARNING));
} else {
  logWarning(validationReport
      .getMessagesByType(Type.WARNING));
  Customer customer = buildCustomer(customerMap,
      results);
  bankingService.add(customer); // runs validation
  }
}
```

Code listing 23: Executing the transformation rules and retrieving transformed customer data (`DataTransformationServiceImpl` file).

A new `validationReport` is created, rules are executed in a stateless session, and the customer map is passed in. If the validation report contains any errors, all of the messages are logged and this method terminates. In case there is no error, only warnings are logged, and the customer is built and added to the system. The `buildCustomer` method takes `ExecutionResults`, that contains the results of our queries, as argument. The `add` service call validates the customer (represented in our domain model in this case) before saving.

An excerpt from the `buildCustomer` method can be seen below. It creates all accounts for the customer. The accounts are retrieved from the knowledge session with the `getAccountByCustomerId` query.

```
QueryResults accountQueryResults = (QueryResults)
  results.getValue("accounts");
for (QueryResultsRow accountQueryResult :
  accountQueryResults) {
Map accountMap = (Map) accountQueryResult
    .get("$accountMap");

Account account = new Account();
account.setNumber((Long) accountMap.get("number"));
account.setBalance((BigDecimal) accountMap
    .get("balance"));
//..
customer.addAccount(account);
```

Code listing 24.: Execution of the parameterized query (`DataTransformationServiceImpl` file).

Note that the query command bound all of the account maps under name `accounts` (from code listing 23: `CommandFactory.newQuery("accounts", "getAccountByCustomerId", new Object[] { customerMap })`).

The method retrieves collection of account maps (`results.getValue("accounts")`), and for each `accountMap`, creates a new `Account` object. These accounts are then added to the `Customer` object (`customer.addAccount(account)`).

Implementation of the data loading

In this section, we'll look closer at getting the data from the legacy system. If you're not interested in trying out this example, you can skip this section.

Database setup

The data can come from various sources – database, XML, CSV, and so on. Our application will pull data from a database, however it shouldn't be a problem to work with any other data source. The table structure looks as follows:

```
CREATE TABLE  'droolsBook'.'customer' (
  'customer_id' bigint(20) NOT NULL,
  'first_name' varchar(255) NOT NULL,
  'last_name' varchar(255) NOT NULL,
  email' varchar(255) NOT NULL,
  PRIMARY KEY  ('customer_id')
)
```

Code listing 25: Table structure for legacy customers in a MySQL Database.

```
CREATE TABLE  'droolsBook'.'address' (
  'address_id' bigint(20) NOT NULL default '0',
  'parent_id' bigint(20) NOT NULL,
  'street' varchar(255) NOT NULL,
  'area' varchar(255) NOT NULL,
  'town' varchar(255) NOT NULL,
  'country' varchar(255) NOT NULL,
  PRIMARY KEY  ('address_id')
)
```

Code listing 26: Table structure for legacy addresses in a MySQL Database.

The column `parent_id` from the code listing above represents a foreign key to the customer's primary key. The same applies for the `customer_id` column in the following code:

```
CREATE TABLE  'droolsBook'.'account' (
  'account_id' bigint(20) NOT NULL,
  'name' varchar(255) NOT NULL,
  'currency' varchar(100) NOT NULL,
  'balance' varchar(255) NOT NULL,
  'customer_id' bigint(20) NOT NULL,
  PRIMARY KEY  ('account_id')
)
```

Code listing 27: Table structure for legacy account in a MySQL Database.

As can be seen from the table structures, there is a *one-to-many* relationship between customer and addresses/accounts. Note that the table column names are different than the property names used in our domain model.

You need to set up a database, create the tables from above, and populate them with some sample data.

Project setup

For loading data from database we'll use **iBatis**. (More information about the project iBatis can be found at `http://ibatis.apache.org/`). It is an easy to use data mapper framework. iBatis has rich set of functionalities; we'll use it only for a simple task—to load the data from the database as `java.util.Map` objects. Our rules will then reason over these objects.

We'll need additional libraries on the classpath. They are:

- `ibatis-2.3.3.720.jar`—binary distribution of iBatis.

- JDBC driver for your database; in case of MySQL it is `mysql-connector-java-5.1.6-bin.jar` (MySQL database driver for Java can be downloaded from `http://dev.mysql.com/downloads/connector/j/`).

iBatis configuration

Before any data can be loaded, iBatis needs to be configured. It needs to know about the database and its structure. This is configured in the `SqlMapConfig.xml` file as follows:.

```xml
<?xml version="1.0" encoding="UTF-8" ?>
<!DOCTYPE sqlMapConfig
    PUBLIC "-//ibatis.apache.org//DTD SQL Map Config 2.0//EN"
    "http://ibatis.apache.org/dtd/sql-map-config-2.dtd">
<sqlMapConfig>
    <transactionManager type="JDBC" commitRequired="false">
        <dataSource type="SIMPLE">
            <property name="JDBC.Driver"
                    value="com.mysql.jdbc.Driver" />
            <property name="JDBC.ConnectionURL"
                    value="jdbc:mysql://localhost/droolsBook?createDat
                        abaseIfNotExist=true&amp;useUnicode=true&amp
                        ;characterEncoding=utf-8" />
            <property name="JDBC.Username" value="root" />
            <property name="JDBC.Password" value="" />
        </dataSource>
    </transactionManager>
    <sqlMap resource="Banking.xml" />
</sqlMapConfig>
```

Code listing 28: iBatis main configuration file—`SqlMapConfig.xml`.

The configuration is straightforward. JDBC driver, connection URL, username, and password are given. Further down the configuration, the `sqlMap` element refers to external file (`Banking.xml`) that specifies the table structure.

```xml
<?xml version="1.0" encoding="UTF-8" ?>
<!DOCTYPE sqlMap
    PUBLIC "-//ibatis.apache.org//DTD SQL Map 2.0//EN"
    "http://ibatis.apache.org/dtd/sql-map-2.dtd">
<sqlMap namespace="Banking">
  <select id="findAllCustomers"
      resultClass="java.util.HashMap">
```

```
        select * from customer
    </select>
    <select id="findAddressByCustomerId" parameterClass="long"
        resultClass="java.util.HashMap" >
      select * from address where parent_id = #id#
    </select>
    <select id="findAccountByCustomerId" parameterClass="long"
        resultClass="java.util.HashMap" >
      select * from account where customer_id = #id#
    </select>
  </sqlMap>
```

Code listing 29: iBatis configuration file—`Banking.xml`.

The `sqlMap` element defines three `select` statements: one for loading all customers, one for loading customer's addresses, and one for customer's accounts. All of the `select` statements specify `java.util.HashMap` as the result class. When `select` executes, it creates and populates this map. Each row in a table will be represented by one `HashMap` instance. Table column names are mapped to the map's keys and values to the map's values. The two other `select` elements, `findAddressByCustomerId` and `findAccountByCustomerId`, take one parameter of type, `long`. This parameter is used in the `where` clause of `select`. It represents the foreign key to the customer table.

Running iBatis

The main interface that will be used to interact with iBatis is `com.ibatis.sqlmap.client.SqlMapClient`. An instance of this class can be obtained as follows:

```
Reader reader = Resources
    .getResourceAsReader("SqlMapConfig.xml");
SqlMapClient sqlMapClient = SqlMapClientBuilder
    .buildSqlMapClient(reader);
reader.close();
```

Code listing 30: iBatis set up—building the `SqlMapClient` instance.

After we have the `SqlMapClient` instance, it can be used to load data from the database as follows:

```
List customers = sqlMapClient
    .queryForList("findAllCustomers");
List addresses = sqlMapClient.queryForList(
    "findAddressByCustomerId", new Long(654258));
```

Code listing 31: Running iBatis queries.

The second query shows how we can pass parameters to iBatis. The returned object is in both cases of type `java.util.List`. The list contains zero or many `HashMap` instances. Remember? Each map represents one database record.

We can now write the implementation of the `LegacyBankService` interface from code listing 1. The implementation is straightforward. It simply delegates to `sqlMapClient` as we've seen for example in code listing 30 and code listing 31.

Alternative data loading

Drools supports various data loaders—Smooks (`http://milyn.codehaus.org/Smooks`), JAXB (`https://jaxb.dev.java.net/`), and so on. They can be used as alternatives to iBatis. For example, Smooks can load data from various sources—XML, CSV, Java, and others. It is itself a powerful **ETL (Extract Transform Load)** tool. However, we can use it to do just the data loading part, probably with some minor transformations.

Summary

In this chapter, we saw how to use rules to perform more complex data transformation tasks. These rules are easy to read and can be expanded without increasing the overall complexity. However, it should be noted that Drools is probably not the best option if we want to carry out high throughput/high performance data transformations.

We saw how to write rules over a generic data type such as a `java.util.Map`. You should try to avoid using this kind of generic data type. However, it is not always possible, especially when you are doing data transformation and you don't know much about the data.

Some testing approaches were shown. Use of `AgendaFilter` as a way to isolate the individual rule tests was also demonstrated. Please note that upon execution, all of the rules are matched and placed onto the agenda. However, only those that pass this filter are executed. `ObjectFilter` was used to filter facts from the knowledge session when we were verifying test assertions.

Finally, some examples were given on how to use Drools queries. They represent very convenient way of accessing facts in the knowledge session.

5

Human-readable Rules

Business rules implementations presented so far were aimed mostly at developers. However, it is sometimes needed that these rules are readable and understandable by the business analysts. Ideally, they should be able to change the rules or even write new ones. An important aspect of business rules is their readability and user friendliness. Looking at a rule, you should immediately have an idea of what it is about. In this chapter, we'll look at **Domain Specific Languages (DSLs)**, decision tables, and rule flows to create human-readable rules.

Domain Specific Language

The **domain** in this sense represents the business area (for example, life insurance or billing). Rules are expressed with the terminology of the problem domain. This means that domain experts can understand, validate, and modify these rules more easily.

You can think of DSL as a translator. It defines how to translate sentences from the problem-specific terminology into rules. The translation process is defined in a `.dsl` file. The sentences themselves are stored in a `.dslr` file. The result of this process must be a valid `.drl` file.

Building a simple DSL might look like:

```
[condition][]There is a Customer with firstName
{name}=$customer : Customer(firstName == {name})
[consequence][]Greet Customer=System.out.println("Hello " +
$customer.getFirstName());
```

Code listing 1: Simple DSL file `simple.dsl`.

The code listing above contains only two lines (each begins with [). However, because the lines are too long, they are wrapped effectively creating four lines. This will be the case in most of the code listings.

When you are using the Drools Eclipse plugin to write this DSL, enter the text before the first equal sign into the field called **Language expression**, the text after equal sign into **Rule mapping**, leave the **object** field blank and select the correct scope.

The previous DSL defines two DSL mappings. They map a DSLR sentence to a DRL rule. The first one translates to a condition that matches a `Customer` object with the specified first name. The first name is captured into a variable called `name`. This variable is then used in the rule condition. The second line translates to a greeting message that is printed on the console. The following `.dslr` file can be written based on the previous DSL:

```
package droolsbook.dsl;
import droolsbook.bank.model.*;
expander simple.dsl
rule "hello rule"
  when
    There is a Customer with firstName "David"
  then
    Greet Customer
end
```

Code listing 2: Simple `.dslr` file (`simple.dslr`) with rule that greets a customer with name `David`.

As can be seen, the structure of a `.dslr` file is the same as the structure of a `.drl` file. Only the rule conditions and consequences are different. Another thing to note is the line containing `expander simple.dsl`. It informs Drools how to translate sentences in this file into valid rules. Drools reads the `simple.dslr` file and *tries to translate/expand each line by applying all mappings* from the `simple.dsl` file (it does it in a single pass process, line-by-line from top to bottom). The *order of lines is important* in a `.dsl` file. Please note that one condition/consequence must be written on one line, otherwise the expansion won't work (for example, the condition after the `when` clause, from the rule above, must be on one line).

When you are writing `.dslr` files, consider using the Drools Eclipse plugin. It provides a special editor for `.dslr` files that has an editing mode and a read-only mode for viewing the resulting `.drl` file. A simple DSL editor is provided as well.

The result of the translation process will look like the following screenshot:

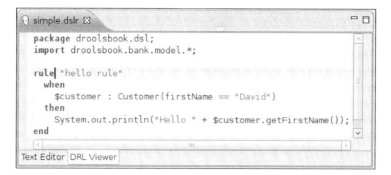

This translation process happens in memory and no `.drl` file is physically stored. We can now run this example. First of all, a knowledge base must be created from the `simple.dsl` and `simple.dslr` files. The process of creating a package using a DSL is as follows (only the package creation is shown, the rest is the same as we've seen in Chapter 2, *Basic Rules*):

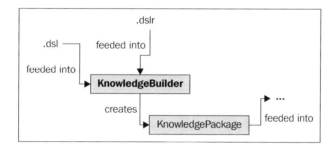

`KnowledgeBuilder` acts as the translator. It takes the `.dslr` file, and based on the `.dsl` file, creates the DRL. This DRL is then used as normal (we don't see it; it's internal to `KnowledgeBuilder`). The implementation is as follows:

```
private KnowledgeBase createKnowledgeBaseFromDSL()
    throws Exception {
  KnowledgeBuilder builder =
      KnowledgeBuilderFactory.newKnowledgeBuilder();
  builder.add(ResourceFactory.newClassPathResource(
      "simple.dsl"), ResourceType.DSL);
  builder.add(ResourceFactory.newClassPathResource(
      "simple.dslr"), ResourceType.DSLR);
  if (builder.hasErrors()) {
    throw new RuntimeException(builder.getErrors()
        .toString());
  }
  KnowledgeBase knowledgeBase = KnowledgeBaseFactory
```

```
      .newKnowledgeBase();
  knowledgeBase.addKnowledgePackages(
      builder.getKnowledgePackages());
  return knowledgeBase;
}
```

Code listing 3: Creating knowledge base from `.dsl` and `.dslr` files.

The `.dsl` and subsequently the `.dslr` files are passed into `KnowledgeBuilder`. The rest is similar to what we've seen before.

DSL as an interface

DSLs can be also looked at as another level of indirection between your `.drl` files and business requirements. It works as shown in the following figure:

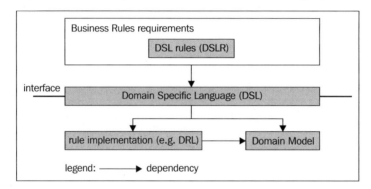

The figure above shows DSL as an interface (dependency diagram). At the top are the business requirements as defined by the business analyst. These requirements are represented as DSL sentences (`.dslr` file). The DSL then represents the interface between DSL sentences and rule implementation (`.drl` file) and the domain model. For example, we can change the transformation to make the resulting rules more efficient without changing the language. Further, we can change the language, for example, to make it more user friendly, without changing the rules. All this can be done just by changing the `.dsl` file.

DSL for validation rules

The first three implemented object/field required rules from Chapter 2, *Basic Rules*, can be rewritten as:

- If the Customer does not have an address, then Display warning message
- If the Customer does not have a phone number or it is blank, then Display error message

- If the Account does not have an owner, then Display error message for Account

We can clearly see that all of them operate on some object (Customer/Account), test its property (address/phone/owner), and display a message (warning/error) possibly with some context (account). Our `validation.dslr` file might look like the following code:

```
expander validation.dsl

rule "address is required"
    when
        The Customer does not have address
    then
        Display warning
end

rule "phone number is required"
    when
        The Customer does not have phone number or it is blank
    then
        Display error
end

rule "account owner is required"
    when
        The Account does not have owner
    then
        Display error for Account
end
```

Code listing 4: First DSL approach at defining the required object/field rules (`validation.dslr` file).

The conditions could be mapped like this:

```
[condition][]The {object} does not have {field}=${object} : {object}(
{field} == null )
```

Code listing 5: `validation.dsl`.

This covers the address and account conditions completely. For the phone number rule, we have to add the following mapping at the beginning of the `validation.dsl` file:

```
[condition][] or it is blank =  == "" ||
```

Code listing 6: Mapping that checks for a blank phone number.

As it stands, the phone number condition will be expanded to:

```
$Customer : Customer( phone number  == "" || == null )
```

Code listing 7: Unfinished phone number condition.

To correct it, `phone number` has to be mapped to `phoneNumber`. This can be done by adding the following at the end of the `validation.dsl` file:

```
[condition][]phone number=phoneNumber
```

Code listing 8: Phone number mapping.

The conditions are working. Now, let's focus on the consequences. The following mapping will do the job:

```
[consequence][]Display {message_type} for {object}={message_type}(
    kcontext, ${object} );
[consequence][]Display {message_type}={message_type}( kcontext );
```

Code listing 9: Consequence mappings.

The three validation rules are now being expanded to the same `.drl` representation as we've seen in Chapter 2.

File formats

Before we go further, we'll examine each file format in more detail.

DSL file format

A line in a `.dsl` file has the following format:

```
[<scope>][<Type>]<language expression>=<rule mapping>
```

Code listing 10: The format of one line in a `.dsl` file.

As we've already seen, an example of a line in DSL file might look like this:

```
[condition][droolsbook.bank.model.Customer]The Customer does not have
address=Customer(address == null)
```

Code listing 11: Sample line from DSL file (note that it is just one line that has been wrapped).

The scope can have the following values:

- `condition`: Specifies that this mapping can be used in the condition part of a rule.
- `consequence`: Specifies that this mapping can be used in the consequence part of a rule.
- `*`: Specifies that this mapping can be used in both the condition and the consequence part of a rule.
- `keyword`: This mapping is applied to the whole file (not just the condition or the consequence part). Used mainly when writing DSLs in languages other than English or to hide the package/import/global statements at the beginning of the file behind a business friendly sentence.

Type can be used to further limit the scope of the mapping. Scope and Type are used by the Drools Eclipse plugin to provide auto-completion when writing `.dslr` files (when pressing *Ctrl + Space*, only relevant choices are offered). This is especially useful with the multiple constraints feature (refer to the section, *DSL for multiple constraints in a condition*).

DSL supports comments by starting the line with the hash character, #. For example:

```
#this is a comment in a .dsl file
```

DRL file format

As a side note, in a `.drl` file, it is valid to write the whole rule on a single line. This allows us to write more complex DSLs because one sentence in `.dslr` file can be translated into multiple conditions—even the whole rule. For example, these are valid rules on a single line:

```
rule "addressRequired" when Customer( address == null ) then
warning(kcontext); end
```

Code listing 12: `addressRequired` rule *on one line.*

Make sure that you add spaces between Drools keywords. Another more complex example of a rule on one line:

```
rule "studentAccountCustomerAgeLessThan" when Customer( eval (year
sPassedSince(dateOfBirth) >= 27) ) and $account : Account( type ==
Account.Type.STUDENT ) then error(kcontext, $account); System.out.
println("another statement"); end
```

Code listing 13: `studentAccountCustomerAgeLessThan` rule *on one line.*

The preceding rule contains two conditions and two Java statements in the consequence block. There is also an optional and keyword between the conditions to make it more readable.

DSLR file format

A .dslr file contains the sentences written using the DSL. The .dslr file is very similar to the .drl file. One thing to note is that by prepending a line with a '>', we can turn off the expander for the line. This allows us to write a hybrid .dslr file that contains traditional DRL rules and DSL rules. For example, if we are not yet sure how to map some complex rule, we can leave it in its original .drl file format.

DSL for multiple constraints in a condition

We'll go through more complex DSLs. Let's look at a standard condition for example:

```
Account( owner != null, balance > 100, currency == "EUR" )
```

Code listing 14: Condition that matches some account.

It is difficult to write DSL that will allow us to create conditions with any subset of constraints from the code listing above (without writing down all possible permutations). The '-' feature comes to the rescue:

```
[condition][]There is an Account that=$account : Account( )
[condition][]-has owner=owner != null
[condition][]-has balance greater than {amount}=balance > {amount}
[condition][]-has currency equal to {currency}=currency == {currency}
```

Code listing 15: DSL using the '-' feature. This can create seven combinations of the constraints.

When the DSL condition starts with '-', the DSL parser knows that this constraint should be added to the last condition (in a .dslr file). With the preceding DSL, the following condition can be created:

```
There is an Account that
-   has currency equal to "USD"
"has balance greater than 2000"
```

Code listing 16: Condition using the '-' feature (in a .dslr file).

The '-' feature increases the flexibility of the resulting language. It works just fine for simple cases involving only one pair of brackets. In case of multiple brackets in the condition, Drools always adds the constraint to the last pair of brackets. This may not always be what we want. We have to find a different way of specifying multiple constraints in a condition. We can also write our DSL in the following manner:

```
[condition] [] There is an Account that {constraints} = Account (
{constraints} )
[condition] [] has {field} equal to {value}={field} == {value}
[condition] [] and has {field} equal to {value}=, {field} == {value}
```

Code listing 17: Flexible DSL that can be expanded to a condition with two field constraints.

With this DSL, the following DSLR can be written:

```
There is an Account that has owner equal to null and has balance equal
to 100
```

Code listing 18: DSLR that describes an account with two constraints.

If we want to have more conditions, we can simply duplicate the last line in the DSL. Remember? Translation is a single pass process.

Named capture groups

Sometimes, when a more complex DSL is needed, we need to be more precise at specifying what a valid match is. We can use named capture groups with regular expressions to give us the needed precision. For example:

```
{name:[a-zA-Z]+}
```

Code listing 19: Name that matches only characters.

Regular expressions (java.util.regex.Pattern) can be used not only for capturing variables but also within the DSL. For example, in order to carry out case insensitive matching. If we look at the DSL from code listing 15, the users should be allowed to type Account, account, ACCOUNT, or even aCcount in their .dslr files. This can be done by enabling the embedded case insensitive flag expression — (?i):
```
[condition] [] There is an (?i:account) that ....
```
Another useful example is sentences that are sensitive to gender — (s)?he to support "he" and "she", and so on.

In order to make the sentences space insensitive, Drools automatically replaces all spaces with \s+. Each \s+ matches one or more spaces. For example, the following line in a .dslr file will be successfully expanded by the DSL from code listing 15:
```
There     is          an          Account that ....
```

DSL for data transformation rules

We'll now implement DSL for the data transformation rules from Chapter 4, *Data Transformation*. We'll reuse our rule unit tests to verify that we don't change the functionality of the rules but only their representation. The unit test class will be extended and the method for creating `KnowledgeBase` will be overridden to use the `.dsl` file and `.dslr` file as inputs. Rule names will stay the same. Let's start with the `twoEqualAddressesDifferentInstance` rule:

```
rule twoEqualAddressesDifferentInstance
    when
        There is legacy Address-1
        There is legacy Address-2
        - same as legacy Address-1
    then
        remove legacy Address-2
        Display WARNING for legacy Address-2
end
```

Code listing 20: Rule for removing redundant addresses (`dataTransformation.dslr` file).

The conditions can be implemented with the following DSL:

```
[condition][] legacy {object}-{id} = {object}-{id}
[condition][] There is {object}-{id} = ${object}{id} : Map( this["_
type_"] == "{object}" )
[condition][]- same as {object}-{id} = this == ${object}{id}, eval(
${object}1 != ${object}2 )
```

Code listing 21: DSL for conditions (`dataTransformation.dsl` file).

The first mapping is a simple translation rule, where we remove the word `legacy`. The next mapping captures a map with its type. The last mapping includes the equality test with the object identity test. Mapping for consequences is as follows:

```
[consequence][] legacy {object}-{id} = ${object}{id}
[consequence][]Display {message_type_enum} for {object}=validationRepo
rt.addMessage(reportFactory.createMessage(Message.Type.{message_type_
enum}, kcontext.getRule().getName(), {object}));
[consequence][]remove {object} = retract( {object} );
```

Code listing 22: DSL for consequences.

The first mapping just removes the word `legacy`. The second mapping adds a message to `validationReport`. Finally, the last mapping removes an object from the knowledge session. This is all we need for the `twoEqualAddressesDifferentInstance` rule.

As you can see, we started with the sentence in the domain specific language (code listing 1) and then we've written the transformation to reflect the rules (from Chapter 4). In reality, this is an iterative process. You'll modify the `.dslr` and `.dsl` files until you are happy with the results. It is also a good idea to write your rules in standard `.drl` first and only then try to write a DSL for them.

We'll move to the next rule, `addressNormalizationUSA`:

```
rule addressNormalizationUSA
    when
        There is legacy Address-1
        - country is one of "US", "U.S.", "USA", "U.S.A"
    then
        for legacy Address-1 set country to USA
end
```

Code listing 23: DSLR rule for normalizing address country field.

The rule just needs another constraint type:

```
[condition][]- country is one of {country_list} = this["country"] in
({country_list})
```

Code listing 24: Another condition mapping.

The consequence is defined with two mappings. The first one will translate the country to an `enum` and the second will then perform the assignment.

```
[consequence][]set country to {country}=set country to Address.
Country.{country}
[consequence][]for {object}set {field} to {value} = modify( {object} )
\{ put("{field}", {value} ) \}
```

Code listing 25: Consequence mapping for the country normalization rule.

Please note that the curly brackets are escaped. Moreover, the original rule used `mvel` dialect. It is a good idea to write your rules using the same dialect. It makes the DSL easier. Otherwise, the DSL will have to be "dialect aware".

The other country normalization rule can be written without modifying the DSL. We'll now continue with `unknownCountry` rule:

```
rule unknownCountry
Apply after address normalizations
    when
        There is legacy Address-1
        - country is not normalized
```

```
    then
        Display ERROR for legacy Address-1
    end
```

Code listing 26: DSLR representation of the `unknownCountry` rule.

The whole sentence `Apply after address normalizations` is mapped as a keyword mapping:

```
    [keyword][] Apply after address normalizations = salience -10
```

Code listing 27: `salience` keyword mapping.

Now, we can use the other rule attributes to achieve the same goal just by changing the DSL.

Additional mapping that is needed:

```
    [condition][]- country is not normalized = eval(!($Address1.
    get("country") instanceof Address.Country))
```

Code listing 28: Another condition mapping.

In the condition mapping, the `$Address1` is hard-coded. This is fine for the rules that we have.

As you can imagine, the rest of the rules follow similar principles.

What we have achieved by writing this DSL is better readability. A business analyst can verify the correctness of these rules more easily. We could push this further by defining a complete DSL that can represent any concept from the problem domain. The business analyst will then be able to express any business requirement just by editing the `.dslr` file.

Decision tables

Decision tables are another form of human-readable rules that are useful when there are lots of similar rules with different values. Rules that share the same conditions with different parameters can be captured in a decision table. Decision tables can be represented in an Excel spreadsheet (`.xls` file) or a comma separated values (`.csv` file) format. Starting from version 5.0, Drools supports web-based decision tables as well. They won't be discussed in this book; however, they are very similar. Let's have a look at a simple decision table in `.xls` format.

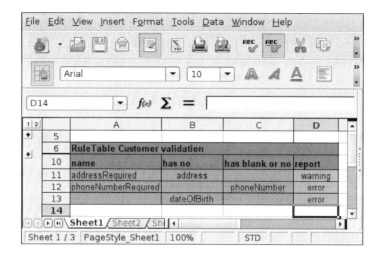

The preceding screenshot shows a decision table in `validation.xls` opened with OpenOffice Calc editor. It shows one decision table for validating a customer. Line **10** shows four columns. The first one defines rule name, the next two define conditions, and the last one is for defining actions/consequences. The next three lines (**11-13**) represent the individual rules—one line per rule. Each cell defines parameters for conditions/consequences. If a cell doesn't have a value, that condition/action is ignored. Some rows in the spreadsheet are grouped and hidden (see the two plus (**+**) signs in the left). This makes the decision tables more user-friendly, especially for business users. Please note that tables don't have to start on the first column. The full `validation.xls` file is as follows:

	A	B	C	D
1	**RuleSet**	droolsbook.decisiontables.validation		
2	**Import**	droolsbook.bank.model.*, droolsbook.bank.service.*, function droolsbook.bank.service.ValidationHelper.error, function droolsbook.bank.service.ValidationHelper.warning,		
3	**Variables**	ValidationReport validationReport, ReportFactory reportFactory, BankingInquiryService inquiryService		
4	**Notes**	Decision tables for customer validation		
5				
6	**RuleTable Customer validation**			
7	NAME	CONDITION	CONDITION	ACTION
8		$customer : Customer		
9		$param == null	$param == null || == ""	$param(kcontext);
10	name	has no	has blank or no	report
11	addressRequired	address		warning
12	phoneNumberRequired		phoneNumber	error
13		dateOfBirth		error

Every file for defining decision tables start with a global configuration section. The configuration consists of name-value pairs. As can be seen from the screenshot above:

- `RuleSet` defines the package
- `Import` specifies the classes used, including static imported functions
- `Variables` is used for global variables
- `Notes` can be any text

Further:

- `Functions` can be used to write local functions as in `.drl` format
- `Worksheet` specifies the sheet to be used; by default only the first sheet is checked for rules

The `RuleTable` then denotes the start of the decision table. It has no specific purpose. It is used only to group rules that operate on the same objects and share conditions. The next line defines column types. The following column types are available:

- `CONDITION`—defines a single rule condition or constraint, the following row can contain type for this condition, if it doesn't, then the next row must define full condition (with a type, not just a constraint as in the preceding case).
- `ACTION`—rule action. Similar to condition, the next line can contain any global or bound variable. Drools will then assume that the next line is a method that should be called on this global or bound variable.
- `PRIORITY`—for defining rule salience.
- `NAME`—by default rule names are auto generated, `NAME` can be used to explicitly specify the name.
- `No-loop` or `Unloop`—specifies the rule no-loop attribute.
- `XOR-GROUP`—specifies rule activation-group (this will be discussed in the upcoming section, *Drools Flow*).

For full configuration options, please consult the Drools manual (`http://www.jboss.org/drools/documentation.html`).

The next line from the preceding screenshot looks similar to what we see in a `.drl` file. It is a simple condition that matches any `Customer` object and exposes this object as the `$customer` variable. The only difference is that there are no brackets. They will be added automatically by Drools at parsing time. Please note that this line contains only two columns. The first two columns are **merged** into one column. This is because they operate on the same type (`Customer`). If we don't merge the two columns, they'll match two separate objects (which may or may not be the same instance).

The next line then defines individual constraints (in case of conditions) or code blocks (in case of actions). Special parameters can be used as `$param` or `$1`, `$2`, `$3`, and so on. The first one is used if our constraint needs only one parameter; otherwise, the `$n` format should be used.

The following line (corresponds to line 10 in the preceding screenshot showing a decision table in `validation.xls` file) is for pure informational purposes. It should contain some meaningful description of the column/action so that we don't have to always look at how it is implemented (by expanding/collapsing rows).

Finally, the actual values follow in subsequent rows. Each line represents one rule. For example, the first line gets translated behind the scenes to the following `.drl` rule:

```
#From row number: 11
rule "addressRequired"
    when
        $customer : Customer(address == null)
    then
        warning(kcontext);
end
```

Code listing 29: Generated rule from a decision table.

The `.drl` rule is exactly the same as we've implemented in Chapter 3, *Validation*. We can even reuse the same unit test to test this rule.

Advantages of a decision table

Here are the advantages of a decision table:

- It is easy to read and understand.
- Refactoring is quicker because we just have to change a column definition to change a group of related rules (that is, it is easy to change conditions across group of rules).
- Isolation is similar to DSL; decision tables can hide the rule implementation details.
- Provides separation between the rules and data (they are still in one file but separated).
- Any formatting available in a spreadsheet editor can be applied to present these data in a more readable manner (for example, using a drop-down for a list of values. It can reduce errors from mistyping a value into a cell by allowing only valid values).
- Eclipse Drools plugin can also validate a spreadsheet. This is very useful when writing rules. The **Problems** view in Eclipse shows what exactly is wrong with the generated `.drl` file.

Disadvantages of a decision table

- It can be awkward to debug/write these rules. Sometimes it helps to convert the spreadsheet to a `.drl` file, save this file, and fix it, as we're used to.

- Decision tables shouldn't be used if the rules don't share many conditions. Further, the order of conditions is important. In a decision table, the order of a condition is given by the order of a column. Care should be taken if you want to convert the existing DRL rules into decision tables, as the order of conditions may change (to take advantage of the reuse).

- XLS is a binary format which makes version management more difficult.

Calculating the interest rate

As an example, we'll calculate the interest rate based on the account `balance`, `currency`, `duration`, and `type`. This calculation is ideal for a decision table because we have a lot of constraints that are reused across rules with different data. The decision table looks as follows:

	A	B	C	D	E
1	**RuleSet**	droolsbook.decisiontables			
2	**Import**	droolsbook.decisiontables.bank.model.*, droolsbook.bank.model.Customer, droolsbook.bank.model.Account.Type, java.math.*,			
3	**Notes**	Decision tables for calculating interest rates.			
4					
5	RuleTable Interest Calculation				
6	CONDITION	CONDITION	CONDITION	CONDITION	ACTION
7	$a:Account				
8	type == Account.Type. $param	currency	balance >= $1 && < $2	monthsBetweenStartAnd EndDate >= $1 && < $2	$a.setInterestRate(new BigDecimal($param));
9	type	currency	balance <min, max)	months	set interest rate
10	TRANSACTIONAL	EUR			"0.01"
11	STUDENT	EUR	0, 2000		"1.00"
12	SAVINGS	EUR	0, 100	0, 1	"0.00"
13	SAVINGS	EUR	0, 100	1, 3	"0.10"
14	SAVINGS	EUR	0, 100	3, 12	"2.00"
15	SAVINGS	EUR	100, 1000	0, 1	"0.10"
16	SAVINGS	EUR	100, 1000	1, 3	"3.00"
17	SAVINGS	EUR	100, 1000	3, 12	"3.25"
18	SAVINGS	EUR	1000, 5000	0, 1	"0.10"
19	SAVINGS	EUR	1000, 5000	1, 3	"3.25"
20	SAVINGS	EUR	1000, 5000	3, 12	"3.50"
21	SAVINGS	EUR	5000, 10000	0, 1	"0.10"
22	SAVINGS	EUR	5000, 10000	1, 3	"3.50"
23	SAVINGS	EUR	5000, 10000	3, 12	"3.75"
24	SAVINGS	USD	0, 100	0, 1	"0.00"

Please note that the `Account` object is used in every condition so the CONDITION columns are merged. We can see the use of parameters `$1` and `$2`. The first line can be read as: *For every transactional account with currency EUR, set its interest rate to 0.01 percent (regardless of the balance)*. Another line can be read as: *For every savings account whose balance is between 100 EUR and 1000 EUR that is opened for one to three months, set its interest rate to 3 percent*. The following rule will be generated:

```
#From row number: 16
rule "Interest Calculation_16"
    when
        $a:Account(type == Account.Type.SAVINGS,
            currency == "EUR", balance >= 100 && < 1000,
            monthsBetweenStartAndEndDate >= 1 && < 3)
    then
        $a.setInterestRate(new BigDecimal("3.00"));
end
```

Code listing 30: Generated rule for calculating the interest rate.

If we had not used a decision table, we would have to write such rules by hand. Please note that the second condition column in the decision table above doesn't have any operator or operand. It simply says `currency`. It is a special feature and this is automatically translated to `currency == $param`.

The last condition column uses `getMonthsBetweenStartAndEndDate` method of the `Account` class.

```
    private DateMidnight startDate;
    private DateMidnight endDate;

    /**
     * @return number of months between start and end date
     */
    public int getMonthsBetweenStartAndEndDate() {
      if (startDate == null || endDate == null) {
        return 0;
      }
      return Months.monthsBetween(startDate, endDate)
          .getMonths();
    }
```

Code listing 31: Implementation of `getMonthsBetweenStartAndEndDate` method of `Account`.

The implementation uses the Joda-Time library to do the calculation.

Project setup

The following libraries are needed on the classpath:

- `drools-decisiontables-5.0.1.jar`: used for compiling spreadsheets into `.drl` file format; it knows how to handle `.xls` and `.csv` formats.

- `jxl-2.4.2.jar` XLS API: used for parsing `.xls` spreadsheets.

Testing

For testing the interest calculation rules, we'll use a stateless knowledge session, an account, and a date object. All tests will reuse the stateless session. The test can be set up as follows:

```
static StatelessKnowledgeSession session;
Account account;
static DateMidnight DATE;

@BeforeClass
public static void setUpClass() throws Exception {
  KnowledgeBase knowledgeBase =
    createKnowledgeBaseFromSpreadsheet();
  session = knowledgeBase.newStatelessKnowledgeSession();
  DATE = new DateMidnight(2008, 1, 1);
}

@Before
public void setUp() throws Exception {
  account = new Account();
}
```

Code listing 32: Setup of the decision table test.

The date will be used to set deposit durations. An account is created for every test method. The `createKnowledgeBaseFromSpreadsheet` method is implemented as follows:

```
private static KnowledgeBase createKnowledgeBaseFromSpreadsheet()
    throws Exception {
  DecisionTableConfiguration dtconf =KnowledgeBuilderFactory
    .newDecisionTableConfiguration();
  dtconf.setInputType( DecisionTableInputType.XLS );
  //dtconf.setInputType( DecisionTableInputType.CSV );
  KnowledgeBuilder knowledgeBuilder =
    KnowledgeBuilderFactory.newKnowledgeBuilder();
  knowledgeBuilder.add(ResourceFactory.newClassPathResource(
```

```
                "interest calculation.xls"), ResourceType.DTABLE,
                dtconf);
        //knowledgeBuilder.add(ResourceFactory
        //  .newClassPathResource("interest calculation.csv"),
        //  ResourceType.DTABLE, dtconf);

        if (knowledgeBuilder.hasErrors()) {
          throw new RuntimeException(knowledgeBuilder.getErrors()
              .toString());
        }

        KnowledgeBase knowledgeBase = KnowledgeBaseFactory
          .newKnowledgeBase();
        knowledgeBase.addKnowledgePackages(
            knowledgeBuilder.getKnowledgePackages());
        return knowledgeBase;
    }
```

Code listing 33: Creating a `knowledgeBase` from a spreadsheet.

As opposed to the other knowledge definitions, the decision table needs a special configuration that is encapsulated in `DecisionTableConfiguration` class. This configuration specifies the type of decision table and it is then passed on to the knowledge builder. The commented lines show how to create a knowledge base from a `.csv` format. The rest should be familiar.

Note if you want to see the generated `.drl` source, you can get it like this:

```
        String drlString = DecisionTableFactory
            .loadFromInputStream(ResourceFactory
                .newClassPathResource("interest calculation.xls")
                .getInputStream(), dtconf);
```

Code listing 34: Getting the `.drl` representation of the decision table.

It is stored in a `drlString` string variable; it can be printed to the console and used for debugging purposes.

We'll now write a test for depositing 125 EUR for 40 days:

```
    @Test
    public void deposit125EURfor40Days() throws Exception {
        account.setType(Account.Type.SAVINGS);
        account.setBalance(new BigDecimal("125.00"));
        account.setCurrency("EUR");
        account.setStartDate(DATE.minusDays(40));
        account.setEndDate(DATE);
```

```
        session.execute(account);

        assertEquals(new BigDecimal("3.00"), account
            .getInterestRate());
    }
```

Code listing 35: Test for depositing 125 EUR for 40 days.

The preceding test verifies that the correct interest rate is set on the `account`.

And one test for default transactional account rate:

```
    @Test
    public void defaultTransactionalRate() throws Exception {
        account.setType(Account.Type.TRANSACTIONAL);
        account.setCurrency("EUR");

        session.execute(account);

        assertEquals(new BigDecimal("0.01"), account
            .getInterestRate());
    }
```

Code listing 36: Test for the default transactional account rate.

The test above, again, verifies that the correct interest rate is set.

Comma Separated values

The XLS spreadsheet can be easily converted into CSV format. Just select **Save as CSV** in your spreadsheet editor. However, there is one caveat — CSV format doesn't support merging of columns by default. For overcoming this, Drools has the following workaround: if we add three dots at the end of type declarations, they will be merged into one. It can be seen in the last line of the following CSV excerpt:

```
"RuleTable Interest Calculation",,,,
"CONDITION","CONDITION","CONDITION","CONDITION","ACTION"
"$a:Account...","$a:Account...","$a:Account...","$a:Account...",
```

Code listing 37: Excerpt from the `interest calculation.csv` file.

It is the only change that needs to be done. Tests should pass for CSV format as well.

CSV is a text format as opposed to XLS, which is a binary format. Binary format makes version management harder. For example, it is very difficult to merge changes between two binary files. CSV doesn't have these problems. On the other hand, the presentation suffers.

Rule Templates

If you like the concept of decision tables, you may want to look at **Drools Rule Templates**. They are similar to the decision tables but more powerful. With Rule Templates, the data is fully separated from the rule (for example, it can come from a database and have different templates over the same data). You have more power in defining the resulting rule. The data can define any part of rule (for example, condition operator, class, or property name). For more information, refer to the *Rule Templates* section of the *Drools Experts User Guide* (available at `http://www.jboss.org/drools/documentation.html`).

Drools Flow

Drools Flow (or **ruleflow** in short) is another way we can have human readable rules. It is not a substitute to rules as was the case with DSLs and decision tables. It is a way of defining the execution flow between complex rules. The rules are then easier to understand.

Drools Flow can *externalize the execution order from the rules*. The execution order can be then managed externally. Potentially, you may define more execution orders for one `KnowledgeBase`.

Drools Flow can be even used as a workflow engine replacement. It can execute arbitrary actions or user-defined work items at specific points within the flow. It can be even persisted as we'll see in Chapter 8, *Drools Flow*, which shows a bigger example of using ruleflows.

Drools Agenda

Before we talk about how to manage rule execution order, we have to understand Drools Agenda. When an object is inserted into the knowledge session, Drools tries to match this object with all of the possible rules. If a rule has all of its conditions met, its consequence can be executed. We say that a rule is **activated**. Drools records this event by placing this rule onto its agenda (it is a collection of activated rules). As you may imagine, many rules can be activated, and also deactivated, depending on what objects are in the rule session. After the `fireAllRules` method call, Drools *picks* one rule from the agenda and executes its consequence. It may or may not cause further activations or deactivations. This continues until the Drools Agenda is empty.

The purpose of the agenda is to manage the execution order of rules.

Methods for managing rule execution order

The following are the methods for managing the rule execution order (from the user's perspective). They can be viewed as alternatives to ruleflow. All of them are defined as rule attributes.

- `salience`: This is the most basic one. Every rule has a salience value. By default it is set to `0`. Rules with higher salience value will fire first. The problem with this approach is that it is hard to maintain. If we want to add new rule with some priority, we may have to shift the priorities of existing rules. It is often hard to figure out why a rule has certain salience, so we have to comment every salience value. It creates an invisible dependency on other rules.

- `activation-group`: This used to be called **xor-group**. When two or more rules with the same activation group are on the agenda, Drools will fire just one of them.

- `agenda-group`: Every rule has an agenda group. By default it is `MAIN`. However, it can be overridden. This allows us to partition Drools Agenda into multiple groups that can be executed separately.

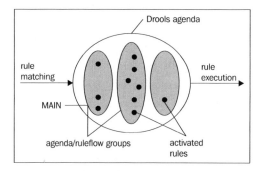

The figure above shows partitioned Agenda with activated rules. The matched rules are coming from left and going into Agenda. One rule is chosen from the Agenda at a time and then executed/fired.

At runtime we can programmatically set the active Agenda group (through the `getAgenda().getAgendaGroup(String agendaGroup).setFocus()` method of `KnowledgeRuntime`), or declaratively, by setting the rule attribute `auto-focus` to `true`. When a rule is activated and has this attribute set to `true`, the active agenda group is automatically changed to rule's agenda group. Drools maintains a **stack** of agenda groups. Whenever the focus is set to a different agenda group, Drools adds this group onto this stack. When there are no rules to fire in the current agenda group, Drools pops from the stack and sets the agenda group to the next one. Agenda groups are similar to ruleflow groups with the exception that ruleflow groups are not stacked.

Note that only one instance of each of these attributes is allowed per rule (for example, a rule can only be in one `ruleflow-group`; however, it can also define a `salience` within that group).

Ruleflow

As we've already said, ruleflow can externalize the execution order from the rule definitions. Rules just define a `ruleflow-group` attribute, which is similar to `agenda-group`. It is then used to define the execution order. A simple ruleflow (in the `example.rf` file) is shown in the following screenshot:

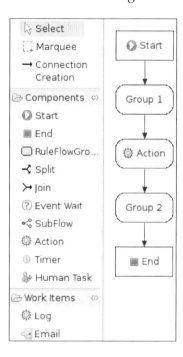

The preceding screenshot shows a ruleflow opened with the Drools Eclipse plugin. On the lefthand side are the components that can be used when building a ruleflow. On the righthand side is the ruleflow itself. It has a **Start** node which goes to ruleflow group called **Group 1**. After it finishes execution, an **Action** is executed, then the flow continues to another ruleflow group called **Group 2**, and finally it finishes at an **End** node.

Ruleflow definitions are stored in a file with the `.rf` extension. This file has an XML format and defines the structure and layout for presentational purposes.

Another useful rule attribute for managing which rules can be activated is lock-on-active. It is a special form of the no-loop attribute. It can be used in combination with ruleflow-group or agenda-group. If it is set to true, and an agenda/ruleflow group becomes active/focused, it discards any further activations for the rule until a different group becomes active. Please note that activations that are already on the agenda will be fired.

A ruleflow consists of various nodes. Each node has a name, type, and other specific attributes. You can see and change these attributes by opening the standard **Properties** view in Eclipse while editing the ruleflow file. The basic node types are as follows:

- **Start**
- **End**
- **Action**
- **RuleFlowGroup**
- **Split**
- **Join**

They are discussed in the following sections.

Start

It is the initial node. The flow begins here. Each ruleflow needs one start node. This node has no incoming connection—just one outgoing connection.

End

It is a terminal node. When execution reaches this node, the whole ruleflow is terminated (all of the active nodes are canceled). This node has one incoming connection and no outgoing connections.

Action

Used to execute some arbitrary block of code. It is similar to the rule consequence—it can reference global variables and can specify dialect.

RuleFlowGroup

This node will activate a ruleflow-group, as specified by its RuleFlowGroup attribute. It should match the value in ruleflow-group rule attribute.

Split

This node splits the execution flow into one or many branches. It has two properties—name and type. Name is just for display purposes. Type can have three values: **AND**, **OR**, and **XOR**:

- **AND**: The execution continues through all of the branches.

- **OR**: Each branch has a condition. The condition is basically same as a rule condition. If the condition is true, the ruleflow continues through this branch. There must be at least one condition that is true; otherwise, an exception will be thrown.

- **XOR**: Similar to OR type, each branch has a condition, but in this case, with a priority. The ruleflow continues through just **one** branch, whose condition is true and it has the lowest value in the priority field. There must be at least one condition that is true; otherwise, an exception will be thrown.

The dialog for defining OR and XOR split types looks like the following screenshot:

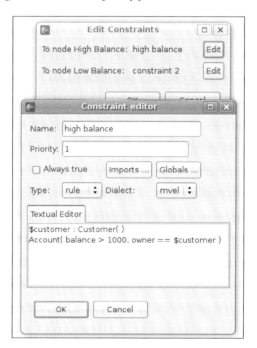

The screenshot above shows Drools Eclipse plugin ruleflow constraint editor. It is accessible from the standard Eclipse **Properties** view.

Join

It joins multiple branches into one. It has two properties—name and a type. Name is for display purposes. Type decides when the execution will continue. It can have following values:

- **AND**: Join waits for all the incoming branches. The execution then continues.
- **XOR**: Join node waits for one incoming branch.

Please consult the Drools manual for further node types.

Example

If you look at data transformation rule in Chapter 4, *Data Transformation*, you'll see that in some rules we've used salience to define rule execution order. For example, all of the addresses needed to be normalized (that is, converted to enum) before we could report the unknown countries. The unknown country rule used salience of -10, which meant that it would fire only after all address normalization rules. We'll now extract this execution order logic into a ruleflow to demonstrate how it works. The ruleflow might look like the following screenshot:

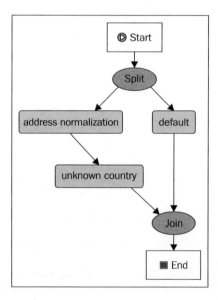

When the execution starts, it goes through the **Start** node straight into the **Split** node. In this case, it is an *and* type split node. It basically creates two parallel branches that will be executed concurrently (note that this doesn't mean multiple threads). We can see that the flow is explicitly specified. **address normalization** happens before **unknown country** reporting. Parallel to this branch is a **default** ruleflow group. It contains the other rules. Finally, a join node of type *and* is used to block until all branches complete and then the flow continues to the terminal node. We had to use the **Join** node (instead of going straight to the **End** node), because as soon as some branch in a ruleflow reaches the **End** node, it terminates the whole ruleflow (that is, our branches may be canceled before competition, which is not what we want).

The process ID is set to `dataTransformation`. Click on the canvas in the ruleflow editor and then in the **Properties** view (Eclipse Properties plugin), set the ID to this value.

Rules

Next we create copy of `dataTransformation.drl` file from Chapter 4 and we'll name it `dataTransformation-ruleflow.drl`. We'll make the following changes:

- Each rule gets new attribute: `ruleflow-group "default"`

- Except the address normalization rules for example:

  ```
  rule addressNormalizationUSA
  ruleflow-group "address normalization"
  ```

  Code listing 37: Top part of the USA address normalization rule.

- Unknown country rule gets the `"unknown country"` ruleflow group.

KnowledgeBase setup

We can now create a knowledge base out of the ruleflow file and the `.drl` file.

```
static KnowledgeBase createKnowledgeBaseFromRuleFlow()
    throws Exception {
  KnowledgeBuilder builder = KnowledgeBuilderFactory
    .newKnowledgeBuilder();
  builder.add(ResourceFactory.newClassPathResource(
      "dataTransformation-ruleflow.drl"), ResourceType.DRL);
  builder.add(ResourceFactory.newClassPathResource(
      "dataTransformation.rf"), ResourceType.DRF);
  if (builder.hasErrors()) {
    throw new RuntimeException(builder.getErrors()
        .toString());
  }
```

```
KnowledgeBase knowledgeBase = KnowledgeBaseFactory
    .newKnowledgeBase();
knowledgeBase.addKnowledgePackages(builder
    .getKnowledgePackages());
return knowledgeBase;
}
```

Code listing 38: Method that creates `KnoweldgeBase` with a ruleflow.

> A knowledge base is created from both files `.drl` and `.rf`. To achieve true isolation of unit tests, consider constructing the knowledge base only from the `.drl` file or `.rf` file. That way, the unit tests can focus only on the relevant part.

Tests

The test setup needs to be changed as well. Ruleflows are fully supported only for stateful sessions. Stateful sessions can't be shared across tests because they maintain state. We need to create a new stateful session for each test. We'll move the session initialization logic from the `setUpClass` method that is called once per test class into the `intialize` method that will be called once per test method:

```
static KnowledgeBase knowledgeBase;
StatefulKnowledgeSession session;

@BeforeClass
public static void setUpClass() throws Exception {
    knowledgeBase = createKnowledgeBaseFromRuleFlow();
}
@Before
public void initialize() throws Exception {
    session = knowledgeBase.newStatefulKnowledgeSession();
```

Code listing 39: Excerpt from the unit test initialization.

Once the stateful session is initialized, we can use it.

We'll write a test that will create a new address map with an unknown country. This address map will be inserted into the session. We'll start the ruleflow and execute all of the rules. The test will verify that the `unknownCountry` rule has been fired:

```
@Test
public void unknownCountryUnknown() throws Exception {
    Map addressMap = new HashMap();
    addressMap.put("_type_", "Address");
```

```
        addressMap.put("country", "no country");

        session.insert(addressMap);
        session.startProcess("dataTransformation");
        session.fireAllRules();

        assertTrue(validationReport.contains("unknownCountry"));
    }
```

Code listing 40: Test for the unknown country rule with an unknown country.

Note that the order of the three `session` methods is important. All of the facts need to be in the session before the ruleflow can be started and rules can be executed.

Please note that in order to test this scenario, we didn't use any agenda filter. This test is more like an integration test where we need to test more rules cooperating together.

Another test verifies that the ruleflow works with a known country:

```
    @Test
    public void unknownCountryKnown() throws Exception {
        Map addressMap = new HashMap();
        addressMap.put("_type_", "Address");
        addressMap.put("country", "Ireland");

        session.startProcess("dataTransformation");
        session.insert(addressMap);
        session.fireAllRules();

        assertFalse(validationReport.contains("unknownCountry"));
    }
```

Code listing 41: Test for the unknown country rule with a known country.

As a stateful session is being used, every test should call the `dispose` method on the session after it finishes. It can be done in the following manner:

```
    @After
    public void terminate() {
        session.dispose();
    }
```

Code listing 42: Calling the `session.dispose` method after every test.

Summary

In this chapter we've learned about writing more user-friendly rules using DSLs, decision tables, and ruleflows. You can mix and match these approaches. It makes sense to write some rules using DSL, some using decision tables, and more complex rules using pure `.drl` file format. `KnowledgeBase` can be created from multiple sources.

DSLs are very useful if there is a need for the business analyst to read and understand the existing rules and even write new rules. The resulting language uses businesses terminologies making it more natural for the business analyst. DSL provides an abstraction layer that hides complicated rule implementations. The Eclipse editor brings auto competition so that the rules are easier to write.

Decision tables, on the other hand, are useful when we have a lot of similar rules that use different values as was the case in the interest rate calculation example. It makes it easy to change such rules because the rule implementation is decoupled from the values they use. Spreadsheet format is also more concise. We can fit more rules into one screen, which makes it easier to understand the overall picture.

In the last section, we've learned about Drools Flow, Agenda, and various ways of managing rule execution order. Drools Flow managed the execution order in a nice human-readable graphical representation.

6
Stateful Session

In this chapter, we'll look at using a stateful knowledge session for executing validation rules from Chapter 3, *Validation*. We'll discuss the advantages and disadvantages that this brings. As a stateful session maintains a state, we'll go through various serialization modes that are supported. We'll also cover logical assertions, fact handles, and a new rule conditional element called collect.

Introduction to stateful session

Drools supports two kinds of knowledge sessions for executing rules: stateful and stateless. The names might be a bit misleading at first, because both the sessions maintain a state. The difference is that a stateful session also maintains its state *between session invocations* (calls to the `fireAllRules` method). This is useful when we need to call rules multiple times over a period of time while making iterative changes to its state.

Another use case is if we need to execute the same set of rules over the same facts that don't change very often over time. It would be a waste of computer resources to insert all facts over and over again. Instead, we should use a stateful session and tell it about the facts that have been changed since the last execution.

The disadvantage is that this session is not thread safe because it maintains a state. Working with this session is more complex because we have to take into account its state unlike a stateless session where a new state is formed with each session invocation. A stateful session needs to be destroyed when we finish working with it. Only then can the garbage collector reclaim the resources it holds.

Generally speaking, if a task can be done just with a stateless session, this should be preferred. It is in line with the **Keep it Short and Simple (KISS)** principle.

org.drools.runtime.StatefulKnowledgeSession

StatefulKnowledgeSession is the interface for all Drools stateful sessions. A stateful knowledge session keeps state between session invocations. It can be created by calling the newStatefulKnowledgeSession method on KnowledgeBase. By default, KnowledgeBase keeps a transient reference to all the stateful sessions. By keeping the references, the sessions can be updated when a new rule is added or an existing rule is removed. In case a new rule is added to the knowledge base, it notifies all of the existing sessions, and all of the objects/facts are automatically matched with rule's conditions as if the rule was always there. If an existing rule is removed from the knowledge base, it is removed from each knowledge session as well. If we've finished working with the session, the engine should be notified by calling the dispose() method on the StatefulKnowledgeSession. The rule engine can then disassociate this session from KnowledgeBase, free all of the session's memories and remove attached event listeners so that the session can be garbage collected. If a lot of stateful sessions were created and we forgot to call the dispose method, the program may soon run out of memory.

StatefulKnowledgeSession implements the BatchExecutor interface in a similar manner as StatelessKnowledgeSession does. It allows us to execute commands that implement the Command interface. The only difference in StatelessKnowledgeSession is that stateless session automatically executes FireAllRulesCommand if we haven't done it explicitly. Note that there is a special command—CommandFactory.newBatchExecution—that allows us to execute multiple commands at once.

It should be noted that from the rules perspective, it makes no difference if we use a stateful or stateless session. We can switch from stateless to stateful and vice versa without changing the rules.

Validation using stateful session

Our implementation of validation service from Chapter 3, *Validation*, is working seamlessly, but it is doing more work than needed. The state of the session isn't kept, and so, all of the rules have to be processed every time. Imagine a web application where a user logs into his/her bank account and wants to do a couple of changes. Every change needs to leave the system in a consistent state. The validation must run as a part of every request. However, with the validation implementation that we have, all of the objects will have to be inserted into a new stateless knowledge session over and over again which is unnecessary. With a stateful session, we just need to insert all of the objects once and then simply update only those that changed. This can save us computing time, especially if we have lots of facts that need to be inserted. Of course, one needs to know which objects did change, but this shouldn't be a problem. If, for example, a customer is changing his/her demographic data, only the `Customer` and `Address` objects need to be updated. The client of this service API can make these decisions and update only `Customer` and `Address` objects.

Design overview

If we think about the implementation, there are at least two approaches to stateful sessions. The first one is to have the stateful session in the domain model itself. The advantage is that you'll get a rich model that knows how to validate itself. Domain objects can even be intelligent enough to know if they've been changed, and only then call `session.update`, removing the burden from the user of this API. Every domain object will have a `FactHandle`, which is a handle to its representation in the knowledge session. `FactHandle` is needed for external (that is, not from within a DRL file) interactions with the knowledge session. The disadvantage is that the model will depend on the Drools API or at least some abstraction of it. Moreover, each object will need to have access to the knowledge session probably through its parent. This is not ideal from the point of domain modeling.

The second option is to separate this logic completely from the domain model by having a separate stateful service. The disadvantage of this approach is that we'll get a more anemic domain model (where business logic is implemented outside of domain model). The stateful service will have to maintain a map of fact to `FactHandle`. Alternatively, it could use such an existing map that Drools maintains internally—that is, delegate to session's `getFactHandle` method for retrieval of `FactHandle`. By default, it retrieves `FactHandle` by fact identity. It works fine as long as the identities don't change. If they do, then we have to re-populate the session.

Stateful validation service

We'll implement the second option (note that both of the options are valid and it shouldn't be much different to perform the first option). Let's start with a stateful service interface. Firstly, the service needs to know about our domain objects probably through some register method. Then it needs to be notified when an object has been changed. Finally, it needs to generate a validation report. The interface is as follows:

```
public interface StatefulService {
    /**
     * registers new objects with this service or notifies this
     * service that an object has been modified
```

```
    */
    void insertOrUpdate(Object object);

    /**
     * same as insertOrUpdate(Object object); plus this method
     * calls insertOrUpdate on child objects
     */
    void insertOrUpdateRecursive(Customer customer);

    /**
     * executes validation rules and returns report
     */
    ValidationReport executeRules();

    /**
     * releases all resources held by this service
     */
    void terminate();
}
```

Code listing 1: Stateful validation service interface (`StatefulService.java` file).

The stateful service works in a similar manner as a stateful session. New objects can be inserted into the stateful service and existing objects can be updated. The first two methods of this service are exactly for this purpose. The second method is a convenience method that will traverse the tree of objects starting with the `Customer` (argument of the method). We can use this approach because all of our domain objects are traversable or reachable from the `Customer` object.

After all of the needed objects have been inserted/updated, the `executeRules` method can be called. It will execute all the rules and return a validation report. If the validation fails, this report can be displayed to the user. The user can make changes, which translates to inserting new or updating an existing object by using the two methods mentioned earlier. Then the rules are executed again and the process may continue until the user is happy with the validation result (for example, validation report has no errors). When we've finished working with the stateful service, we should call its `terminate` method to properly release all of the resources it holds. The following is a graphical representation of this whole process (state diagram of `StatefulService`).

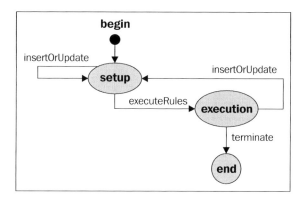

Let's now start implementing this service. It will use some classes that we should be familiar with from Chapter 3, *Validation*:

```
public class StatefulServiceImpl implements StatefulService,
    Serializable {
  private transient KnowledgeBase knowledgeBase;
  private transient StatefulKnowledgeSession statefulSession;
  private transient ReportFactory reportFactory;
  public StatefulServiceImpl(KnowledgeBase knowledgeBase,
      ReportFactory reportFactory,
      BankingInquiryService inquiryService) {
    this.reportFactory = reportFactory;
    this.knowledgeBase = knowledgeBase;
    statefulSession = createKnowledgeSession(inquiryService);
  }
```

Code listing 2: Service constructor and properties (StatefulServiceImpl.java file).

The service implements StatefulService interface and also the java.io.Serializable interface. It has three properties: knowledgeBase, the session itself, and reportFactory. They are all declared as transient, which means they won't be serialized by default. We'll talk about serialization later in this chapter. The constructor sets the properties and delegates the creation of the stateful knowledge session to the createKnowledgeSession method. This method is as follows:

```
private StatefulKnowledgeSession createKnowledgeSession(
    BankingInquiryService inquiryService) {
  StatefulKnowledgeSession session = knowledgeBase
    .newStatefulKnowledgeSession();
  session.setGlobal("reportFactory", reportFactory);
  session.setGlobal("inquiryService", inquiryService);
  return session;
}
```

Code listing 3: Method for creating and setting up the stateful knowledge session (StatefulServiceImpl.java file).

The createKnowledgeSession method also sets the global variables as required by the validation rules. knowledgeBase will be created from the same file—validation.drl.

The following code listing shows the implementation of the two setup methods:

```java
public void insertOrUpdate(Object fact) {
    if (fact == null) {
        return;
    }

    FactHandle factHandle = statefulSession
        .getFactHandle(fact);

    if (factHandle == null) {
        statefulSession.insert(fact);
    } else {
        statefulSession.update(factHandle, fact);
    }
}

public void insertOrUpdateRecursive(Customer customer) {
    insertOrUpdate(customer);
    insertOrUpdate(customer.getAddress());
    if (customer.getAccounts() != null) {
        for (Account account : customer.getAccounts()) {
            insertOrUpdate(account);
        }
    }
}
```

Code listing 4: Two stateful service setup methods (StatefulServiceImpl.java file).

The insertOrUpdate generic method takes a fact and checks if this fact already exists in the knowledge session. If it exists, it updates this fact, and if it doesn't exist, it inserts this fact into the session. The statefulSession.getFactHandle method is used to check the fact existence. It takes the fact and returns FactHandle.

org.drools.runtime.rule.FactHandle

As the name suggests, it is a handle to an already inserted fact in the knowledge session. When a fact is inserted, the insert method returns FactHandle. An object inside the knowledge session can be modified only through its FactHandle. The session's modify/update method actually takes two parameters: FactHandle and the updated object. You may be wondering why the modify/update method worked in the rule consequences that we've written so far. It is because behind the scenes, Drools provides FactHandle for us, as it is known in the rule consequence.

Drools supports two fact insertion modes: *equality* and *identity*. They can be set at KnowledgeBase creation time in the org.drools. KnowledgeBaseConfiguration. Identity mode means that no two objects with the same JVM object reference can be inserted into the knowledge session. Equality mode works based on the equals method. The default is identity. Changing the insertion mode also changes the way how session.getFactHandle method behaves (if it is changed to equality mode, it will retrieve facts based on the equals method).

The rule engine needs FactHandle to correctly identify the fact we're referring to. Let's say that the insertion mode is set to identity and we want to change the value of some immutable object (for example, java.math.BigDecimal). The only way to change it is to create a new instance. Then, if the session.update method is called, by passing in the FactHandle together with the object, the engine can correctly update itself. Another example is if the insertion mode is set to equality and we're changing the object state that is part of the equals contract. Only through the FactHandle will the engine recognize the object.

Note that FactHandle is not serializable out of the box.

The insertOrUpdateRecursive method takes Customer and simply calls the insertOrUpdate method for the Customer object and all its descending objects.

The method that represents the second state of the stateful service (execution of validation rules) is as follows:

```
public ValidationReport executeRules() {
    ValidationReport validationReport =
        reportFactory.createValidationReport();
    statefulSession.setGlobal("validationReport",
        validationReport);
    statefulSession.fireAllRules();
    return validationReport;
}
```

Code listing 5: Method for rule execution (StatefulServiceImpl.java file).

It creates a validation report, sets it as a global variable, fires all rules, and returns this validation report. A new validation report is created for every rule execution.

Finally, the method that handles the termination of this service is as follows:

```
public void terminate() {
   statefulSession.dispose();
}
```

Code listing 6: Method for terminating the service (`StatefulServiceImpl.java` file).

It calls the session's `dispose` method, which releases all of the resources held by this session.

Integration testing

If we run the tests implemented in the validation Chapter 2, *Basic Rules*, they would run just fine. However, the purpose of this section is to test the interactions that include multiple user requests. The test will cover the following scenario: the user logs in, performs multiple operations, and then logs out.

The setup of `StatefulServiceIntegrationTest` is similar to what we've done before:

```
public class StatefulServiceIntegrationTest {
   StatefulServiceImpl statefulService;
   static KnowledgeBase knowledgeBase;
   @BeforeClass
   public static void setUpClass() throws Exception {
      knowledgeBase = DroolsHelper.createKnowledgeBase(
         "validation-stateful.drl");
   }
   @Before
   public void initialize() throws Exception {
      ReportFactory reportFactory = new DefaultReportFactory();
      BankingInquiryService inquiryService =
         new BankingInquiryServiceImpl();
      statefulService = new StatefulServiceImpl(knowledgeBase,
         reportFactory, inquiryService);
   }
   @After
   public void terminate() {
      statefulService.terminate();
   }
}
```

Code listing 7: `StatefulServiceIntegrationTest` setup.

In the `setUpClass` method, the `knowledgeBase` is created from the file `validation-stateful.drl`. This file is, for now, a pure copy of the `validation.drl` file. The `initialize` method will run before every test method and it will create `statefulService` that we'll test. After each test method, `statefulService` will be discarded by calling the `terminate` method.

Before writing the test, a helper method for creating a valid customer will be needed:

```
private Customer createValidCustomer() {
    Customer customer = new Customer();
    customer.setPhoneNumber("123 456 789");
    customer.setAddress(new Address());

    statefulService.insertOrUpdateRecursive(customer);
    ValidationReport report = statefulService.executeRules();
    assertEquals(0, report.getMessages().size());
    return customer;
}
```

Code listing 8: Helper method for creating a valid customer (`StatefulServiceIntegrationTest.java` file).

This method creates a new valid `Customer` and sets the required fields. This customer is then passed into the `insertOrUpdateRecursive` method which, behind the scenes, inserts the customer and address object into a stateful session. As this is a valid customer, the method verifies that the validation report has no messages.

Let's write a test method. It will use the previous method to create a valid `Customer`. Since we'll be testing a full user session interaction, the test method will be split into three sections. The first part is shown in the following code listing. It will blank the customer phone number, notify the service, and verify that it contains the correct report.

```
@Test
public void statefulValidation() throws Exception {
    Customer customer = createValidCustomer();

    customer.setPhoneNumber("");
    statefulService.insertOrUpdate(customer);
    ValidationReport report = statefulService.executeRules();
    assertEquals(1, report.getMessages().size());
    assertTrue(report.contains("phoneNumberRequired"));
```

Code listing 9: First part of `statefulValidation` test method (`StatefulServiceIntegrationTest.java` file).

As we've modified the customer object, `statefulService` is notified about this by calling the `insertOrUpdate` method and passing in the `customer` object. After executing the rules, the test verifies that there is one message in the validation report.

Let's imagine that the user now creates a new account. The next part tests this scenario:

```
Account account = new Account();
account.setOwner(customer);
customer.addAccount(account);
statefulService.insertOrUpdate(customer);
statefulService.insertOrUpdate(account);
report = statefulService.executeRules();
assertEquals(3, report.getMessages().size());
assertTrue(report.contains("accountNumberUnique"));
assertTrue(report.contains("accountBalanceAtLeast"));
assertTrue(report.contains("phoneNumberRequired"));
```

Code listing 10: Second part of `statefulValidation` test method (`StatefulServiceIntegrationTest.java` file).

After creating the new `Account` object and setting its properties, `statefulService` is notified. Please note that the notification is done not only for the new `Account` object, but also for the `Customer` object, because it has **changed**.

Our expectation is that there will be three messages in the report. The `balance` hasn't been set. The customer's phone number is still missing. The `accountNumberUnique` rule should fire because our stub implementation of `bankingInquiryService.isAccountNumberUnique` method simply always returns `false`.

If we run this, everything else works as expected. Let's continue with the last part of this test method. It will set the account owner to null and expect one more message in the validation report (`accountOwnerRequired`).

```
account.setOwner(null);
statefulService.insertOrUpdate(account);
report = statefulService.executeRules();
assertEquals(4, report.getMessages().size());
assertTrue(report.contains("accountNumberUnique"));
assertTrue(report.contains("accountOwnerRequired"));
assertTrue(report.contains("accountBalanceAtLeast"));
assertTrue(report.contains("phoneNumberRequired"));
}
```

Code listing 11: Third and last part of `statefulValidation` test method (`StatefulServiceIntegrationTest.java` file).

Again, the `statefulService` is notified that the `account` fact has been changed. Please note that only the account object has changed this time. Our expectation is that there will be four messages in the report (four validation rules are violated). However, after running the test, only three account validation messages are in the report. The `phoneNumberRequired` message is missing. If we look at the rule, we'll see that it has only one condition: `Customer (phoneNumber == null || == "")`. As we had not updated the `Customer` object, the rule didn't fire.

The problem is that a new report is created every time the `executeRules` method is called. It contains only messages from rules that fired during the last execution. You may ask "Why do we create a new report with each rule execution?" If we had a report for the whole duration of the `statefulService`, we wouldn't know when an error had been corrected (for example, in this case, the customer's phone number has been set). There are no rules that remove messages from the report. Logical assertions provide a nice solution to this problem.

Logical assertions

Similar to standard assertions (we're previously referring to them as `inserts`), a logical assertion adds facts into the knowledge session. If the same fact is logically inserted by more rules, *only one equal instance will be physically present in the session*. Furthermore, a logically inserted fact will be automatically retracted when the conditions of all rules that inserted it are no longer true. Enough of theory, let's explain this with the help of an example.

Imagine that we have couple of rules for checking fraudulent transactions. We'll create a special type—`SuspiciousTransaction`—to mark that the transaction is suspicious.

```
rule notification
    when
        $transaction : Transaction( )
        Notification( transaction == $transaction )
    then
        insertLogical(new SuspiciousTransaction($transaction))
end
```

Code listing 12: Rule that triggers on user notifications and adds `SuspiciousTransaction` logical assertion (`fraudulent-transactions.drl` file).

The `Notification` above may, for example, represent a customer service department receiving a notification of some sort. The rule consequence inserts the logical fact, `SuspiciousTransaction`.

There can be many of such rules that insert `SuspiciousTransaction`. For example:

```
rule unusualLocation
    when
        $transaction : Transaction( )
        RiskFactor( unusualLocation > 10,
            transaction == $transaction )
    then
        insertLogical(new SuspiciousTransaction($transaction))
end
```

Code listing 13: Rule that adds `SuspiciousTransaction` logical assertion based on unusual location risk factor (`fraudulent-transactions.drl` file).

This rule will fire if a risk factor is greater than a certain value (in this case, `10`). This `RiskFactor` fact can be calculated and updated by many other rules.

Each logically inserted fact has a counter, which is incremented every time an equal fact is inserted (our suspicious transaction facts are 'equal' if they refer to the same transaction). If the conditions of this rule are no longer true—for example, the `unusualLocation` value of `RiskFactor` is changed to 5 and the `RiskFactor` fact is updated—the counter for this logically inserted fact will be decremented. If the value reaches zero, the fact will be automatically retracted. The transaction is no longer considered suspicious if the risk factor is small.

Next, we may have a different set of rules with very low priority firing at the end that react to the presence of a `SuspiciousTransaction` fact. If there is a suspicious transaction, the account will be put on hold.

```
rule freezeAccount
salience -1000
    when
        $from : Account( )
        $transaction : Transaction( from == $from )
        SuspiciousTransaction( transaction == $transaction)
    then
        $from.setStatus(Account.Status.ON_HOLD);
end
```

Code listing 14: Rule that puts an account on hold if there is a suspicious transaction originating from it (`fraudulent-transactions.drl` file).

The introduction of the `SuspiciousTransaction` fact provides a level of insulation between two set of rules—rules that identify a threat and rules that react to it.

If we logically insert a fact, we can override it with a standard insert. It then becomes an ordinary fact that was inserted using the standard `insert` method. For more information about logical assertions, please see the Drools documentation (Drools Expert—section, *Truth Maintenance with Logical Objects*).

Keeping the validation report up-to-date

Let's now move back to our validation example. Logical assertions can be used to keep the report up-to-date. Instead of adding messages to a global validation report, we can insert them into the session just as another fact. A logical insert will be used so that messages that are no longer valid will be automatically retracted. A query can be used to fetch all of the messages and create the validation report.

In Chapter 3, *Validation*, all of the messages were created and added to the validation report in the `ValidationHelper` utility class by `error` and `warning` methods. We'll now create another version of `ValidationHelper` that will insert all the messages into the knowledge session by calling the `insertLogical` method. The `error` method of the utility class is as follows:

```
public class ValidationHelper {
  /**
    * inserts new logical assertion - a message
    * @param drools KnowledgeHelper that is accessible from
    *   rule condition
    * @param context for the message
    */
  public static void error(KnowledgeHelper drools,
      Object... context) {
    KnowledgeRuntime knowledgeRuntime = drools
        .getKnowledgeRuntime();
    ReportFactory reportFactory = (ReportFactory)
        knowledgeRuntime.getGlobal("reportFactory");

    drools.insertLogical(reportFactory.createMessage(
        Message.Type.ERROR, drools.getRule().getName(),
        context));
  }
```

Code listing 15: `ValidationHelper` utility class that uses logical assertions.

Instead of using `RuleContext`, we're using its old deprecated counterpart — `KnowledgeHelper`. We need to use `KnowledgeHelper` because `RuleContext` doesn't support logical assertions, yet (they will be supported in Drools 5.1+). As part of this change, we have to replace all occurrences of `kcontext` with `drools` in the `validation-stateful.drl` file.

Modify the `validation-stateful.drl` file to import these two helper functions instead of the old ones. Next, add the following query for message retrieval to the `.drl` file:

```
query getAllMessages
    $message : Message( )
end
```

Code listing 16: Query for retrieving all the messages (`validation-stateful.drl` file).

The global variable `validationReport` can be removed completely from this file. The validation report will be created inside the stateful service. Just modify the `executeRules` method to call `fireAllRules`, then create a blank validation report and populate it with the messages fetched by the query above. Finally, the report is returned. The test should now pass without any error. The "phone number required" message will still be present in the knowledge session even though the stateful service hasn't been notified to update the `customer object`.

Collect conditional element

With the solution above, the report creation has been moved outside the rule engine, which is acceptable. However, with a new `collect` conditional element, we can put it back into the rule engine. `collect` can gather multiple objects, in a stateful or stateless session, into one collection. One can use it to gather all the messages in the knowledge session and then put them into the validation report. Only one validation report will be used throughout the lifetime of the stateful knowledge session (even service). This report will be created in the service's constructor. We also need a way to clear this validation report between `executeRules` calls.

```
/**
 * clears this report
 */
public void reset() {
  messagesMap.clear();
}
```

Code listing 17: Method of `ValidationReport` that clears the report.

Add the method above to the service implementation (and interface).The global variable `validationReport` needs to be put back into the `validation-stateful. drl` file. A new rule for creating the validation report will be added as shown in the following code:

```
rule createValidationReport
salience -1000 //should be the last rule to fire
    when
        $messages : ArrayList( ) from collect( Message() )
    then
        validationReport.reset();
        for(Message message : (List<Message>) $messages) {
            validationReport.addMessage(message);
        }
end
```

Code listing 18: Rule that collects all messages in the knowledge session and updates the report (`validation-stateful.drl` file).

The condition of this rule is interesting. It matches on `$messages` collection, which is created by collecting all of the facts of type `Message`. The collection is then traversed inside the rule consequence and all of the messages are added into already cleared validation report. The rule has a negative salience, which ensures that it will be the last one to fire. It only makes sense to create the report after all of the validation rules fired. Please note that the `java.util.ArrayList` and `java.util.List` types need to be imported in the `.drl` file.

The `executeRules` method of stateful service will then simply call `statefulSession.fireAllRules` and will return the `validationReport` local property. Our tests should pass as before.

Collect

As we've seen in Code listing 18, `collect` can be used together with `from` to group facts that meet the given constraints. The result can be any object that implements the `java.util.Collection` interface and provides a public no argument constructor. In our example, we were collecting any `Message`, but we could have easily collected only warning by adding the following type constraint:

```
$messages : ArrayList( size >= 2 ) from collect( Message( type ==
Message.Type.WARNING ) )
```

Code listing 19: Condition that matches on a collection of at least two warning messages.

Variables bound in conditions before `collect` are visible inside the collect pattern. Collect can accept nested `from`, `collect`, and `accumulate` elements, for example:

```
$destinationAccount : Account ( )
$transactions : LinkedList ( ) from collect ( Transaction(
    to == $destinationAccount, $currency : currency )
    from bankService.getTransactions() )
```

Code listing 20: Nested `from` conditional element which groups all of the transactions that have the specified destination `Account` from a service.

However, any variables bound inside the `collect` conditional element are not visible outside it, for example, in this case, `$currency`. It is quite logical.

Serialization

Imagine that we have a web application. The stateful service is stored within the HTTP session. The user makes multiple HTTP requests throughout the lifetime of the stateful service. This is all perfect as long as it all happens within one server. However, as soon as we begin talking about scalability and fault tolerance, we need to think about serialization. For example, we may need to serialize all of the objects in the HTTP session and transfer this session to another server. As it is currently, `StatefulService` fails to serialize. Let's fix it.

Of course this implies that the rule engine will run in the presentation tier. If you don't like this approach, the stateful service can reside within the service tier, alternatively. However, with this approach, we would have to maintain its life cycle (creation and termination). An identifier can be passed from the presentation tier to identify the instance of the stateful service. The service tier would then maintain a map of identifiers and their associated stateful services.

Also, as stateful service is not thread safe, only single threaded access is possible. This is something to keep in mind when designing the application. If an object is inside the HTTP session, there is the potential that two threads may access it at the same time. You could, for example, declare all of the service methods as synchronized. (There will still be a possibility of a single user doing multiple requests at the same time which may cause the validation results to interleave.)

Knowledge session re-creation

Our first approach will simply re-create the knowledge session upon stateful service de-serialization. This approach is fine for sessions with a small number of facts where the facts can be easily re-inserted.

The stateful service already implements the `java.io.Serializable` marker interface. All that needs to be done is to implement the `readObject` and `writeObject` methods. The following implementation will serialize just `KnowledgeBase` as that is the only state we want to maintain.

```
private void writeObject(ObjectOutputStream out)
    throws IOException {
  out.defaultWriteObject();

  DroolsObjectOutputStream droolsOut =
      new DroolsObjectOutputStream((OutputStream) out);
  droolsOut.writeObject(knowledgeBase);
}
```

Code listing 21: `writeObject` method for serializing the stateful service (`StatefulServiceImpl.java` file).

As good practice, the `defaultWriteObject` is called first. A special type of `ObjectOutputStream` – `DroolsObjectOutputStream` is needed to serialize the `KnowledgeBase`. It acts as a wrapper around the `ObjectOutputStream`.

The following is the `readObject` method which is mirroring the `writeObject` method:

```
private void readObject(ObjectInputStream in)
    throws IOException, ClassNotFoundException {
  in.defaultReadObject();

  DroolsObjectInputStream droolsIn =
      new DroolsObjectInputStream((InputStream) in);
  this.knowledgeBase = (KnowledgeBase)droolsIn.readObject();

  this.reportFactory = new DefaultReportFactory();
  statefulSession = createKnowledgeSession(
      new BankingInquiryServiceImpl());
}
```

Code listing 22: `readObject` method for de-serializing the stateful service (`StatefulServiceImpl.java` file).

The `readObject` method de-serializes `KnowledgeBase`, and creates a new report factory and a banking inquiry service. A better solution would be to use some static service locator to locate them as they are singletons. These objects are used by the `createKnowledgeSession` method to create and initialize a new stateful knowledge session. The `createKnowledgeSession` method also sets a new validation report. Note that the report and the session are empty.

Testing

The following test will demonstrate that the serialization of the stateful service works:

```
@Test
public void testSerialization() throws Exception {
    Customer customer = createValidCustomer();
    statefulService.insertOrUpdateRecursive(customer);

    ByteArrayOutputStream baos = new ByteArrayOutputStream();
    ObjectOutputStream out = new ObjectOutputStream(baos);
    out.writeObject(statefulService);
    out.close();

    byte[] bArray = baos.toByteArray();
    ObjectInputStream in = new ObjectInputStream(
        new ByteArrayInputStream(bArray));
    statefulService = (StatefulServiceImpl) in.readObject();
    in.close();
    statefulService.insertOrUpdateRecursive(customer);

    ValidationReport report = statefulService.executeRules();
    assertEquals(0, report.getMessages().size());

    customer.setPhoneNumber(null);
    statefulService.insertOrUpdate(customer);
    report = statefulService.executeRules();
    assertEquals(1, report.getMessages().size());
    assertTrue(report.contains("phoneNumberRequired"));
}
```

Code listing 23: Test method that exercises serialization of stateful service (`StatefulServiceIntegrationTest.java` file).

The test above creates a valid customer, and adds this customer and all his dependent objects into the stateful service. The stateful service is then serialized into an array of bytes. These bytes can be transferred, for example, to a remote machine. The stateful service is then de-serialized from this array. An important thing to note is that after de-serializing the `statefulService`, it needs to be re-populated by calling the `insertOrUpdateRecursive` method and passing in the `customer`. Rules are executed and the test verifies that there are no messages. The customer is then invalidated by clearing his phone number. After updating the stateful session and running the rules, the test verifies that there is exactly one message about the missing phone number.

Session serialization

This section will discuss a complete stateful session serialization (full state including internal memories, agenda, ruleflow instances and so on.). A stateful session cannot be serialized out of the box (for example, you cannot just pass it to `java.io.ObjectOutputStream`). Drools currently supports two modes of stateful session serialization. Each mode is an implementation of the interface—`org.drools.marshalling.ObjectMarshallingStrategy`. It defines methods for writing and reading object to/from `java.io.ObjectOutputStream/ObjectInputStream`. An `accept` method, which returns a `boolean` value, can be used to make more complex decisions about which objects to serialize with which strategy. Both the implementations of this interface take `ObjectMarshallingStrategyAcceptor` as a constructor argument and simply delegate to its `accept` method to do the accept logic. `Marshaller` then takes an array of marshaling strategies and can serialize the stateful session.

A class diagram of the Drools serialization is as follows:

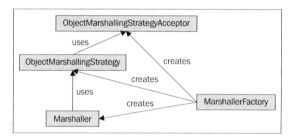

The following strategies are supported:

- **Identity mode**: It is implemented by the `IdentityPlaceholderResolverStrategy` class. This is a stateful mode, which means that exactly the same instance of this strategy is needed at both serialization and de-serialization time. Each fact is assigned an ID. These IDs are stored together with their associated facts in a map. It is a map of type `Map<Integer, Object>`. This map is the actual state of this `ObjectMarshallingStrategy` implementation. None of the facts are serialized—only the IDs are. This means that when reconstructing the stateful session from the serialized stream of data, all of the objects need to be present in memory (that is, the session must be de-serialized in the same JVM). This strategy can be used for the so-called *session templates* where you pre-populate session with immutable facts, serialize it, and then simply de-serialize it as many times as you want. The session may then be used as usual. This is especially useful if you are creating a lot of session with the same immutable facts and you're experiencing long fact insertion times (due to a lot of facts, rules, and so on).

- **Full serialization mode**: It is implemented by the `SerializablePlaceholderResolverStrategy` class. Everything is serialized, including facts. This strategy can be used for backup, and session pause/resume when moving the session to another server. Please keep in mind that upon de-serialization of a knowledge session, all of the facts will have a new identity. Alternatively, you could serialize the fact together with the session in one `ObjectOutputStream`. This way, the object references will be preserved. This is, for example, the case when a HTTP session is serialized.

In both cases, the stateful session's agenda, action queue, process instances, work items, and timers are serialized. Global variables are not serialized, so we need to take care of them.

Full session serialization

We'll now look at serializing the stateful session using the full serialization mode. We'll implement the standard `writeObject` and `readObject` methods. Let's start with the `writeObject` method:

```
private void writeObject(ObjectOutputStream out)
    throws IOException {
  out.defaultWriteObject();

  DroolsObjectOutputStream droolsOut =
      new DroolsObjectOutputStream((OutputStream) out);
  droolsOut.writeObject(knowledgeBase);

  Marshaller marshaller = createSerializableMarshaller(
      knowledgeBase);
  marshaller.marshall(droolsOut, statefulSession);
}
```

Code listing 24: Implementation of the `writeObject` method of the stateful service (`StatefulServiceImpl.java` file).

Firstly, the default object state is serialized followed by `knowledgeBase`. A new `Marshaller` is created by the `createSerializableMarshaller` method. It is then used to serialize the stateful knowledge session into the same output stream.

Please note that currently the stateful serialization mode changes identities of objects even though they are saved to the same output stream. This should be fixed in future versions of Drools (see `https://jira.jboss.org/jira/browse/JBRULES-2048` for more details).

The marshaller will use only one serializable marshaller strategy that will accept all objects, *.*. The first star represents the package name and the second start represents the class name. The `createSerializableMarshaller` method is as follows:

```
private Marshaller createSerializableMarshaller(
    KnowledgeBase knowledgeBase) {
  ObjectMarshallingStrategyAcceptor acceptor =
      MarshallerFactory.newClassFilterAcceptor(
      new String[] { "*.*" } );
  ObjectMarshallingStrategy strategy = MarshallerFactory
      .newSerializeMarshallingStrategy( acceptor );
  Marshaller marshaller = MarshallerFactory.newMarshaller(
      knowledgeBase, new ObjectMarshallingStrategy[] {
      strategy } );
  return marshaller;
}
```

Code listing 25: A method for creating a full serialization marshaller (`StatefulServiceImpl.java` file).

Note that in the example above, we're using only one pattern for our strategy acceptor; however, many can be defined, if needed.

The method that takes care of the de-serialization process (`readObject`) is shown in the following code. It will create a marshaller and will use it to de-serialize the stateful knowledge session. Further, it will initialize its global variables.

```
private void readObject(ObjectInputStream in)
    throws IOException, ClassNotFoundException {
  in.defaultReadObject();

  DroolsObjectInputStream droolsIn =
      new DroolsObjectInputStream((InputStream) in);
  this.knowledgeBase = (KnowledgeBase)droolsIn.readObject();

  Marshaller marshaller = createSerializableMarshaller(
      knowledgeBase);
  statefulSession = marshaller.unmarshall(droolsIn);

  this.reportFactory = new DefaultReportFactory();
  statefulSession.setGlobal("reportFactory", reportFactory);
  statefulSession.setGlobal("inquiryService",
      new BankingInquiryServiceImpl());
}
```

Code listing 26: Implementation of the `readObject` method of the stateful service for de-serialization (`StatefulServiceImpl.java` file).

Note that if we had used the identity mode serialization, the same marshaller instance would have to be used for both serialization and de-serialization, as the identity marshaller is stateful.

Summary

In this chapter, we've learned about stateful sessions, what are they used for, and how they keep their state between session invocations. This is especially useful in long iterative interaction scenarios, for example, in a web application where a user logs into the system, makes couple of changes in multiple HTTP requests, and logs out of the system.

Logical assertions were discussed. We saw that they are automatically retracted when none of the conditions that inserted them are true. This was useful as it kept the validation report updated all the time.

Finally, the serialization section discussed two options of serializing a stateful session — Identity and Serialized. An example was given of how to serialize the stateful service which contained a stateful session.

7
Complex Event Processing

Rules usually operate on a more or less static set of data (facts). However, for some systems, it is necessary to define the relationships between facts over the time. This is often called **Complex Event Processing (CEP)** or **Event Stream Processing (ESP)**. Drools, more specifically **Drools Fusion**, starting with version 5.0, provides this support together with sliding windows, temporal operators, and type declarations.

In this chapter, we'll look at implementing a banking fraud detection system. It is an ideal candidate for CEP. The volume of events in a banking system is huge and we need to be able to do complex decisions based on these events.

CEP and ESP

CEP and ESP are styles of processing in an **Event Driven Architecture** (General introduction to Event Driven Architecture can be found at: `http://elementallinks.typepad.com/bmichelson/2006/02/eventdriven_arc.html`). One of the core benefits of such an architecture is that it provides loose coupling of its components. A component simply publishes events about actions that it is executing and other components can subscribe/listen to these events. The producer and the subscriber are completely unaware of each other. A subscriber listens for events and doesn't care where they come from. Similarly, a publisher generates events and doesn't know anything about who is listening to those events. Some orchestration layer then deals with the actual wiring of subscribers to publishers.

An event represents a significant change of state. It usually consists of a header and a body. The header contains meta information such as its name, time of occurrence, duration, and so on. The body describes what happened. For example, if a transaction has been processed, the event body would contain the transaction ID, the amount transferred, source account number, destination account number, and so on.

CEP deals with complex events. A complex event is a set of simple events. For example, a sequence of large withdrawals may raise a suspicious transaction event. The simple events are considered to infer that a complex event has occurred.

ESP is more about real-time processing of huge volume of events. For example, calculating the real-time average transaction volume over time.

More information about CEP and ESP can be found on the web site, `http://complexevents.com/` or in a book written by Prof. David Luckham, *The Power of Events*. This book is considered the milestone for the modern research and development of CEP.

There are many existing pure CEP/ESP engines, both commercial and open source. Drools Fusion enhances the rule based programming with event support. It makes use of its Rete algorithm and provides an alternative to existing engines.

Drools Fusion

Drools Fusion is a Drools module that is a part of the Business Logic Integration Platform. It is the Drools event processing engine covering both CEP and ESP (these terms will be used interchangeably in this book). Each event has a type, a time of occurrence, and possibly, a duration. Both point in time (zero duration) and interval-based events are supported. Events can also contain other data like any other facts—properties with a name and type. All events are facts but not all facts are events. An event's state should not be changed. However, it is valid to populate the unpopulated values. Events have clear life cycle windows and may be transparently garbage collected after the life cycle window expires (for example, we may be interested only in transactions that happened in the last 24 hours). Rules can deal with time relationships between events.

Fraud detection

It will be easier to explain these concepts by using an example—a fraud detection system. Fraud in banking systems is becoming a major concern. The amount of online transactions is increasing every day. An automatic system for fraud detection is needed. The system should analyze various events happening in a bank and, based on a set of rules, raise an appropriate alarm.

This problem cannot be solved by the standard Drools rule engine. The volume of events is huge and it happens asynchronously. If we simply inserted them into the knowledge session, we would soon run out of memory. While the Rete algorithm behind Drools doesn't have any theoretical limitation on number of objects in the session, we could use the processing power more wisely. Drools Fusion is the right candidate for this kind of task.

Problem description

Let's consider the following set of business requirements for the fraud detection system:

1. If a notification is received from a customer about a stolen card, block this account and any withdrawals from this account.

2. Check each transaction against a blacklist of account numbers. If the transaction is transferring money from/to such an account, then flag this transaction as suspicious with the **maximum** severity.

3. If there are two large debit transactions from the same account within a ninety second period and each transaction is withdrawing more than 300% of the average monthly (30 days) withdrawal amount, flag these transactions as suspicious with **minor** severity.

4. If there is a sequence of three consecutive, increasing, debit transactions originating from a same account within a three minute period and these transactions are together withdrawing more than 90% of the account's average balance over 30 days, then flag those transactions as suspicious with **major** severity and suspend the account.

5. If the number of withdrawals over a day is 500% higher than the average number of withdrawals over a 30 day period and the account is left with less than 10% of the average balance over a month (30 days), then flag the account as suspicious with **minor** severity.

6. Duplicate transactions check — if two transactions occur in a time window of 15 seconds that have the same source/destination account number, are of the same amount, and just differ in the transaction ID, then flag those transactions as duplicates.

Monitoring:

1. Monitor the average withdrawal amount over all of the accounts for 30 days.

2. Monitor the average balance across all of the accounts.

Design and modeling

Looking at the requirements, we'll need a way of flagging a transaction as suspicious. This state can be added to an existing `Transaction` type, or we can externalize this state to a new event type. We'll do the latter. The following new events will be defined:

- `TransactionCreatedEvent` — An event that is triggered when a new transaction is created. It contains a transaction identifier, source account number, destination account number, and the actual amount transferred.

- `TransactionCompletedEvent` — An event that is triggered when an existing transaction has been processed. It contains the same fields as the `TransactionCreatedEvent` class.

- `AccountUpdatedEvent` — An event that is triggered when an account has been updated. It contains the account number, current balance, and the transaction identifier of a transaction that initiated this update.

- `SuspiciousAccount` — An event triggered when there is some sort of a suspicion around the account. It contains the account number and severity of the suspicion. It is an enumeration that can have two values `MINOR` and `MAJOR`. This event's implementation is shown in the following code.

- `SuspiciousTransaction` — Similar to `SuspiciousAccount`, this is an event that flags a transaction as suspicious. It contains a transaction identifier and severity level.

- `LostCardEvent` — An event indicating that a card was lost. It contains an account number.

One of events described — `SuspiciousAccount` — is shown in the following code. It also defines `SuspiciousAccountSeverity` enumeration that encapsulates various severity levels that the event can represent. The event will define two properties. One of them is already mentioned `severity` and the other one will identify the account — accountNumber.

```
/**
 * marks an account as suspicious
 */
public class SuspiciousAccount implements Serializable {
  public enum SuspiciousAccountSeverity {
    MINOR, MAJOR
  }

  private final Long accountNumber;
  private final SuspiciousAccountSeverity severity;

  public SuspiciousAccount(Long accountNumber,
      SuspiciousAccountSeverity severity) {
    this.accountNumber = accountNumber;
    this.severity = severity;
  }

  private transient String toString;

  @Override
  public String toString() {
    if (toString == null) {
      toString = new ToStringBuilder(this).appendSuper(
```

```
        super.toString()).append("accountNumber",
        accountNumber).append("severity", severity)
        .toString();
    }
    return toString;
}
```

Code listing 1: Implementation of `SuspiciousAccount` event.

Please note that the `equals` and `hashCode` methods in `SuspiciousAccount` from the preceding code listing are not overridden. This is because an event represents an active entity, which means that each instance is unique. The `toString` method is implemented using `org.apache.commons.lang.builder.ToStringBuilder`. All of these event classes are lightweight, and they have no references to other domain classes (no object reference; only a number — `accountNumber` — in this case). They are also implementing the `Serializable` interface. This makes them easier to transfer between JVMs. As best practice, this event is immutable. The two properties above (`accountNumber` and `severity`) are marked as final. They can be set only through a constructor (there are no `set` methods — only two `get` methods). The `get` methods were excluded from this code listing.

The events themselves don't carry a time of occurrence — a time stamp (they easily could, if we needed it; we'll see *how* in the next set of code listings). When the event is inserted into the knowledge session, the rule engine assigns such a time stamp to `FactHandle` that is returned. (Remember? `session.insert(..)` returns a `FactHandle`). In fact, there is a special implementation of `FactHandle` called `EventFactHandle`. It extends the `DefaultFactHandle` (which is used for normal facts) and adds few additional fields, for example — `startTimestamp` and `duration`. Both contain millisecond values and are of type `long`.

Ok, we now have the event classes and we know that there is a special `FactHandle` for events. However, we still don't know how to tell Drools that our class represents an event. Drools *type declarations* provide this missing link. It can define new types and enhance existing types. For example, to specify that the class `TransactionCreatedEvent` is an event, we have to write:

```
declare TransactionCreatedEvent
    @role( event )
end
```

Code listing 2: Event role declaration (`cep.drl` file).

This code can reside inside a normal `.drl` file. If our event had a time stamp property or a duration property, we could map it into `startTimestamp` or `duration` properties of `EventFactHandle` by using the following mapping:

```
@duration( durationProperty )
```

Code listing 3: Duration property mapping.

The name in brackets is the actual name of the property of our event that will be mapped to the `duration` property of `EventFactHandle`. This can be done similarly for `startTimestamp` property.

 As an event's state should not be changed (only unpopulated values can be populated), think twice before declaring existing beans as events. Modification to a property may result in an unpredictable behavior.

In the following examples, we'll also see how to define a new *type declaration* (as shown in code listing 16).

Fraud detection rules

Let's imagine that the system processes thousands of transactions at any given time. It is clear that this is challenging in terms of time and memory consumption. It is simply not possible to keep all of the data (transactions, accounts, and so on) in memory. A possible solution would be to keep all of the accounts in memory as there won't be that many of them (in comparison to transactions) and *keep only transactions for a certain period*. With Drools Fusion, we can do this very easily by declaring that a `Transaction` is an event.

The transaction will then be inserted into the knowledge session through an `entry-point`. Each entry point defines a partition in the input data storage, reducing the match space and allowing patterns to target specific partitions. Matching data from a partition requires explicit reference at the pattern declaration. This makes sense, especially if there are large quantities of data and only some rules are interested in them. We'll look at entry points in the following example.

If you are still concerned about the volume of objects in memory, this solution can be easily partitioned, for example, by account number. There might be more servers, each processing only a subset of accounts (simple routing strategy might be: `accountNumber module totalNumberOfServersInCluster`). Then each server would receive only appropriate events.

Notification

The requirement we're going to implement here is essentially to block an account whenever a `LostCardEvent` is received. This rule will match two facts: one of type `Account` and one of type `LostCardEvent`. The rule will then set the the status of this account to blocked. The implementation of the rule is as follows:

```
rule notification
    when
        $account : Account( status != Account.Status.BLOCKED )
        LostCardEvent( accountNumber == $account.number )
            from entry-point LostCardStream
    then
        modify($account) {
            setStatus(Account.Status.BLOCKED)
        };
    end
```

Code listing 4: Notification rule that blocks an account (`cep.drl` file).

As we already know, `Account` is an ordinary fact from the knowledge session. The second fact—`LostCardEvent`—is an event from an entry point called `LostCardStream`. Whenever a new event is created and goes through the entry point, `LostCardStream`, this rule tries to match (checks if its conditions can be satisfied). If there is an `Account` in the knowledge session that didn't match with this event yet, and all conditions are met, the rule is activated. The consequence sets the status of the account to *blocked* in a modify block.

As we're updating the account in the consequence and also matching on it in the condition, we have to add a constraint that matches only the non-blocked accounts to prevent looping (see above: `status != Account.Status.BLOCKED`).

Test configuration setup

Following the best practice that every code/rule needs to be tested, we'll now set up a class for writing unit tests. All of the rules will be written in a file called `cep.drl`. When creating this file, just make sure it is on the classpath. The creation of `knowledgeBase` won't be shown. It is similar to the previous tests that we've written. We just need to change the default knowledge base configuration slightly:

```
KnowledgeBaseConfiguration config = KnowledgeBaseFactory
    .newKnowledgeBaseConfiguration();
config.setOption( EventProcessingOption.STREAM );
```

Code listing 5: Enabling STREAM event processing mode on knowledge base configuration.

This will enable the STREAM event processing mode. KnowledgeBaseConfiguration from the preceding code is then used when creating the knowledge base — KnowledgeBaseFactory.newKnowledgeBase(config).

Part of the setup is also clock initialization. We already know that every event has a time stamp. This time stamp comes from a clock which is inside the knowledge session. Drools supports several clock types, for example, a *real-time clock* or a *pseudo clock*. The real-time clock is the default and should be used in normal circumstances. The pseudo clock is especially useful for testing as we have complete control over the time. The following initialize method sets up a pseudo clock. This is done by setting the clock type on KnowledgeSessionConfiguration and passing this object to the newStatefulKnowledgeSession method of knowledgeBase. The initialize method then makes this clock available as a test instance variable called clock when calling session.getSessionClock(), as we can see in the following code:

```
public class CepTest {
    static KnowledgeBase knowledgeBase;
    StatefulKnowledgeSession session;
    Account account;
    FactHandle accountHandle;
    SessionPseudoClock clock;
    TrackingAgendaEventListener trackingAgendaEventListener;
    WorkingMemoryEntryPoint entry;

    @Before
    public void initialize() throws Exception {
        KnowledgeSessionConfiguration conf =
            KnowledgeBaseFactory.newKnowledgeSessionConfiguration();
        conf.setOption( ClockTypeOption.get( "pseudo" ) );
        session = knowledgeBase.newStatefulKnowledgeSession(conf,
            null);
        clock = (SessionPseudoClock) session.getSessionClock();
        trackingAgendaEventListener =
            new TrackingAgendaEventListener();
        session.addEventListener(trackingAgendaEventListener);
        account = new Account();
        account.setNumber(1234561);
        account.setBalance(BigDecimal.valueOf(1000.00));
        accountHandle = session.insert(account);
```

Code listing 6: Unit tests setup (CepTest.java file).

The preceding initialize method also creates an event listener and passes it into the session. The event listener is called TrackingAgendaEventListener. It simply tracks all of the rule executions. It is useful for unit testing to verify whether a rule fired or not. Its implementation is as follows:

```
public class TrackingAgendaEventListener extends
    DefaultAgendaEventListener {
  List<String> rulesFiredList = new ArrayList<String>();

  @Override
  public void afterActivationFired(
      AfterActivationFiredEvent event) {
    rulesFiredList.add(event.getActivation().getRule()
        .getName());
  }

  public boolean isRuleFired(String ruleName) {
    for (String firedRuleName : rulesFiredList) {
      if (firedRuleName.equals(ruleName)) {
        return true;
      }
    }
    return false;
  }
  public void reset() {
    rulesFiredList.clear();
  }
}
```

Code listing 7: Agenda event listener that tracks all rules that have been fired.

DefaultAgendaEventListener comes from the org.drools.
event.rule package that is part of drools-api.jar file as opposed
to the org.drools.event package that is part of the old API in
drools-core.jar.

All of the Drools agenda event listeners must implement the AgendaEventListener
interface. TrackingAgendaEventListener in the preceding code extends
DefaultAgendaEventListener so that we don't have to implement all of the
methods defined in the AgendaEventListener interface. Our listener just overrides
the afterActivationFired method that will be called by Drools every time a rule's
consequence has been executed. Our implementation of this method adds the fired
rule name into a list of fired rules—rulesFiredList. Then the convenience method
isRuleFired takes a ruleName as a parameter and checks if this rule has been
executed/fired. The reset method is useful for clearing out the state of this listener,
for example, after session.fireAllRules is called.

Now, back to the test configuration setup. The last part of the `initialize` method from code listing 6 is account object creation (`account = new Account(); ...`). This is for convenience purposes so that every test does not have to create one. The account balance is set to `1000`. The account is inserted into the knowledge session and its `FactHandle` is stored so that the account object can be easily updated.

Testing the notification rule

The test infrastructure is now fully set up and we can write a test for the `notification` rule from code listing 4 as follows:

```
@Test
public void notification() throws Exception {
    session.fireAllRules();
    assertNotSame(Account.Status.BLOCKED,account.getStatus());

    entry = session
        .getWorkingMemoryEntryPoint("LostCardStream");
    entry.insert(new LostCardEvent(account.getNumber()));
    session.fireAllRules();
    assertSame(Account.Status.BLOCKED, account.getStatus());
}
```

Code listing 8: Notification rule's unit test (`CepTest.java` file).

The test verifies that the account is not blocked by accident first. Then it gets the `LostCardStream` entry point from the session by calling: `session.getWorkingMem oryEntryPoint("LostCardStream")`. Then the code listing demonstrates how an event can be inserted into the knowledge session through an entry-point—`entry. insert(new LostCardEvent(...))`.

In a real application, you'll probably want to use Drools Pipeline for inserting events into the knowledge session. It can be easily connected to an existing **ESB (Enterprise Service** Bus) or a JMS topic or queue.

Drools entry points are thread-safe. Each entry point can be used by a different thread; however, no two threads can concurrently use the same entry point. In this case, it makes sense to start the engine in `fireUntilHalt` mode in a separate thread like this:

```
new Thread(new Runnable() {
    public void run() {
        session.fireUntilHalt();
    }
}).start();
```

Code listing 9: Continuous execution of rules.

The engine will then continuously execute activations until the `session. halt()` method is called.

The test then verifies that the status of the account is blocked. If we simply executed `session.insert(new LostCardEvent(..));` the test would fail because the rule wouldn't see the event.

Monitoring—averageBalanceQuery

In this section, we'll look at how to write some monitoring rules/queries over the data that is in the knowledge session. Let's say that we want to know what is the average balance across all accounts. As all of them are in the knowledge session, we could use `collect` (that was introduced in Chapter 6, *Stateful Session*) to collect all of the accounts into a collection and then iterate over this collection, sum up all of the balances, and then divide it by the number of accounts. Another, more preferred solution is to use *neighbor* of `collect – accumulate`. The following is a query that calculates the average balance across all accounts:

```
query averageBalanceQuery
   Number( $averageBalance : doubleValue ) from accumulate(
      $account : Account($balance : balance), average($balance))
end
```

Code listing 10: Query for calculating the average balance over all accounts (`cep.drl` file).

`accumulate` has two forms. This is a simple one. Similar to `collect`, it iterates over objects in the knowledge session that meet the given criteria; however, in case of `accumulate`, it performs some action on each of the individual objects before returning the result. In our example, the action is: `average($balance)`. Finally, the result is returned as $averageBalance variable. The average balance is updated whenever there is a new account or an existing account is updated or retracted from the knowledge session. Similar to `collect`, you can think of it as a **continuous query**. Other useful functions that can be used within accumulate are:

- `count` – for counting objects
- `min/max` – for finding the minimum/maximum value
- `sum` – for calculating the sum of all the values and others

Some of them will be shown in the following examples. We'll also define a new one.

> The accumulate function can take any code block (written in the current dialect). This means that it is, for example, valid to write: `sum($account.getBalance().multiply($account.getInterestRate()))`

Testing the averageBalanceQuery

The test for this `averageBalanceQuery` query is shown in the following code. First, it will use the default setup, which includes one account in the knowledge session that has balance of `1000`. Then, it will add another account into the knowledge session and verify that the average balance is correct.

```
@Test
public void averageBalanceQuery() throws Exception {
    session.fireAllRules();
    assertEquals(account.getBalance(), getAverageBalance());

    Account account2 = new Account();
    account2.setBalance(BigDecimal.valueOf(1400));
    session.insert(account2);
    session.fireAllRules();
    assertEquals(BigDecimal.valueOf(1200.00),
        getAverageBalance());
}

BigDecimal getAverageBalance() {
    QueryResults queryResults = session
        .getQueryResults("averageBalanceQuery");
    return BigDecimal.valueOf((Double) queryResults
        .iterator().next().get("$averageBalance"));
}
```

Code listing 11: Test for the `averageBalanceQuery` (`CepTest.java` file).

The `getAverageBalance` method gets the query results and extracts the `$averageBalance` variable.

Two large withdrawals

We'll now look at the next rule. A rule that will flag two transactions as suspicious if they are withdrawing more than 300% of the average withdrawn amount over 30 days. The problem is how to find out the average withdrawn amount for an account over 30 days. This is when *sliding time windows* or *sliding length windows* come in handy. They allow us to match only those events that originated within the window. In case of time windows, the session clock's time minus event's time stamp must be within the window time. In case of length windows, only the N most recent events are taken into account. Time/Length windows also have another very important reason. When running in STREAM mode, Drools can *automatically retract events that are no longer needed* — those that are outside the window. (This applies to all of the events that were inserted into the knowledge session).

The average withdrawn amount can be calculated by averaging the amount of TransactionCompletedEvent. We are only interested in transactions that have already been successfully completed. We can now match only those transactions that happened within the last 30 days: over window:time(30d) from entry-point TransactionStream. If we, for example, wanted 10 most recent events, we'd write over window:length(10) from entry-point TransactionStream.

We know how to calculate the average withdrawn amount. All that remains now is to find two transactions happening over ninety seconds that are withdrawing 300% or more. TransactionCreatedEvent can be used to find those transactions. The implementation is as follows:

```
rule twoLargeWithdrawals
dialect "mvel"
  when
    $account : Account( )
    Number( $averageAmount : doubleValue ) from accumulate(
      TransactionCompletedEvent( fromAccountNumber ==
      $account.number, $amount : amount )
      over window:time( 30d ) from entry-point
      TransactionStream, average( $amount ) )
    $t1 : TransactionCreatedEvent( fromAccountNumber ==
      $account.number, amount > ($averageAmount * 3.00) ) over
      window:time(90s) from entry-point TransactionStream
    $t2 : TransactionCreatedEvent( this != $t1,
      fromAccountNumber == $account.number,
      amount > ($averageAmount * 3.00) ) over
      window:time(90s) from entry-point TransactionStream
  then
    insert(new SuspiciousAccount($account.number,
      SuspiciousAccountSeverity.MINOR));
    insert(new SuspiciousTransaction($t1.transactionUuid,
      SuspiciousTransactionSeverity.MINOR));
    insert(new SuspiciousTransaction($t2.transactionUuid,
      SuspiciousTransactionSeverity.MINOR));
end
```

Code listing 12: Implementation of the twoLargeWithdrawals rule (cep.drl file).

The rule is matching an `Account`, calculating `$averageAmount` for this account, and finally matching two different `TransactionCreatedEvents` (we make sure that they are different by executing `this != $t1`). These events represent transactions from this account which have an amount 300% larger than `$averageAmount`. This is enforced with the constraint: `amount > ($averageAmount * 3.00)`. These events must occur in a time window of 90 seconds as can be seen above—`over window: time(90s)` from `entry-point TransactionStream`. The consequence then inserts three new events into the knowledge session. They flag the account and transactions as suspicious with severity, `MINOR`.

As you may have noticed, in this rule, we've used one stream—`TransactionStream`—for getting two types of events. This is completely valid. Note that performance is directly proportional to the number of partial matches. Drools is capable of handling heterogeneous streams with extreme performance. You will see no performance difference between homogeneous and heterogeneous streams.

If you are using a real-time clock, think twice about the length of the time window. Under a heavy load, the CPU might be so busy, that the event won't be processed in the expected time window. In that case, the sliding length window makes more sense.

Testing the twoLargeWithdrawals rule

As usual, our unit test will exercise some of the corner cases where the rule is most likely to break. It will follow the sequence of events presented in the following time line diagram:

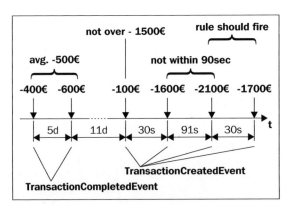

Each event is represented by an arrow pointing down. At the base of the arrow is the amount that is being withdrawn. The first two events are of type `TransactionCompletedEvent` and their task is to build the average amount that was withdrawn. The average will be 500. The following events are of type

`TransactionCreatedEvent` and they are the ones we want to keep an eye on. The first two of them meet the time constraint of 90 seconds, but the first isn't three times greater than the average. Therefore, our rule won't be activated. The next event comes after 91 seconds, which doesn't meet the time window constraint. Finally, the last two events meet all of the constraints and we can verify that the rule fired, and that the account and transactions were marked as suspicious. The test implementation is as follows:

```
@Test
public void twoLargeWithdrawals() throws Exception {
    entry = session
        .getWorkingMemoryEntryPoint("TransactionStream");
    transactionCompletedEvent(400);
    clock.advanceTime(5, TimeUnit.DAYS);
    transactionCompletedEvent(600);
    clock.advanceTime(11, TimeUnit.DAYS);

    transactionCreatedEvent(100);
    clock.advanceTime(30, TimeUnit.SECONDS);
    transactionCreatedEvent(1600);
    assertNotFired("twoLargeWithdrawals");

    clock.advanceTime(91, TimeUnit.SECONDS);
    transactionCreatedEvent(2100);
    assertNotFired("twoLargeWithdrawals");

    clock.advanceTime(30, TimeUnit.SECONDS);
    transactionCreatedEvent(1700);
    assertFired("twoLargeWithdrawals");
}
```

Code listing 13: Test for the `twoLargeWithdrawals` rule (file `CepTest.java`).

For brevity, commonly used code snippets have been re-factored into helper methods. For example, the creation of `TransactionCompletedEvent` and its insertion into the session has been re-factored into the following method — `transactionCompletedEvent` — as follows:

```
private void transactionCompletedEvent(
    double amountTransferred) {
    entry.insert(new TransactionCompletedEvent(BigDecimal
        .valueOf(amountTransferred), account.getNumber()));
}
```

Code listing 14: Helper method that creates `TransactionCompletedEvent` and inserts it into the knowledge session (`CepTest.java` file).

The event is initialized with the transferred amount and source account number. As you may imagine, the `transactionCreatedEvent` method from code listing 13 is similar.

Another helper method—`assertFired`—takes a rule name as an argument, fires rule that matches this name, and verifies that the rule fired using `trackingAgendaEventListener`:

```
private void assertFired(String ruleName) {
  session.fireAllRules(new RuleNameEqualsAgendaFilter(
      ruleName));
  assertTrue(trackingAgendaEventListener
      .isRuleFired(ruleName));
}
```

Code listing 15: Helper method for verifying that a rule with specified name has fired (`CepTest.java` file).

The Agenda filter—`RuleNameEqualsAgendaFilter`—was already used in Chapter 4, *Data Transformation*. Do not use the deprecated `org.drools.base.` `RuleNameEqualsAgendaFilter`, otherwise, you'll get compilation errors. The logic is the same; however, the deprecated Agenda filter doesn't use the new API.

As you may imagine, the `assertNotFired` method is similar to `assertFired` method. If we now run the `twoLargeWithdrawals` test, everything should pass as expected.

Sequence of increasing withdrawals

We'll now focus on the next requirement from the list. Among other things, it talks about an account's average balance over 30 days. We shouldn't have any problem in calculating this. Thinking about the implementation of the rule, it seems that more rules are calculating these averages. We should be able to separate this logic into another rule that will calculate this information and store it into some common data structure. Other rules will just match on this data structure and use the calculated averages. We have a plan! Now, let's define this data structure. Drools *type declarations* can be used for this purpose. The declaration may look as follows:

```
declare AccountInfo
    number : Long
    averageBalance : BigDecimal
    averageAmount : BigDecimal
end
```

Code listing 16: `AccountInfo` type declaration (`cep.drl` file).

Please note that in this use of the `declare` keyword, we're not modifying the existing type (as was the case in code listing 2) but adding a completely new one. `AccountInfo` is a simple POJO that resides in the same package as the `.drl` file package that it is declared in. `equals/hashCode` of `AccountInfo` are inherited from the `java.lang.Object` class. If we'd like to add some fields to the `equals/hashCode` contract, we can declare it with `@key()` metadata, for example: `number : Long @key`.

The common data structure is there, we can write the rule that will populate it. Our rule will match an `Account` object, calculate its average balance over 30 days, and will set this calculated amount into the `AccountInfo` object.

```
rule averageBalanceOver30Days
no-loop true
  when
    $account : Account( )
    $averageBalance : BigDecimal( ) from accumulate(
      AccountUpdatedEvent( accountNumber == $account.number,
      $balance : balance ) over window:time( 30d )
      from entry-point AccountStream, average( $balance ) )
    $accountInfo : AccountInfo( number == $account.number )
  then
    modify($accountInfo) {
        setAverageBalance($averageBalance)
    };
  end
```

Code listing 17: Rule that calculates average balance for an account over 30 days (`cep.drl` file).

The `averageBalanceOver30Days` rule accumulates `AccountUpdateEvents` in order to calculate the average balance over 30 days. Finally, the consequence sets calculated `$averageBalance` into `$accountInfo`.

Average balance test

The `AccountInfo` object needs to be added into the knowledge session before the `averagebalanceover30days` rule is activated. As it is an internal type, we cannot simply make a new instance of this class (for example, to call `new AccountInfo()`). This type will only be created at runtime, when the knowledge package is compiled. The Drools team thought about this and they have added a method to `KnowledgeBase` called `getFactType`, which returns an object implementing the `org.drools.definition.type.FactType` interface. This interface encapsulates the type information about an internal type. It allows us to create new instances, get list of fields, set/get their properties, and even get a map of field-value pairs and set the values from such map.

The `AccountInfo` bean may be used by many rules, so we'll add it into our unit test `initialize` method that is called before every test method execution. First, let's add types to our test class that will be needed:

```
FactType accountInfoFactType;
Object accountInfo;
FactHandle accountInfoHandle;
```

Code listing 18: `CepTest` unit test class properties (`CepTest.java` file).

Now, the following `AccountInfo` setup logic can be added at the end of the `initialize` method. The following code listing will demonstrate how a new instance of an internal type can be created and its properties can be set:

```
accountInfoFactType = knowledgeBase.getFactType(
    "droolsbook.cep", "AccountInfo");
accountInfo = accountInfoFactType.newInstance();
accountInfoFactType.set(accountInfo, "number",
    account.getNumber());
accountInfoFactType.set(accountInfo, "averageBalance",
    BigDecimal.ZERO);
accountInfoFactType.set(accountInfo, "averageAmount",
    BigDecimal.ZERO);
accountInfoHandle = session.insert(accountInfo);
```

Code listing 19: `AccountInfo` internal type setup (`CepTest.java` file).

The first line gets the fact type from the knowledge session. The `getFactType` method takes the `.drl` file package name and name of the fact type. Then a new instance is created—`accountInfoFactType.newInstance()`. `accountInfoFactType` is then used to set properties on the `accountInfo` instance. Finally, `accountInfo` is inserted into the session and its fact handle is kept.

Similarly, `AccountInfo`'s initialization code might be needed in a real application. When the application starts up, `AccountInfo` should be pre-initialized with some reasonable data.

The unit test of `averagebalanceover30days` follows. It will create some `AccountUpdatedEvent` events and verify that they are used to calculate the correct average balance.

```
@Test
public void averageBalanceOver30Days() throws Exception {
  entry = session
        .getWorkingMemoryEntryPoint("AccountStream");
  accountUpdatedEvent(account.getNumber(), 1000.50,1000.50);
  accountUpdatedEvent(account.getNumber(), -700.40, 300.10);
  accountUpdatedEvent(account.getNumber(), 500, 800);
```

```
    accountUpdatedEvent(112233441, 700, 1300);
    assertFired("averageBalanceOver30Days");
    assertEquals(BigDecimal.valueOf(700.20).setScale(2),
       accountInfoFactType.get(accountInfo,"averageBalance"));
}
```

Code listing 20: Unit test for the `averageBalanceOver30Days` rule
(`CepTest.java` file).

The test first obtains the `AccountStream` entry point for inserting the events. It uses `accountUpdateEvent` helper method to create `AccountUpdatedEvents`. This method takes the account number, amount transferred, and balance. These parameters are passed directly into the event's constructor as was the case in the previous unit test. The test also creates one unrelated `AccountUpdatedEvent=` to verify that it won't be included in the calculation. Finally, the test verifies that the rule has been fired and the average is of expected value `700.20` ((1000.50 + 300.10 + 800)/3 = 2100.60 / 3 = 700.20).

However, when we run the test, it fails as soon as `fireAllRules` method is called with the error: `org.drools.spi.ConsequenceException: java.lang.ClassCastException: java.lang.Double cannot be cast to java.math.BigDecimal`

Drools is informing us that there is a problem with the invocation of the rule's consequence. The consequence uses `$averageBalance` that was calculated by `accumulate`. Luckily, Drools is open source so we can look under the hood. As was mentioned in the preceding sections, accumulate supports pluggable functions (`average`, `sum`, `count`, and so on). These functions are implementations of the `org.drools.runtime.rule.AccumulateFunction` interface.

If we look at the average function's implementation in class `AverageAccumulateFunction`, we'll notice that its state consists of two fields; `count` of type `int` and `total` of type `double`. Here lies the problem. Our domain model uses `BigDecimal`, as best practice when working with floating point numbers. However, `average` casts all of the numbers to primitive `double`. We will now write our own implementation of `AccumulateFunction` that knows how to work with `BigDecimal`. This function will be called `bigDecimalAverage` and will be used as follows (note the last line):

```
$averageBalance : BigDecimal( ) from accumulate(
   AccountUpdatedEvent( accountNumber == $account.number,
   $balance : balance ) over window:time( 30d ) from
   entry-point AccountStream, bigDecimalAverage($balance))
```

Code listing 21: Part of `averageBalanceOver30Days` rule, that calculates the average balance using the new `bigDecimalAverage` accumulate function (`cep.drl` file).

The knowledge base setup needs to be modified, so that Drools knows about our new `accumulate` function implementation. A new `KnowledgeBuilderConfiguration` will hold this information.

```
KnowledgeBuilderConfiguration builderConf =
   KnowledgeBuilderFactory.newKnowledgeBuilderConfiguration();
builderConf.setOption(AccumulateFunctionOption.get(
   "bigDecimalAverage",
   new BigDecimalAverageAccumulateFunction()));
```

Code listing 22: Section of unit test's `setupClass` method (`CepTest.java` file).

`AccumulateFunctionOption` is set with the new accumulate function—`BigDecimalAverageAccumulateFunction`—on the knowledge builder configuration. This configuration can be passed to the `KnowledgeBuilderFactory.newKnowledgeBuilder(builderConf)` factory method that is used to create the knowledge base.

> Another way to configure our accumulate function is to use a configuration file—`META-INF/drools.packagebuilder.conf`—with the following contents (all on one line):
>
>   drools.accumulate.function.
>   bigDecimalAverage = droolsbook.accumulate.
>   BigDecimalAverageAccumulateFunction
>
> Make sure this file is on the classpath. This configuration works not only for Drools, but also for the Drools Eclipse plugin. The Eclipse plugin will acknowledge the existence of the accumulate function and will not raise errors in the IDE.

Let's move to the implementation of the accumulate function. We'll first need some value holder for `count` and `total` fields. This value holder will encapsulate all of the information that the accumulate function invocation needs. The function itself must be *stateless*.

```
/**
 * value holder that stores the total amount and how many
 * numbers were aggregated
 */
public static class AverageData implements Externalizable {
  public int count = 0;
  public BigDecimal total = BigDecimal.ZERO;

  public void readExternal(ObjectInput in)
      throws IOException, ClassNotFoundException {
    count = in.readInt();
```

```
        total = (BigDecimal) in.readObject();
      }
      public void writeExternal(ObjectOutput out)
          throws IOException {
        out.writeInt(count);
        out.writeObject(total);
      }
    }
```

Code listing 23: `AverageData` value holder
(`BigDecimalAverageAccumulateFunction.java` file).

Note that `AverageData` holder is a static member class of
`BigDecimalAverageAccumulateFunction`. The value holder implements the
`Externalizable` interface so that it can be serialized. Finally, its the implementation
of the `BigDecimalAverageAccumulateFunction` that defines the behavior of our
custom function:

```
public class BigDecimalAverageAccumulateFunction implements
    AccumulateFunction {
  /**
   * creates and returns a context object
   */
  public Serializable createContext() {
    return new AverageData();
  }
  /**
   * initializes this accumulator
   */
  public void init(Serializable context) throws Exception {
    AverageData data = (AverageData) context;
    data.count = 0;
    data.total = BigDecimal.ZERO;
  }
  /**
   * @return true if this accumulator supports reverse
   */
  public boolean supportsReverse() {
    return true;
  }
  /**
   * accumulate the given value, increases count
   */
```

```
public void accumulate(Serializable context, Object value) {
  AverageData data = (AverageData) context;
  data.count++;
  data.total = data.total.add((BigDecimal) value);
}

/**
 * retracts accumulated amount, decreases count
 */
public void reverse(Serializable context, Object value)
    throws Exception {
  AverageData data = (AverageData) context;
  data.count++;
  data.total = data.total.subtract((BigDecimal) value);
}

/**
 * @return currently calculated value
 */
public Object getResult(Serializable context)
    throws Exception {
  AverageData data = (AverageData) context;
  return data.count == 0 ? BigDecimal.ZERO : data.total
      .divide(BigDecimal.valueOf(data.count),
          RoundingMode.HALF_UP);
}
```

Code listing 24: Custom accumulate function —
`BigDecimalAverageAccumulateFunction`.

The `createContext` method (at the beginning of the preceding code listing) creates a new instance of the `AverageData` value holder. The `init` method initializes the accumulate function. `supportsReverse` informs the rule engine whether this accumulate function supports the retracting of objects. (when a fact is being removed from the knowledge session — `session.retract(..)` or an existing fact is

modified — `session.update(..)`) If it doesn't, the rule engine will have to do more work if an object is being retracted and the calculation will have to start over. The `accumulate`/`reverse` methods are there to execute/reverse the accumulate action (in this case, the calculation of `count` and `total`). The `getResult` method calculates the result. Our implementation uses hard-coded rounding mode of type `HALF_UP`. This can be easily customized if needed.

Most, if not all, Drools pluggable components implement the `Externalizable` interface. This is also the case with the `AccumulateFunction` interface. We have to implement the two methods that this interface defines. As `BigDecimalAverageAccumulateFunction` is stateless, its `readExternal` and `writeExternal` methods are empty (they are not shown in the code listing).

If we now run the test for the `averageBalanceOver30Days` rule, it should pass without any errors.

 Instead of defining a custom accumulate function, we could have used the full (enhanced) version of accumulate. Please look into the Drools documentation for more information.

After a little side trip, we can now continue with writing the `sequenceOfIncreasingWithdrawals` rule. To refresh our memory: it is about three consecutive increasing debit transactions. With the arsenal of Drools keywords that we've learned so far, it should not be a problem to implement this rule. To make it even easier, we'll use *temporal operators*. Temporal operator (see in the following code listing — `after` and `before`) is a special type of operator that knows how to work with events (their time stamp and duration properties). In our case, we'll simply match three transactions that happened one after another (with no transactions in between).

```
rule sequenceOfIncreasingWithdrawals
  when
    $account:Account($number : number)
    $t1:TransactionCreatedEvent(fromAccountNumber == $number)
      from entry-point TransactionStream
    $t2:TransactionCreatedEvent(amount > $t1.amount,
      fromAccountNumber == $number, this after[0, 3m] $t1)
      from entry-point TransactionStream
    not (TransactionCreatedEvent(fromAccountNumber == $number,
      this after $t1, this before $t2 )
      from entry-point TransactionStream)
    $t3:TransactionCreatedEvent(amount > $t2.amount,
      fromAccountNumber == $number, this after[0, 3m] $t2 )
      from entry-point TransactionStream
    not (TransactionCreatedEvent(fromAccountNumber == $number,
      this after $t2, this before $t3 )
      from entry-point TransactionStream)
    $ai : AccountInfo(number == $number, eval($t1.amount.add(
      $t2.amount).add($t3.amount).compareTo(BigDecimal.
      valueOf(0.90).multiply(averageBalance)) > 0))
  then
```

```
insert(new SuspiciousAccount($number,
  SuspiciousAccountSeverity.MAJOR));
insert(new SuspiciousTransaction($t1.transactionUuid,
  SuspiciousTransactionSeverity.MAJOR));
insert(new SuspiciousTransaction($t2.transactionUuid,
  SuspiciousTransactionSeverity.MAJOR));
insert(new SuspiciousTransaction($t3.transactionUuid,
  SuspiciousTransactionSeverity.MAJOR));
end
```

Code listing 25: Implementation of the `sequenceOfIncreasingWithdrawals` rule (`cep.drl` file).

For example, as shown in the code above, `$t2` is a `TransactionCreatedEvent` that is withdrawing more than `$t1`, they are from the same account and temporal operator — after (`this after[0, 3m] $t1`) — ensures that the event `$t2` occurred after event `$t1` but within three minutes. The next line — not (`TransactionCreatedEvent( this after $t1, this before $t2 ) from ... )` is making sure that no event occurred between events `$t1` and `$t2`.

> Instead of using sliding time windows to check that two events happened within three minutes (`over window:time(3m)`), we're using temporal operators (`this after[0, 3m] $t1`). They are much cheaper in terms of the resources used. Also note that the example above tried to demonstrate several Drools features; however, if we want to reason over a sequence of N events, a more efficient way would be to use a "length" sliding window.

Operators in Drools are pluggable. This means that the temporal operators we've seen above are simply one of many implementations of the `org.drools.runtime.rule.EvaluatorDefinition` interface. Others are, for example, `soundslike`, `matches`, `coincides`, `meets`, `metby`, `overlaps`, `overlappedby`, `during`, `includes`, `starts`, `startedby`, `finishes`, or `finishedby`. Please see the appendix for defining a custom operator.

As we've seen, operators support parameters that can be specified within the square brackets. Each operator can interpret these parameters differently. It may also depend on the event's time stamp and duration (events we've used in our examples are so-called point in time events; they don't have any duration). For example, `this before[1m30s, 2m] $event2` means that the time when `this` event finished and `$event2` started is between `1m30s` and `2m`. Please consult the documentation of Drools Fusion for more details on each operator.

The last line of the `sequenceOfIncreasingWithdrawals` rule's condition tests whether the three matched transactions are withdrawing more than 90% of the average balance. The rule's consequence marks these transactions and account as suspicious.

Testing the sequenceOfIncreasingWithdrawals rule

The unit test for the `sequenceOfIncreasingWithdrawals` rule will follow this sequence of events:

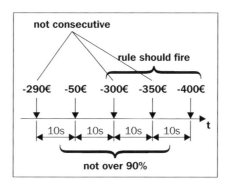

All withdrawals fit into the time window of three minutes. The first three withdrawals are not increasing and their sum is not over 90% of the average balance. The first, third, and fourth events meet all constraints (they are increasing and they are over 90%) except one (they are not consecutive). The second, third, and fourth events are not over 90%. Finally, the last three events meet all constraints and the rule should fire. The test method implementation is as follows:

```
@Test
public void sequenceOfIncreasingWithdrawals()
    throws Exception {
  entry = session
      .getWorkingMemoryEntryPoint("TransactionStream");
  accountInfoFactType.set(accountInfo, "averageBalance",
      BigDecimal.valueOf(1000));
  session.update(accountInfoHandle, accountInfo);

  transactionCreatedEvent(290);
  clock.advanceTime(10, TimeUnit.SECONDS);
  transactionCreatedEvent(50);
  clock.advanceTime(10, TimeUnit.SECONDS);
  transactionCreatedEvent(300);
  assertNotFired("sequenceOfIncreasingWithdrawals");

  clock.advanceTime(10, TimeUnit.SECONDS);
  transactionCreatedEvent(350);
  assertNotFired("sequenceOfIncreasingWithdrawals");
```

```
    clock.advanceTime(10, TimeUnit.SECONDS);
    transactionCreatedEvent(400);
    clock.advanceTime(1, TimeUnit.MICROSECONDS);
    assertFired("sequenceOfIncreasingWithdrawals");
}
```

Code listing 26: Unit test for the `sequenceOfIncreasingWithdrawals` rule
(`CepTest.java` file).

At the beginning of the `averageBalance` test, the property of `accountInfo` is set to
`1000`. The knowledge session is updated. The test executes successfully.

High activity

The next rule should catch fraudulent activities involving lots of small transactions.
For example, the number of transactions over a day is more than 500% of the
average number of transactions and the account's balance is less than 10% of the
average balance. Let's pretend that the `AccountInfo` has all the averages that we
need already calculated and ready to be used in other rules. We'll be able to use just
`AccountInfo` to see if the conditions are met for an `Account`.

```
rule highActivity
  when
    $account : Account ( )
    $accountInfo : AccountInfo ( number == $account.number,
      numberOfTransactions1Day > (averageNumberOfTransactions.
      multiply(BigDecimal.valueOf(5.00))), averageBalance >
      ($account.getBalance().multiply(
      BigDecimal.valueOf(10.00))) )
  then
    insert(new SuspiciousAccount($account.getNumber(),
      SuspiciousAccountSeverity.MINOR));
end
```

Code listing 27: Implementation of the `highActivity` rule (`cep.drl` file).

Thanks to decomposition, the rule looks simple. It will fire if
`numberOfTransactions1Day > averageNumberOfTransactions*500%`
(the number of transactions per one day is greater than 500% of the average number
of transactions per one day over 30 days) and if `averageBalance*10% > account's
balance` (10% of the average balance over 30 days is greater than account's balance).

Testing the highActivity rule

The test for the `highActivity` rule is divided into four parts. The first one tests the cases with a low number of transactions and a low average balance. The second part tests cases with a low number of transactions, the third part tests cases with a low average balance, and the fourth part tests the successful execution of the rule. The account's balance is set to `1000` by the `initialize` method. `averageNumberOfTransactions` of `AccountInfo` is set to `10`. That means, for a successful rule execution, `averageBalance` of `accountInfo` needs to be over 10000 and `numberOfTransactions1Day` needs to be over 50.

```
@Test
public void highActivity() throws Exception {
  accountInfoFactType.set(accountInfo,
      "averageNumberOfTransactions",BigDecimal.valueOf(10));
  accountInfoFactType.set(accountInfo,
      "numberOfTransactions1Day", 40l);
  accountInfoFactType.set(accountInfo, "averageBalance",
      BigDecimal.valueOf(9000));
  session.update(accountInfoHandle, accountInfo);
  assertNotFired("highActivity");

  accountInfoFactType.set(accountInfo, "averageBalance",
      BigDecimal.valueOf(11000));
  session.update(accountInfoHandle, accountInfo);
  assertNotFired("highActivity");

  accountInfoFactType.set(accountInfo,
      "numberOfTransactions1Day", 60l);
  accountInfoFactType.set(accountInfo, "averageBalance",
      BigDecimal.valueOf(6000));
  session.update(accountInfoHandle, accountInfo);
  assertNotFired("highActivity");

  accountInfoFactType.set(accountInfo, "averageBalance",
      BigDecimal.valueOf(11000));
  session.update(accountInfoHandle, accountInfo);
  assertFired("highActivity");
}
```

Code listing 28: Unit test for the `highActivity` rule (`CepTest.java` file).

This concludes rule implementations for the fraud detection system. We haven't implemented all of the rules specified in the requirements section, but they shouldn't be hard to do. I am sure that you can now implement a lot more sophisticated rules.

Summary

In this chapter, we've learned about Drools stream mode for Complex Event Processing. Events in Drools are immutable objects with strong time-related relationships. CEP has a great value, especially, if we need to make complex decisions over a high number of events. The engine automatically detects when an event is no longer needed and makes sure that it can be garbage collected. We've seen the use of time/length sliding windows and temporal operators.

This chapter also discussed the Drools type declarations which can define metadata on top of the existing types or define new types. As was demonstrated, new types are useful for rule decomposition.

Various examples of rules from a fictive fraud detection system were presented.

Drools is a very extensible tool. The development team tries to make almost every feature pluggable and customizable. Custom operators and custom accumulate functions are just a few examples of this plugability. The usage of some of the temporal operators was demonstrated.

8
Drools Flow

Every non-trivial business process needs to make complex decisions. A rule engine is the ideal place for these decisions to happen. However, it is impractical to invoke a rule engine from a standard workflow engine. Instead, if we take a rule engine and add workflow capabilities, we have an ideal tool to model complex business processes—Drools Flow.

The basics of Drools Flow were already covered in Chapter 5, *Human-readable Rules* (section, *Drools Flow*). We've learned about methods for managing rules execution order. Basic components/nodes of a ruleflow—start, end, action, ruleflow group, split, and join.

In this chapter, we'll look at Drools flow in more detail. We'll build a loan approval process and cover the following advanced concepts of a ruleflow: work items, human tasks, faults, subflows, events, and others.

Loan approval service

Loan approval is a complex process starting with customer requesting a loan. This request comes with information such as amount to be borrowed, duration of the loan, and destination account where the borrowed amount will be transferred. Only the existing customers can apply for a loan. The process starts with validating the request. Upon successful validation, a customer rating is calculated. Only customers with a certain rating are allowed to have loans. The loan is processed by a bank employee. As soon as an approved event is received from a supervisor, the loan is approved and money can be transferred to the destination account. An email is sent to inform the customer about the outcome.

Model

If we look at this process from the domain modeling perspective, in addition to model that we already have, we'll need a `Loan` class. An instance of this class will be a part of the context of this process.

The screenshot above shows Java Bean, `Loan`, for holding loan-related information. The `Loan` bean defines three properties. `amount` (which is of type `BigDecimal`), `destinationAccount` (which is of type `Account`; if the loan is approved, the amount will be transferred to this account), and `durationYears` (which represents a period for which the customer will be repaying this loan).

Loan approval ruleflow

We'll now represent this process as a ruleflow. It is shown in the following figure. Try to remember this figure because we'll be referring back to it throughout this chapter.

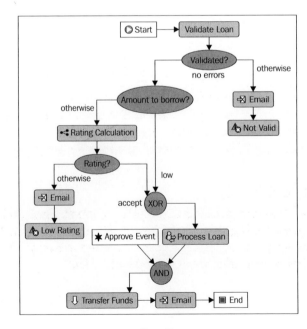

The preceding figure shows the loan approval process — `loanApproval.rf` file. You can use the **Ruleflow Editor** that comes with the Drools Eclipse plugin to create this ruleflow. The rest of the chapter will be a walk through this ruleflow explaining each node in more detail.

The process starts with **Validate Loan** ruleflow group. Rules in this group will check the loan for missing required values and do other more complex validation. Similar to what we've done before, each validation rule simply inserts `Message` into the knowledge session. The next node called **Validated?** is an **XOR** type split node. The ruleflow will continue through the **no errors** branch if there are no error or warning messages in the knowledge session — the split node constraint for this branch says:

```
not Message()
```

Code listing 1: **Validated?** split node **no errors** branch constraint (`loanApproval.rf` file).

For this to work, we need to import the `Message` type into the ruleflow. This can be done from the **Constraint editor**, just click on the **Imports...** button. The import statements are common for the whole ruleflow. Whenever we use a new type in the ruleflow (constraints, actions, and so on), it needs to be imported.

The **otherwise** branch is a "catch all" type branch (it is set to 'always true'). It has higher priority number, which means that it will be checked after the **no errors** branch.

 The `.rf` files are pure XML files that conform with a well formed XSD schema. They can be edited with any XML editor.

Invalid loan application form

If the validation didn't pass, an email is sent to the customer and the loan approval process finishes as **Not Valid**. This can be seen in the **otherwise** branch. There are two nodes — **Email** and **Not Valid**. **Email** is a special ruleflow node called work item.

Email work item

Work item is a node that encapsulates some piece of work. This can be an interaction with other system or some logic that is easier to write using standard Java. Each work item represents a piece of logic that can be reused in many systems. We can also look at work items as a ruleflow alternative to DSLs.

By default, Drools Flow comes with various generic work items, for example, **Email** (for sending emails), **Log** (for logging messages), **Finder** (for finding files on a file system), **Archive** (for archiving files), and **Exec** (for executing programs/system commands).

> In a real application, you'd probably want to use different work item than a generic one for sending an email. For example, a custom work item that inserts a record into your loan repository. Later on we'll see how to define a custom work item.

Each work item can take multiple parameters. In case of email, these are: *From*, *To*, *Subject*, *Text*, and others. Values for these parameters can be specified at ruleflow creation time or at runtime. By double-clicking on the **Email** node in the ruleflow, **Custom Work Editor** is opened (see the following screenshot). Please note that not all work items have a custom editor.

In the first tab (not visible), we can specify recipients and the source email address. In the second tab (visible), we can specify email's subject and body. If you look closer at the body of the email, you'll notice two placeholders. They have the following syntax: #{placeholder}. A placeholder can contain any mvel code and has access to all of the ruleflow variables (we'll learn more about ruleflow variables later in this chapter). This allows us to customize the work item parameters based on runtime conditions. As can be seen from the screenshot above, we use two placeholders: customer.firstName and errorList. customer and errorList are ruleflow variables. The first one represents the current Customer object and the second one is ValidationReport. When the ruleflow execution reaches this email work item, these placeholders are evaluated and replaced with the actual values (by calling the toString method on the result).

Fault node

The second node in the **otherwise** branch in the loan approval process ruleflow is a fault node. Fault node is similar to an end node. It accepts one incoming connection and has no outgoing connections. When the execution reaches this node, a fault is thrown with given name. We could, for example, register a fault handler that will generate a record in our reporting database. However, we won't register a fault handler, and in that case, it will simply indicate that this ruleflow finished with an error.

Test setup

We'll now write a test for the **otherwise** branch. First, let's set up the test environment.

Similar to what was done in Chapter 5, *Human-readable Rules*—a knowledge base needs to be created from multiple files. For now, they are: `loanApproval.drl` and `loanApproval.rf`, and later on we'll add two more: `ratingCalculation.drl` and `ratingCalculation.rf`.

Then a new session is created in the setup method along with some test data. A valid `Customer` with one `Account` is requesting a `Loan`. The setup method will create a valid loan configuration and the individual tests can then change this configuration in order to test various exceptional cases.

```
@Before
public void setUp() throws Exception {
  session = knowledgeBase.newStatefulKnowledgeSession();
  trackingProcessEventListener =
    new TrackingProcessEventListener();
  session.addEventListener(trackingProcessEventListener);
  session.getWorkItemManager().registerWorkItemHandler(
      "Email", new SystemOutWorkItemHandler());

  loanSourceAccount = new Account();

  customer = new Customer();
  customer.setFirstName("Bob");
  customer.setLastName("Green");
  customer.setEmail("bob.green@mail.com");
  Account account = new Account();
  account.setNumber(1234567891);
  customer.addAccount(account);
  account.setOwner(customer);

  loan = new Loan();
  loan.setDestinationAccount(account);
  loan.setAmount(BigDecimal.valueOf(4000.0));
  loan.setDurationYears(2);
```

Code listing 2: Test setup method called before every test execution (`DefaulLoanApprovalServiceTest.java` file).

A tracking ruleflow event listener is created and added to the knowledge session. Similar to `TrackingAgendaEventListener` that was used in the previous chapter, this event listener will record the execution path of a ruleflow—store all of the executed ruleflow nodes in a list. `TrackingProcessEventListener` overrides the `beforeNodeTriggered` method and gets the node to be executed by calling `event.getNodeInstance()`.

`loanSourceAccount` represents the bank's account for sourcing loans.

The setup method also registers an `Email` work item handler. A work item handler is responsible for execution of the work item (in this case, connecting to the mail server and sending out emails). However, the `SystemOutWorkItemHandler` implementation that we've used is only a dummy implementation that writes some information to the console. It is useful for our testing purposes.

Testing the 'otherwise' branch of 'Validated?' node

We'll now test the **otherwise** branch, which sends an email informing the applicant about missing data and ends with a fault. Our test (the following code) will set up a loan request that will fail the validation. It will then verify that the fault node was executed and that the ruleflow process was aborted.

```
@Test
public void notValid() {
   session.insert(new DefaultMessage());
   startProcess();

   assertTrue(trackingProcessEventListener.isNodeTriggered(
      PROCESS_LOAN_APPROVAL, NODE_FAULT_NOT_VALID));
   assertEquals(ProcessInstance.STATE_ABORTED,
      processInstance.getState());
}
```

Code listing 3: Test method for testing **Validated?** node's **otherwise** branch (`DefaultLoanApprovalServiceTest.java` file).

By inserting a message into the session, we're simulating a validation error. The ruleflow should end up in the **otherwise** branch.

Next, the test above calls the `startProcess` method . Its implementation is as follows:

```
private void startProcess() {
   Map<String, Object> parameterMap =
      new HashMap<String, Object>();
   parameterMap.put("loanSourceAccount", loanSourceAccount);
   parameterMap.put("customer", customer);
   parameterMap.put("loan", loan);
```

```
    processInstance = session.startProcess(
        PROCESS_LOAN_APPROVAL, parameterMap);
    session.insert(processInstance);
    session.fireAllRules();
}
```

Code listing 4: Utility method for starting the ruleflow
(`DefaultLoanApprovalServiceTest.java` file).

The `startProcess` method starts the loan approval process. It also sets
`loanSourceAccount`, `loan`, and `customer` as ruleflow variables. The resulting
process instance is, in turn, inserted into the knowledge session. This will enable
our rules to make more sophisticated decisions based on the state of current process
instance. Finally, all of the rules are fired.

We're already supplying three variables to the ruleflow; however, we haven't
declared them yet. Let's fix this. Ruleflow variables can be added through the
Eclipse's **Properties** editor as can be seen in the following screenshot (just click
on the ruleflow canvas, this should give the focus to the ruleflow itself). Each
variable needs a name type and, optionally, a value.

The preceding screenshot shows how to set the loan ruleflow variable. Its **Type** is
set to **Object** and **ClassName** is set to the full type name `droolsbook.bank.model.`
`Loan`. The other two variables are set in a similar manner.

Now back to the test from code listing 3. It verifies that the correct nodes were triggered and that the process ended in aborted state. The isNodeTriggered method takes the process ID, which is stored in a constant called PROCESS_LOAN_APPROVAL. The method also takes the node ID as second argument. This node ID can be found in the properties view after clicking on the fault node. The node ID—NODE_FAULT_ NOT_VALID—is a constant of type long defined as a property of this test class.

```
static final long NODE_FAULT_NOT_VALID = 21;
static final long NODE_SPLIT_VALIDATED = 20;
```

Code listing 5: Constants that holds fault and **Validated?** node's IDs (DefaultLoanApprovalServiceTest.java file).

By using the node ID, we can change node's name and other properties without breaking this test (node ID is least likely to change). Also, if we're doing bigger re-factorings involving node id changes, we have only one place to update—the test's constants.

Ruleflow unit testing

Drools Flow support for unit testing isn't the best. With every test, we have to run the full process from start to the end. We'll make it easier with some helper methods that will set up a state that will utilize different parts of the flow. For example, a loan with high amount to borrow or a customer with low rating.

Ideally we should be able to test each node in isolation. Simply start the ruleflow in a particular node. Just set the necessary parameters needed for a particular test and verify that the node executed as expected.

Drools support for snapshots may resolve some of these issues; however, we'd have to first create all snapshots that we need before executing the individual test methods. Another alternative is to dig deeper into Drools internal API, but this is not recommended. The internal API can change in the next release without any notice.

The size of the loan

All valid loans continue through the **no errors** branch to **Amount to borrow?** split node. It is again a XOR type split node. It works based on amount property of Loan. If it is less than 5000, it continues through the **low** branch, otherwise, it takes the **otherwise** branch. The **otherwise** branch is again a 'catch all' type of branch. Put the following constraint into the split node:

```
Loan( amount <= 5000 )
```

Code listing 6: **Amount to borrow?** split node's **low** branch constraint (loanApproval.rf file).

For all loans that are bigger, a customer rating needs to be calculated.

Test for a small loan

The following method runs a loan with a small amount to borrow through our ruleflow. As can be seen in the following code, the first line of this test sets up a loan with low amount. Next, the process is started and the test verifies that the flow continued through the correct branch.

```
@Test
public void amountToBorrowLow() {
    setUpLowAmount();
    startProcess();

    assertTrue(trackingProcessEventListener.isNodeTriggered(
        PROCESS_LOAN_APPROVAL, NODE_JOIN_RATING));
    assertFalse(trackingProcessEventListener
        .isNodeTriggered(PROCESS_LOAN_APPROVAL,
            NODE_SUBFLOW_RATING_CALCULATION));
}
```

Code listing 7: Test for the **Amount to borrow?** node's **low** branch (`DefaultLoanApprovalServiceTest.java` file).

The test expects the next **XOR** node on the **low** branch to be executed and it also expects that the next node on the **otherwise** branch—**Rating Calculation**—isn't executed.

The `setupLowAmount` method inserts a loan with low amount to borrow into the knowledge session. You could argue that loan could be a global variable instead of a fact. The advantage of having loan as a fact makes it possible to update it later on. Remember? Global variables shouldn't change when we want to reason over them.

Rating Calculation

The first node arising from the **Amount to borrow?** node's **otherwise** branch is a subflow node called **Rating Calculation**. This node will calculate the rating of this customer. It will then be used to decide if a loan should be granted or not.

Subflow

First, some general subflow information. Subflow is a normal ruleflow that can be called from another ruleflow. A subflow is effectively a ruleflow inside a ruleflow. The following are the benefits of doing this:

- A complex flow can be logically separated into multiple simple flows. The problem can be decomposed into sub problems. As the basic principle says—divide and conquer.

- The new subflow can be also reused in different contexts. For example, this rating calculation might be used in mortgage loan approval process. With the help of on-entry/on-exit actions and parameter mappings, the parent flow can supply information to the subflow and then possibly act on the result. The subflow remains independent.

- This subflow can be executed in parallel with the parent flow. This means that after reaching the subflow node, the execution continues in both the parent flow and the subflow (note that this doesn't mean multiple threads). However, this has a disadvantage—we won't be able to use any results from this subflow in our parent flow.

The subflow is executed in the same knowledge session as the parent ruleflow. This means that the subflow can access facts just as its parent ruleflow. The `StatefulKnowledgeSession.getProcessInstances()` method can be used to return collection of all the process instances associated with a knowledge session.

Further, the subflow (and also some other ruleflow nodes) can define in/out parameter mappings and on-entry/on-exit actions. The parent flow will wait on a subflow if the *Wait For Completion* flag is set to `true`. Only in this case, it makes sense to use the out parameter mappings. Another flag that can be set is *independent*. With this flag set to `true`, the subflow will continue executing even if the parent ruleflow finished executing (it is completed or aborted); otherwise, it would be aborted.

Subflow diagram

The following subflow represents the rating calculation flow. After it starts, the execution continues through a split node. This split node is of type **AND**, meaning that the execution will continue in all node's outgoing branches. On the left side there is **Calculate Incomes** ruleflow group, and on the right side there are **Calculate Monthly Repayments** and **Calculate Expenses** ruleflow groups. These ruleflow groups contain rules for accumulating knowledge about customer incomes such as salaries of the customer and his/her spouse, type of occupation they have, for how long they have been employed, for how long they were unemployed, how much funds they have in their accounts, and information about their properties or other asserts. The **Calculate Monthly Repayments** ruleflow group calculates how much will this loan cost by month. The **Calculate Expenses** ruleflow group takes into account expenses such as the size of the family, rent, other loans, mortgages, and obligations.

Finally, these two branches are joined together by an **AND** type join node. This means that the flow won't continue until all of its incoming connections are triggered. The next node is a **Calculate Rating** ruleflow group. This is where all of the acquired information is translated by a set of rules into one number — rating. This ruleflow is as follows:

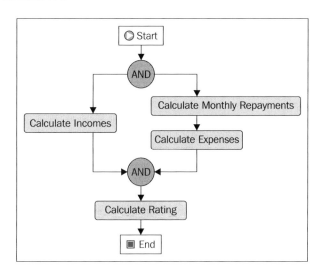

Please note that we've named the split and join nodes as **AND** and **AND**. This may be a good practice to follow. The naming makes their type explicit. We no longer have to examine the node to see its type. The disadvantage is that you have to make sure that both the node's type and its name are updated at the same time. We've also used this naming convention in the parent ruleflow.

One important thing to remember when designing the ruleflow is to make it simple. The ruleflow should describe the core business process. It shouldn't contain every little detail of the process. The rules are ideal for this. They can then fine-tune the business process.

If we take the ruleflow from the preceding figure as an example, we can see that it logically separates the individual calculations in a very nice manner. By looking at this ruleflow diagram, you should immediately get a feeling of what is it trying to achieve.

Now, we know that the subflow uses rules to calculate a rating. This rating is a 'fact' inside the knowledge session. We also know that this rating will somehow be propagated to the parent flow through on exit action.

'On entry'/'On exit' Actions can be defined on various ruleflow nodes—subflow, work item, and human task. As we've seen already in Chapter 5 (the *Ruleflow* section), ruleflow also supports Action as a standalone node. An action is simply a block of dialect-specific code. Action's code can access a `context` variable—`org.drools.runtime.process. ProcessContext`.

org.drools.runtime.process.ProcessContext

`ProcessContext` has various methods for working with the current ruleflow context. `getProcessInstance()` returns the current ruleflow instance. As our action is inside subflow, this method will return the subflow process instance.

In general, when a process starts, a new `ProcessInstance` is created that represents the runtime state of a process. Drools Flow is based on the **PVM** model (**Process Virtual Machine**—more information can be found at `http://docs.jboss.com/jbpm/pvm/article/`).

The `getNodeInstance()` method of `ProcessContext` returns the runtime instance of a currently executing node. The process context can also be used for setting and getting ruleflow variables `getVariable` / `setVariable`. The `getKnowledgeRuntime()` method returns `KnowledgeRuntime` that can be used for interaction with the knowledge session.

Nodes that define both entry/exit actions and also in/out parameter mappings use the following order to evaluate them:

- On-entry actions
- Input parameter mappings
- The node itself
- Output parameter mappings
- On-exit actions.

We'll define an on-exit action with the following body:

```
Rating rating = (Rating)context.getKnowledgeRuntime()
.getObjects(new ClassObjectFilter(Rating.class))
    .iterator().next();
context.setVariable("customerLoanRating", rating.getRating());
update(context.getProcessInstance());
```

Code listing 8: Subflow node's `onExit` action body (`loanApproval.rf` file).

First of all, the action retrieves the calculated `rating` from the knowledge session. It simply iterates over all of the objects in the knowledge session and filters out all of the objects that are not of type `Rating`. `Rating` is a bean that has one property of type `Integer` called `rating`. The code is expecting to find just one `Rating` fact in the knowledge session as can be seen when we call the `next` method.

Next, we set the `customerLoanRating` variable using the `context.setVariable` method, which correctly sets it on the main ruleflow context. Finally, we shouldn't forget to update the `processInstance` because we've modified it.

Rating calculation subflow test

We'll now write a test which verifies that our subflow is being called and the variable is being set.

```
@Test
public void amountToBorrowHighRatingCalculation() {
  setUpHighAmount();
  startProcess();
  assertTrue(trackingProcessEventListener
      .isNodeTriggered(PROCESS_LOAN_APPROVAL,
          NODE_SUBFLOW_RATING_CALCULATION));
  assertTrue(trackingProcessEventListener.isNodeTriggered(
      PROCESS_RATING_CALCULATION,
      NODE_GROUP_CALCULATE_RATING));
  WorkflowProcessInstance process =
      (WorkflowProcessInstance) processInstance;
  assertEquals(1500,
      process.getVariable("customerLoanRating"));
}
```

Code listing 9: Test for the subflow node (`DefaultLoanApprovalServiceTest.java` file).

The test sets up loan request with high amount by calling the setUpHighAmount method. This method inserts a loan (with amount set to 19000) into the knowledge session. Next, the process is started with default parameters, which involve customerLoanRating ruleflow variable set to zero. Next, the test verifies that the subflow node has been executed along with one node from the subflow—**Calculate Rating**. Finally, the test verifies that customerLoanRating variable has been set to 1500—it is a customer loan rating calculated for our test loan. The last couple of lines of the test method also show us how to get variables from the process instance.

 The rules for calculating the rating have been left out. However, for testing purposes you could easily write a rule that inserts a Rating fact into the session with its rating property set to 1500.

Another test for the rating calculation ruleflow may check that all of its nodes are executed, as the flow contains only *and* type split and join nodes.

Decisions on rating

After we've calculated rating and set it as ruleflow variable, the next ruleflow node—**Rating?**—checks if the customer's loan rating is high enough. It is an XOR type split node with the following '**accept**' branch constraint:

```
((Integer)customerLoanRating) >= 1000
```

Code listing 10: **Rating?** node's **accept** branch constraint—code type (loanApproval.rf file).

Set the type of this constraint to code and dialect to mvel. Code constraints have access to all of the ruleflow variables. As can be seen, we're directly referring to the customerLoanRating ruleflow variable and checking if it is greater or equal than 1000. If it is, the loan application can continue to the next step of loan approval process. Note that the variable needs to be cast to Integer; otherwise, an exception will be thrown.

If we need to take more complex decisions, we could use a rule type constraint like we did before:

```
processInstance : WorkflowProcessInstance(
    eval( ((Integer)processInstance.getVariable(
    "customerLoanRating")) >= 1000 ))
```

Code listing 11: **Rating?** node's **accept** branch constraint—rule type (loanApproval.rf file).

The condition uses a special variable name called `processInstance` of type `WorkflowProcessInstance`. It is special because Drools will match *only on the current executing ruleflow instance* even if there were multiple instances in the knowledge session. Through `processInstance`, we can access all of the ruleflow variables. Note that we need to insert the ruleflow instance into the knowledge session as we've done in code listing 4.

Testing the 'Rating?' node

The test will create a loan request for high amount and for a customer that has high rating. It will then execute the ruleflow and verify that the ruleflow execution went through the **Rating?** node through the **accept** branch to the XOR join node.

```
@Test
public void ratingSplitNodeAccept() {
    setUpHighAmount();
    setUpHighRating();
    startProcess();

    assertTrue(trackingProcessEventListener.isNodeTriggered(
        PROCESS_LOAN_APPROVAL, NODE_SPLIT_RATING));
    assertTrue(trackingProcessEventListener.isNodeTriggered(
        PROCESS_LOAN_APPROVAL, NODE_JOIN_RATING));
}
```

Code listing 12: **Rating?** node's **accept** branch constraint (`DefaultLoanApprovalServiceTest.java` file).

The test executes successfully.

Transfer Funds work item

We'll now jump almost to the end of our process. After a loan is approved, we need a way of transferring the specified sum of money to customer's account. This can be done with rules, or even better, with pure Java as this task is procedural in nature. We'll create a custom work item so that we can easily reuse this functionality in other ruleflows. Note that if it was a once-off task, it would probably be better suited to an action node.

The **Transfer Funds** node in the loan approval process is a custom work item. A new custom work item can be defined using the following four steps (later on we'll see how they are accomplished):

1. *Create a work item definition.* This will be used by the eclipse ruleflow editor and by the ruleflow engine to set and get parameters. For example, the following is an extract from the default `WorkDefinitions.conf` file that comes with Drools. It describes '**Email**' work definition. The configuration is written in MVEL. MVEL allows one to construct complex object graphs in a very concise format. This file contains a list of maps—`List<Map<String, Object>>`. Each map defines properties of one work definition. The properties are: `name`, `parameters` (that this work item works with), `displayName`, `icon`, and `customEditor` (these last three are used when displaying the work item in the Eclipse ruleflow editor). A custom editor is opened after double-clicking on the ruleflow node.

```
import org.drools.process.core.datatype.impl.type.StringDataType;
[
    [
        "name" : "Email",
        "parameters" : [
            "From" : new StringDataType(),
            "To" : new StringDataType(),
            "Subject" : new StringDataType(),
            "Body" : new StringDataType()
        ],
        "displayName" : "Email",
        "icon" : "icons/import_statement.gif",
        "customEditor" : "org.drools.eclipse.flow.common.editor.
                         editpart.work.EmailCustomEditor"
    ]
]
```

Code listing 13: Excerpt from the default `WorkDefinitions.conf` file.

Work item's parameters property is a map of `parameterName` and its value wrappers. The value wrapper must implement interface `org.drools.process.core.datatype.DataType`.

2. *Register the work definitions with the knowledge base configuration.* This will be shown in the next section.

3. *Create a work item handler.* This handler represents the actual behavior of a work item. It will be invoked whenever the ruleflow execution reaches this work item node. All of the handlers must extend the `org.drools.runtime.process.WorkItemHandler` interface. It defines two methods. One for executing the work item and another for aborting the work item. Drools comes with some default work item handler implementations, for example, a handler for sending emails: `org.drools.process.workitem.email.EmailWorkItemHandler`. This handler needs a working SMTP server. It must be set through the `setConnection` method before registering the work item handler with the work item manager (next step). Another default work item handler was shown in Code listing 2 - a `SystemOutWorkItemHandler`.

4. *Register the work item handler with the work item manager.*

After reading this you may ask, why doesn't the work item definition also specify the handler? It is because a work item can have one or more work item handlers that can be used interchangeably. For example, in a test case, we may want to use different work item handler than in production environment.

We'll now follow this four-step process and create a **Transfer Funds** custom work item.

Work item definition

Our transfer funds work item will have three input parameters: source account, destination account, and the amount to transfer. Its definition is as follows:

```
import org.drools.process.core.datatype.impl.type.ObjectDataType;
[
  [
    "name" : "Transfer Funds",
    "parameters" : [
        "Source Account" : new ObjectDataType("droolsbook.bank.
                            model.Account"),
        "Destination Account" : new ObjectDataType("droolsbook.bank.
                              model.Account"),
        "Amount" : new ObjectDataType("java.math.BigDecimal")
    ],
    "displayName" : "Transfer Funds",
    "icon" : "icons/transfer.gif"
  ]
]
```

Code listing 14: Work item definition from the `BankingWorkDefinitions.conf` file.

The **Transfer Funds** work item definition from code above declares the usual properties. It doesn't have a custom editor as was the case with email work item. All of the parameters are of the `ObjectDataType` type. This is a wrapper that can wrap any type. In our case, we are wrapping `Account` and `BigDecimal` types. We've also specified an icon that will be displayed in the ruleflow's editor palette and in the ruleflow itself. The icon should be of the size 16x16 pixels.

Work item registration

First make sure that the `BankingWorkDefinitions.conf` file is on your classpath. We now have to tell Drools about our new work item. This can be done by creating a `drools.rulebase.conf` file with the following contents:

```
drools.workDefinitions = WorkDefinitions.conf BankingWorkDefinitions.
conf
```

Code listing 15: Work item definition from the `BankingWorkDefinitions.conf` file (all in one one line).

When Drools starts up, it scans the classpath for configuration files. Configuration specified in the `drools.rulebase.conf` file will override the default configuration. In this case, only the `drools.workDefinitions` setting is being overridden. We already know that the `WorkDefinitions.conf` file contains the default work items such as email and log. We want to keep those and just add ours. As can be seen from the code listing above, `drools.workDefinitions` settings accept list of configurations. They must be separated by a space. When we now open the ruleflow editor in Eclipse, the ruleflow palette should contain our new **Transfer Funds** work item.

If you want to know more about the file based configuration resolution process, you can look into the `org.drools.util.ChainedProperties` class.

Work item handler

Next, we'll implement the work item handler. It must implement the `org.drools.runtime.process.WorkItemHandler` interface that defines two methods: `executeWorkItem` and `abortWorkItem`. The implementation is as follows:

```
/**
 * work item handler responsible for transferring amount from
 * one account to another using bankingService.transfer method
 * input parameters: 'Source Account', 'Destination Account'
 * and 'Amount'
 */
public class TransferWorkItemHandler implements
```

```
    WorkItemHandler {
  BankingService bankingService;

  public void executeWorkItem(WorkItem workItem,
      WorkItemManager manager) {
    Account sourceAccount = (Account) workItem
        .getParameter("Source Account");
    Account destinationAccount = (Account) workItem
        .getParameter("Destination Account");
    BigDecimal sum = (BigDecimal) workItem
        .getParameter("Amount");

    try {
      bankingService.transfer(sourceAccount,
          destinationAccount, sum);
      manager.completeWorkItem(workItem.getId(), null);
    } catch (Exception e) {
      e.printStackTrace();
      manager.abortWorkItem(workItem.getId());
    }
  }
  /**
   * does nothing as this work item cannot be aborted
   */
  public void abortWorkItem(WorkItem workItem,
      WorkItemManager manager) {
  }
```

Code listing 16: Work item handler (`TransferWorkItemHandler.java` file).

The `executeWorkItem` method retrieves the three declared parameters and calls the `bankingService.transfer` method (the implementation of this method won't be shown). If all went OK, the manager is notified that this work item has been completed. It needs the ID of the work item and optionally a result parameter map. In our case, it is set to null. If an exception happens during the transfer, the manager is told to abort this work item.

The `abortWorkItem` method on our handler doesn't do anything because this work item cannot be aborted.

Please note that the work item handler must be thread-safe. Many ruleflow instances may reuse the same work item instance.

Work item handler registration

The transfer work item handler can be registered with a `WorkItemManager` as follows:

```
TransferWorkItemHandler transferHandler =
    new TransferWorkItemHandler();
transferHandler.setBankingService(bankingService);
session.getWorkItemManager().registerWorkItemHandler(
    "Transfer Funds", transferHandler);
```

Code listing 17: `TransferWorkItemHandler` registration
(`DefaultLoanApprovalServiceTest.java` file).

A new instance of this handler is created and the banking service is set. Then it is registered with `WorkItemManager` in a session.

Next, we need to 'connect' this work item into our ruleflow. This means set its parameters once it is executed. We need to set the source/destination account and the amount to be transferred. We'll use the in-parameter mappings of **Transfer Funds** to set these parameters.

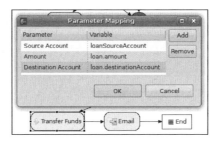

As we can see the **Source Account** is mapped to the `loanSourceAccount` ruleflow variable. The **Destination Account** ruleflow variable is set to the destination account of the `loan` and the **Amount** ruleflow variable is set to `loan`'s amount.

Testing the transfer work item

This test will verify that the **Transfer Funds** work item is correctly executed with all of the parameters set and that it calls the `bankingService.transfer` method with correct parameters. For this test the `bankingService` service will be mocked with **jMock** library (jMock is a lightweight Mock object library for Java. More information can be found at `http://www.jmock.org/`). First we need to set up the banking service mock object in the following manner:

```
mockery = new JUnit4Mockery();
bankingService = mockery.mock(BankingService.class);
```

Code listing 18: jMock setup of `bankingService` mock object
(`DefaultLoanApprovalServiceTest.java` file).

Next, we can write our test. We are expecting one invocation of the `transfer` method with `loanSourceAccount` and loan's `destination` and `amount` properties. Then the test will set up the transfer work item as in code listing 17, start the process, and approve the loan (more about this is discussed in the next section). The test also verifies that the **Transfer Funds** node has been executed. Test method's implementation is as follows:

```
@Test
public void transferFunds() {
  mockery.checking(new Expectations() {
    {
      one(bankingService).transfer(loanSourceAccount,
          loan.getDestinationAccount(), loan.getAmount());
    }
  });

  setUpTransferWorkItem();
  setUpLowAmount();
  startProcess();
  approveLoan();

  assertTrue(trackingProcessEventListener.isNodeTriggered(
      PROCESS_LOAN_APPROVAL, NODE_WORK_ITEM_TRANSFER));
}
```

Code listing 19: Test for the '**Transfer Funds**' work item (`DefaultLoanApprovalServiceTest.java` file).

The test should execute successfully.

Human task

Let's go back to the loan approval ruleflow. We've finished after the **Rating?** node. Our next step is to implement the **Process Loan** node. This is where the human actors will be involved. We've done what we could with our automated process, now is the time for tasks that a computer can't or shouldn't do.

Drools supports human tasks though **Web Services Human Task** specification (**The WS-HumanTask** is an OASIS specification and can be downloaded from `http://download.boulder.ibm.com/ibmdl/pub/software/dw/specs/ws-bpel4people/WS-HumanTask_v1.pdf`). With this specification, we can define human tasks that will be automatically created when the ruleflow reaches this ruleflow node. After they are created, they will appear on the 'task list screen' of designated users than can 'claim' these tasks and start working on them until they are completed. They can also suspend or abort these tasks. Once the task reaches the final state (complete/abort), the ruleflow continues execution. Please note that this is very simplified view; the WS-HumanTask specification defines a more complex life cycle of a task.

From the ruleflow perspective, WS-HumanTask is just a special case of work item. Once it is triggered, the ruleflow simply waits for the end result, be it success or failure. Drools comes with a simple work item handler implementation for human task called WSHumanTaskHandler it is far from implementing all features of WS-HumanTask specification, but it gives us a starting point and a direction.

 Human task support is part of the drools-process-task module.

The human task ruleflow node allows us to specify actorId, which is the ID of a person/group that will have the role of potentialOwner as defined by WS-HumanTask. Also some comment can be specified, which will become the 'subject' and 'description' of a human task. Priority and option if a task can be skipped can be also defined.

The WSHumanTaskHandler provides no support for some WS-HumanTask user roles such as task initiators, excluded owners, task stakeholders, business administrators or recipients. Nor does it support attachments, multiple comments, task delegations, start/end deadlines with their escalations, notifications, and user reassignments. If needed, the WSHumanTaskHandler can be extended to provide the features we need. For the purpose of our loan approval example, we'll use this WSHumanTaskHandler unchanged.

The core part of the WS-HumanTask specification is the server that receives the tasks and manages them. WSHumanTaskHandler is kept lightweight. It is a simple client that creates a task based on properties set in the ruleflow and registers this task with the server together with a callback. As has been said earlier, it then waits for success or failure of the task. It can take some time for a human task to finish; therefore, a more advanced implementation could, for example, persist the ruleflow to some permanent storage in order to free up the resources.

On the other side, the server is a more or less complete implementation of the WS-HumanTask specification. It goes even further by giving us the ability to send standard iCalendar VEVENT notifications (iCalendar is a RFC 2445 standard for calendar exchange. More information about iCalendar VEVENTs can be found at http://en.wikipedia.org/wiki/Icalendar#Events_.28VEVENT.29).

Test for the human task

So far it was only theory—a test will hopefully make it clearer. In order to write some tests for the **Process Loan** human task, we'll need a server that will receive these tasks. Other clients will then connect to this server and work on these tasks and when they are completed our ruleflow will be able to continue.

Due to its size, the test will be divided into three parts—server setup, client setup, and client 'working on the task'.

We'll start with the server setup (see the following code listing). It will initialize the server, register a human task work item handler, and start the loan approval process.

```
@Test
public void processLoan() throws Exception {
  EntityManagerFactory emf = Persistence
      .createEntityManagerFactory("org.drools.task");

  TaskService taskService = new TaskService(emf,
      SystemEventListenerFactory.getSystemEventListener());
  MockUserInfo userInfo = new MockUserInfo();
  taskService.setUserinfo(userInfo);

  TaskServiceSession taskSession = taskService
      .createSession();
  taskSession.addUser(new User("Administrator"));
  taskSession.addUser(new User("123"));
  taskSession.addUser(new User("456"));
  taskSession.addUser(new User("789"));

  MinaTaskServer server = new MinaTaskServer(taskService);
  Thread thread = new Thread(server);
  thread.start();
  Thread.sleep(500);

  WorkItemHandler htHandler = new WSHumanTaskHandler();
  session.getWorkItemManager().registerWorkItemHandler(
      "Human Task", htHandler);
  setUpLowAmount();
  startProcess();
```

Code listing 20: Test for the **Process Loan** node—setup of server and process start-up (`DefaultLoanApprovalServiceTest.java` file).

As part of the server setup, the test creates a JPA `EntityManagerFactory` (**JPA** stands for **Java Persistence API**. More information can be found at `http://en.wikipedia.org/wiki/Java_Persistence_API`) from a persistence unit named `org.drools.task` (the configuration for this persistence unit is inside `drools-process-task.jar` module in `/META-INF/persistence.xml`. By default it uses an in-memory database). It is used for persisting human tasks that are not currently needed. There may be thousands of human task instances running concurrently and each can take minutes, hours, days, or even months to finish. Persisting them will save us resources. In the next chapter, we'll also see how to persist the whole ruleflow.

Next, `TaskService` is created. It takes the EntityManagerFactory and a SystemEventListener.

org.drools.SystemEventListener

The `SystemEventListener` provides callback style logging of various Drools system events. The listener can be set through the `SystemEventListenerFactory`. The default listener prints everything to the console.

The `TaskService` represents the main server process. A `UserInfo` object is set to the `taskService`. It has methods for retrieving various information about users and groups of users in our organisation that the `taskService` needs (it is, for example, used when sending the iCalendar notifications). For testing purposes, we're using only a mock implementation—`MockUserInfo`.

The `TaskService` can be accessed by multiple threads. Next the `TaskServiceSession` represents one session of this service. This session can be accessed by only one thread at a time. We use this session to create some test users. Our **Process Loan** task is initially assigned to actorIds: `123`, `456` and `789`. This is defined in the **Process Loan** ruleflow node's properties. Next, the server thread is started wrapped in a `MinaTaskServer`. It is a lightweight server implementation that listens on a port for clients requests. It is based on **Apache MINA**. (More information about Apache MINA can be found at `http://mina.apache.org/`).

The current thread then sleeps for 500ms, so that the server thread has some time to initialize. Then a default Drools `WSHumanTaskHandler` is registered, a new loan application with low amount is created, and the ruleflow is started. The ruleflow will execute all the way down to **Process Loan** human task where the `WSHumanTaskHandler` takes over. It creates a task from the information specified in the **Process Loan** node and registers this task with the server. It knows how to connect to the server. The ruleflow then waits for the completion of this task.

The next part of this test represents a client (bank employee) that is viewing his/her task list and getting one task. First the client must connect to the server.

Because all of the communication between the client and the server is asynchronous and we want to test it in one test method, we will use some blocking response handlers that will simply block until the response is available. These response handlers are from the drools-process-task module.

Next the `client.getTasksAssignedAsPotentialOwner` method is called and we wait for a list of tasks that the client can start working on. The test verifies that the list contains one task and that the status of this task is `Ready`.

```
MinaTaskClient client = new MinaTaskClient("client 1",
    new TaskClientHandler(
    SystemEventListenerFactory.getSystemEventListener()));
NioSocketConnector connector = new NioSocketConnector();
SocketAddress address = new InetSocketAddress("127.0.0.1",
    9123);
client.connect(connector, address);

BlockingTaskSummaryResponseHandler summaryHandler =
    new BlockingTaskSummaryResponseHandler();
client.getTasksAssignedAsPotentialOwner("123", "en-UK",
    summaryHandler);
List<TaskSummary> tasks = summaryHandler.getResults();
assertEquals(1, tasks.size());
TaskSummary task = tasks.get(0);
assertEquals("Process Loan", task.getName());
assertEquals(3, task.getPriority());
assertEquals(Status.Ready, task.getStatus());
```

Code listing 21: Test for the **Process Loan** node—setup of a client and task list retrieval (`DefaultLoanApprovalServiceTest.java` file).

The final part of this test represents a client (bank employee) that 'claims' one of the task from the task list, then 'starts' this task, and finally 'completes' this task.

```
BlockingTaskOperationResponseHandler operationHandler =
    new BlockingTaskOperationResponseHandler();
client.claim(task.getId(), "123", operationHandler);
operationHandler.waitTillDone(10000);

operationHandler =
    new BlockingTaskOperationResponseHandler();
client.start(task.getId(), "123", operationHandler);
operationHandler.waitTillDone(10000);
```

```
operationHandler =
    new BlockingTaskOperationResponseHandler();
client.complete(task.getId(), "123", null,
    operationHandler);
operationHandler.waitTillDone(10000);

assertTrue(trackingProcessEventListener.isNodeTriggered(
    PROCESS_LOAN_APPROVAL, NODE_JOIN_PROCESS_LOAN));
}
```

Code listing 22: Test for the **Process Loan** node — client is claiming, starting, and completing a task (`DefaultLoanApprovalServiceTest.java` file).

After the task is completed, the test verifies that the ruleflow continues execution through the next join node.

Final Approval

As you may imagine, before any money is paid out to the loan requester, a final check is needed from a supervisor. This is represented in the ruleflow by the **Approve Event** node. It is an event node from the ruleflow palette. It allows a process to respond to the external events. This node has no incoming connection; in fact, the events can be created/signaled through the process instance's `signalEvent` method. The method needs event type and the event value itself.

Parameters of the Event node include event type and variable name that hold this event. The variable must be itself declared as a ruleflow variable.

Test for the 'Approve Event' node

A test will show us how all this works. We'll setup a valid loan request. The dummy `SystemOutWorkItemHandler` will be used to get through the **Transfer Funds** and **Process Loan** work items. The execution should then wait for the approve event. Then we'll signal the event using the `processInstance.signalEvent("LoanApprovedEvent", null)` method and verify that the ruleflow finished successfully.

```
@Test
public void approveEventJoin() {
  setUpLowAmount();
  startProcess();
  assertEquals(ProcessInstance.STATE_ACTIVE, processInstance
      .getState());
  assertFalse(trackingProcessEventListener.isNodeTriggered(
      PROCESS_LOAN_APPROVAL, NODE_WORK_ITEM_TRANSFER));
  approveLoan();
  assertTrue(trackingProcessEventListener.isNodeTriggered(
      PROCESS_LOAN_APPROVAL, NODE_WORK_ITEM_TRANSFER));
```

```
        assertEquals(ProcessInstance.STATE_COMPLETED,
            processInstance.getState());
    }
```

Code listing 23: Test for the **Approve Event** node
(`DefaultLoanApprovalServiceTest.java` file).

Before sending the approved event, we've verified that the process is in active state
and that the **Transfer Funds** work item hasn't been called yet.

After sending the approved event, the test verifies that the **Transfer Funds** work
item was actually executed and the ruleflow reached its final COMPLETED state.

Banking service

The final step is to implement the `approveLoan` service that represents the interface
to our loan approval process. It ties everything that we've done together. The
`approveLoan` method takes a `Loan` and a `Customer`, which is requesting the loan.

```
        KnowledgeBase knowledgeBase;
        Account loanSourceAccount;
        /**
         * runs the  loan approval process for a specified
         * customer's loan
         */
        public void approveLoan(Loan loan, Customer customer) {
          StatefulKnowledgeSession session = knowledgeBase
              .newStatefulKnowledgeSession();
          try {
            //TODO: register workitem/human task handlers
            Map<String, Object> parameterMap =
              new HashMap<String, Object>();
            parameterMap.put("loanSourceAccount",loanSourceAccount);
            parameterMap.put("customer", customer);
            parameterMap.put("loan", loan);
            session.insert(loan);
            session.insert(customer);
            ProcessInstance processInstance =
            session.startProcess("loanApproval", parameterMap);
            session.insert(processInstance);
            session.fireAllRules();
          } finally {
            session.dispose();
          }
        }
```

Code listing 24: `approveLoan` service method of `BankingService`
(`DefaultLoanApprovalService.java` file).

The service creates a new session. It should then set-up and register all of the work item handlers that we've implemented. This part is left out. Normally it would involve setting up configuration parameters such as the IP address of an SMTP server for the email work item handler and so on.

Next, the `loan` and the `customer` are inserted into the `session`, the ruleflow is started, and the rules are fired. When the ruleflow completes, the session is disposed. (Please be aware that with this solution, the knowledge session is held in memory from the time when the ruleflow starts up to the time when it finishes. In the next chapter, we'll see how to persist this ruleflow.)

Disadvantages of a ruleflow

A ruleflow may potentially do more work than it should do. This is a direct consequence of how the algorithm behind Drools works. All of the rule constraints are evaluated at fact insertion time. For example, if we have a ruleflow with many nodes and 80% of the time the ruleflow finishes at the second node, most of the computation is wasted. This will be clearer when we get to Chapter 12, *Performance*.

Another disadvantage is that the business logic is now spread across at least two places. The rules are still in the `.drl` file; however, the ruleflow is in the `.rf` file. The ruleflow file also contains split node conditions and actions. If somebody wants to get the full understanding of a process, he/she has to look back and forth between these files. This may be fixed in future by having better integration in the Drools Eclipse plugin between the `.drl` file editor and the `.rf` file editor (for example, it would be nice to see the rules that belong to a selected ruleflow group).

Summary

In this chapter, we've learned about various Drools Flow features. It represents an interesting approach to business process representation. The vision of Drools Flow is to unify rules and processes into one product. This is a very powerful idea, especially with business processes involving complex decisions because these complexities can be implemented within rules which are ideal for this.

We've designed a loan approval service that involves validation of the loan request, customer rating calculation, approval events from a supervisor, and finally, custom domain specific work item for transferring money between accounts.

We've seen Drools Flow support of human tasks through the WS-HumanTask specification. This allows for greater interoperability between systems from different vendors.

All in all, Drools Flow represents an interesting approach to rules and processes.

9
Sample Application

This chapter will focus on the usage of Drools in a real application. It connects to the previous chapters and will give an overall picture of how it all comes together. We'll look at how Drools can be used in a sample JEE web application covering layered design, persistence, transactions, and others.

This chapter assumes that you have some basic understanding of **JPA** (**Java Persistence API**. More information can be found at `http://java.sun.com/javaee/technologies/persistence.jsp`) and the Spring Framework.

We'll now look at the various aspects of the sample application.

Users

Our application will have three sets of users—normal bank employees, supervisors, and bank customers. Normal bank employees will be able to create new customers. Customers will be able to request loans. Bank employees will then work on these loans. Supervisors will issue final loan approvals.

Architecture

This sample application will consist of three layers. From bottom to top—persistence, service, and presentation. It can be seen in the following diagram. The persistence layer is responsible for storing objects into a database. Transactions guarantee consistency of the database and provide isolation between concurrent requests.

The service layer represents the business logic of this application. It consists of validation service, **Complex Event Processing (CEP)** service, and loan approval service. Finally, the presentation layer uses these services to provide functionality to users in a user-friendly fashion. The sample application architecture diagram is as follows:

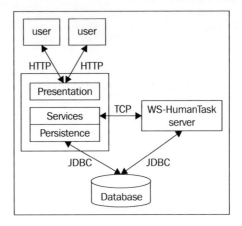

Please note that with some minor configuration changes, the service layer and presentation layer may be deployed on different physical servers and can communicate over the network. With some more configuration changes, it is even possible to have multiple service or presentation layer deployments. However, it won't be covered in this book.

Technologies used

The persistence layer will be implemented using JPA with Hibernate as the persistence provider. JPA is a standard that makes it easier to switch persistence providers. JPA annotations will be used to map our domain objects into persistent entities (for example, database tables). **JTA (Java Transaction API)** will be used for managing database transactions with **BTM (Bitronix transaction manager** — http://docs.codehaus.org/display/BTM/Home) as the transaction manager implementation.

The presentation layer will use Spring MVC framework to define the behavior of the screens. Spring MVC was chosen because of its simplicity. The actual screens will be implemented as traditional **JSP (Java Server Pages)**. Tomcat servlet container version 6.X will host our application.

All three layers will be configured with Spring Framework.

Our application won't use any special features of any technology/framework, so it's easy to use any other technologies/frameworks to do the same job.

Additional Drools projects used

We'll use `drools-process-task` module (as described in Chapter 8, *Drools Flow*) and `drools-persistence-jpa` module that will provide persistence services for our loan approval ruleflow.

Libraries used

Please refer to Appendix C, *Dependencies of Sample Application* for other third party libraries needed. It contains a list of libraries and their versions.

Business logic

We'll use our previously implemented services. Created customers will be validated (described in Chapters 3, *Validation* and Chapter 6, *Stateful Session*) before they are persisted. New loans will go through the loan approval process (described in Chapter 8, *Drools Flow*) and if they meet all criteria, a new 'process loan' human task will be created. Bank employees will see this task on their task lists and will be able to claim a task, start working on it, and when they are done with this task, they will be able to complete it. A supervisor will be able to approve a loan. After approval, the process will finish. Various events will be generated and fed into the CEP service (described in Chapter 7, *Complex Event Processing*) running in the background.

Design

Let's now look in more detail at the individual layers. The following diagram also gives us an overview of what we'll be implementing in this chapter. Again, from bottom to top, we'll have two repositories—one for persisting customers and one for accounts. The services layer will have our three already defined services—validation, loan approval, and CEP service. These services will be hidden behind a public **BankingService**, which will act as a mediator between these services. The presentation tier will use this public service to do all of its tasks. There will be various controllers—each responsible for some unit of work (for example, **CustomerSaveFormController** for saving a customer). The presentation tier will also contain a **WS-HumanTask client** that will be responsible for all communication with the **WS-HumanTask server**. The sample application design diagram is as follows:

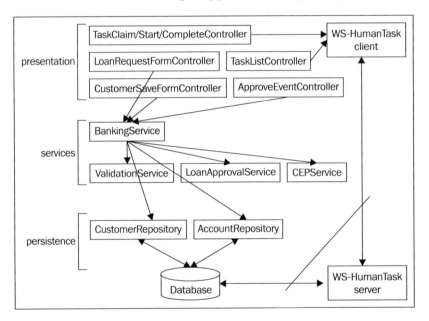

In the **persistence** layer, only the **CustomerRepository** will be normally used. It will persist the whole object graph (customer object, including address and customer's accounts). **AccountRepository** is also shown. It can be used to persist accounts that have no customers (we won't use this repository in our examples).

Configuration

In the following sections, we'll go through some configuration of the various layers. This is necessary before we can write some presentation code and deploy the web application.

JPA annotations for domain objects

We'll start with the persistence layer. All of the objects that are going to be persisted need to be mapped. This includes the Customer, Address, Account, and Loan objects. The validation message objects don't need to be mapped because they are not going to be persisted. Most of the time, the default mapping settings will be used. The @Entity annotation will be used to declare that a class should be persistable and we'll also explicitly specify the table name. Every entity needs an ID. A uuid field of type String will be added to every entity. The @Id annotation will declare that this uuid field is the ID of an entity. Customer's accounts will be mapped with a @OneToMany annotation, which declares that one customer can have many accounts. Let's now look at a mapping of the Customer class:

```
@Entity
@Table(name = "app_customer")
public class Customer implements Serializable {
  @Id private String uuid;
  private String firstName;
  private String lastName;
  private Date dateOfBirth;
  private Address address;

  @OneToMany(mappedBy="owner") private Set<Account> accounts;
  private String phoneNumber;
```

Code listing 1: Code extract from the Customer class (Customer.java file).

Please consult the Hibernate manual for advanced mapping (http://www.hibernate.org/hib_docs/reference/en/html/index.html).

We're using uuid as IDs, because they are much easier to work with. We can assign them at object creation time instead of object persistence time as is the case with database assigned IDs. The standard java.util.UUID class will be used to generate uuid instances. We can define a factory for creating our domain objects that will automatically assign uuid to every new object as follows:

```
public class DefaultBankingFactory implements BankingFactory {
  @Override
  public Customer createCustomer() {
    Customer customer = new Customer();
    customer.setUuid(UUID.randomUUID().toString());
    Set<Account> accounts = new HashSet<Account>();
    customer.setAccounts(accounts);
    return customer;
  }
```

Code listing 2: DefaultBankingFactory class that follows the factory design pattern (DefaultBankingFactory.java file).

Our factory implements the `BankingFactory` interface which contains all of the factory methods such as `createCustomer`, `createAddress`, and `createAccount`. These methods make sure that all of the created objects have their references correctly set—for example, `createAccount` method takes a customer as an argument, adds the newly created account to the collection of customer's accounts, and also sets this customer as the owner of this account. This keeps the referential integrity intact. We can even declare domain object's constructors as `package private` so that new instances can be created only through this factory.

JPA configuration

Next, we'll work on the JPA provider configuration. This configuration also defines the classes that should be made persistable. All of this information will be contained in a so-called `persistence-unit`. This configuration is as follows:

```xml
<?xml version="1.0" encoding="UTF-8" standalone="yes"?>
<persistence version="1.0"
  xsi:schemaLocation="http://java.sun.com/xml/ns/persistence
    http://java.sun.com/xml/ns/persistence/persistence_1_0.xsd
    http://java.sun.com/xml/ns/persistence/orm
    http://java.sun.com/xml/ns/persistence/orm_1_0.xsd"
  xmlns:orm="http://java.sun.com/xml/ns/persistence/orm"
  xmlns:xsi="http://www.w3.org/2001/XMLSchema-instance"
  xmlns="http://java.sun.com/xml/ns/persistence">
  <persistence-unit name="droolsbook.persistence"
      transaction-type="JTA">
   <provider>org.hibernate.ejb.HibernatePersistence</provider>
   <jta-data-source>jdbc/testDS1</jta-data-source>
   <class>droolsbook.bank.model.Customer</class>
   <class>droolsbook.bank.model.Address</class>
   <class>droolsbook.bank.model.Account</class>
   <class>droolsbook.bank.model.LoanApprovalHolder</class>
  </persistence-unit>
</persistence>
```

Code listing 3: JPA configuration (`persistence.xml` file).

The preceding code is stored in a file called `persistence.xml`. This file should be stored on the classpath under `META-INF/` folder. The name of our persistence unit is `droolsbook.persistence`. The transaction type we're using is JTA, which means that our transactions can span one or many local/remote resources. This gives us more possibilities at the cost of performance. Later on, we'll discuss how to avoid JTA transactions by using a simple `RESOURCE_LOCAL` transaction type.

The `<provider>` element specifies the actual provider—in our case, it's `org.hibernate.ejb.HibernatePersistence`. Next, we'll tell the provider to look into `Customer`, `Address`, `Account`, and `LoanApprovalHolder` classes for JPA annotations. These classes are declared to be persistable.

The `jta-data-source` element specifies the location and name of our data source. Note that there is no data source defined, yet. The data source and the transaction manager will be managed outside our application by the application server—Tomcat.

Spring Framework configuration

Now, we'll configure Spring. This can be done in various ways. XML is the most commonly used language. The configuration will reside in three XML files. We'll start with a file called `applicationContext.xml` that will hold configuration related to service layer (persistence, transactions, knowledge base configuration, and individual services configurations).

```
<?xml version="1.0" encoding="UTF-8"?>
<beans xmlns="http://www.springframework.org/schema/beans"
  xmlns:xsi="http://www.w3.org/2001/XMLSchema-instance"
  xmlns:aop="http://www.springframework.org/schema/aop"
  xmlns:tx="http://www.springframework.org/schema/tx"
  xsi:schemaLocation="
      http://www.springframework.org/schema/beans http://www.
springframework.org/schema/beans/spring-beans-2.5.xsd
      http://www.springframework.org/schema/tx http://www.
springframework.org/schema/tx/spring-tx-2.5.xsd
      http://www.springframework.org/schema/aop http://www.
springframework.org/schema/aop/spring-aop-2.5.xsd">
```

Code listing 4: Extract from the Spring configuration (`applicationContext.xml` file).

The various Spring configuration files will use more or less the same 'header' (as shown in the preceding code). They will differ only in the XSD name spaces used. The previous file declares three name spaces that will be used—beans as the default one and aop, and tx. For more information, please consult Spring documentation (`http://static.springframework.org/spring/docs/2.5.x/reference/index.htm`).

We've already defined the persistence configuration in `persistence.xml` file. These were just the very basics. We'll now enhance this configuration in Spring. Spring configuration files will be the ultimate place where everything is configured. The following code is the definition of an `entityManagerFactory` that will be responsible for creating `EntityManager` instances, which will store our objects into the persistent store. `entityManagerFactory` references the `persistence-unit` configuration named `droolsbook.persistence`, which was defined earlier. It also specifies a bunch of properties that will be simply passed to the persistence provider.

```xml
<bean id="entityManagerFactory"
      class="org.springframework.orm.jpa.
LocalContainerEntityManagerFactoryBean">
  <property name="persistenceUnitName"
            value="droolsbook.persistence" />
  <property name="jpaPropertyMap" ref="jpaPropertyMap" />
</bean>

<bean id="jpaPropertyMap" class="org.springframework.beans.factory.
config.MapFactoryBean">
  <property name="sourceMap">
    <map>
      <entry key="hibernate.dialect"
             value="org.hibernate.dialect.H2Dialect" />
      <entry key="hibernate.show_sql"  value="true" />
      <entry key="hibernate.format_sql" value="true" />
      <entry key="hibernate.use_sql_comments" value="true"/>
      <entry key="hibernate.hbm2ddl.auto"
             value="create-drop" />
      <entry key="hibernate.transaction.manager_lookup_class"
             value="org.hibernate.transaction.
             BTMTransactionManagerLookup" />
    </map>
  </property>
</bean>
```

Code listing 5: Extract from the Spring configuration (`applicationContext.xml` file), `entityManagerFactory` bean definition.

`entityManagerFactory` is an instance of `LocalContainerEntityManagerFactoryBean`. It will read contents of the `persistence.xml` file and based on them and value-pairs in `jpaPropertyMap`, it will create `entityManagerFactory`. `jpaPropertyMap` is declared as a separate bean so that it can be easily reused later on.

The first JPA property—`hibernate.dialect` specifies a class that represents the dialect of our database. As you can see, we'll use H2 database (`http://www.h2database.com`). It can run entirely in memory which is ideal for our purposes. The next few properties are self explanatory. The `hibernate.hbm2ddl.auto` property, whose value is set to `create-drop`, specifies that we want to recreate the database (structure and data) every time we start the application. Note that Hibernate also needs to know the location of our transaction manager. It is specified by the last property, `...manager_lookup_class`. Hibernate needs to integrate with the transaction manager to control the life cycle of its sessions and caches.

The `applicationContext.xml` file will also define some beans that we'll use later.

```
<bean name="bankingFactory"
      class="droolsbook.bank.model.DefaultBankingFactory" />
<bean name="reportFactory"
      class="droolsbook.bank.service.impl.DefaultReportFactory" />
<bean class="org.springframework.orm.jpa.support.
PersistenceAnnotationBeanPostProcessor" />
<bean name="customerRepository"
      class="droolsbook.sampleApplication.repository.jpa.
JPACustomerRepository" />
```

Code listing 6: Extract from the Spring configuration (`applicationContext.xml` file), various bean definitions.

The first two are factories. We've already seen `DefaultBankingFactory` in code listing 2 and `DefaultReportFactory` was described in Chapter 3, *Validation*. The next two beans configure a customer repository. We'll see how `PersistenceAnnotationBeanPostProcessor` is responsible for injecting `EntityManagers` into repositories in the next few sections.

Web application setup

The core components of the persistence and service layers are there. We can start working on the presentation layer. We'll start with the web application configuration file, `web.xml`. It is a standard `web-app` configuration file, which defines the basics of a web application such as the name, welcome file list, and some initialization servlets. The initialization servlets will be called when we start the application in a server.

```
<?xml version="1.0" encoding="UTF-8"?>
<web-app xmlns:xsi="http://www.w3.org/2001/XMLSchema-instance"
         xmlns="http://java.sun.com/xml/ns/javaee"
         xmlns:web="http://java.sun.com/xml/ns/javaee/web-app_2_5.xsd"
         xsi:schemaLocation="http://java.sun.com/xml/ns/javaee
                             http://java.sun.com/xml/ns/
                             javaee/web-app_2_5.xsd"
```

```
          id="sampleApplication" version="2.5">
  <display-name>sampleApplication</display-name>
  <servlet>
    <servlet-name>sampleApplication</servlet-name>
    <servlet-class>
      org.springframework.web.servlet.DispatcherServlet
    </servlet-class>
    <load-on-startup>1</load-on-startup>
  </servlet>
  <servlet-mapping>
    <servlet-name>sampleApplication</servlet-name>
    <url-pattern>*.htm</url-pattern>
  </servlet-mapping>
  <welcome-file-list>
    <welcome-file>index.jsp</welcome-file>
  </welcome-file-list>
</web-app>
```

Code listing 7: Web application configuration (`web.xml` file).

As can be seen from code listing 7, Spring's `DispatcherServlet` is loaded at startup. This servlet by default looks for `sampleApplication-servlet.xml` configuration file. We'll soon define this file. Just make sure that it is placed in the `webRoot/WEB-INF/` directory. The configuration also defines a servlet mapping for all resources ending with `.htm` to this `DispatcherServlet`. The welcome file is set to `index.jsp`. This file has to be present in the `webRoot/` directory. For testing purposes, `index.jsp` will contain a listing of various entry points into the application (list all customers, add customer, request loan, and so on).

As promised, the `sampleApplication-servlet.xml` Spring configuration file follows. It will import the already defined configuration file—`applicationContext.xml`.

Further, the configuration file will define a standard 'view resolver'. This view resolver will be set to look for 'views' in `webRoot/WEB-INF/jsp/` directory ('view' as in MVC. MVC stands for model-view-controller—`http://en.wikipedia.org/wiki/Model-view-controller`). This will help us to separate our controllers from the view implementations. We'll see how it works in a few sections.

```
<import resource="classpath:applicationContext.xml" />
<context:annotation-config />
<bean id="viewResolver"
      class="org.springframework.web.servlet.view.
             InternalResourceViewResolver">
  <property name="viewClass"
```

```
            value="org.springframework.web.servlet.view.JstlView" />
    <property name="prefix" value="/WEB-INF/jsp/" />
    <property name="suffix" value=".jsp" />
  </bean>
```

Code listing 8: Extract from the Spring configuration
(`sampleApplication-servlet.xml` file), initial configuration.

The `import resource` elements are simply importing the contents of the resource
into one big Spring application context. The `<context:annotation-config />`
element activates Spring's annotation support for easier configuration of controllers.
For the interface layer, we'll use full Spring annotation auto wiring because the
presentation layer changes more frequently. Whereas, in the persistence and service
layers, reliability is the most important. Hence, we define the wiring ourselves
(we also don't want to depend on Spring API).

Tag library

We'll be using some Spring MVC tags in our JSPs. We have to copy the `tag` library
descriptor called `spring-form.tld` into `webRoot/WEB-INF/tld/` directory. This file
can be obtained from the standard Spring distribution (`http://www.springsource.`
`com/download/community?project=Spring%20Framework`). Download and unzip
the distribution and the file will be located in the `/dist/resources/` directory.

Tomcat setup

We'll now setup the transaction manager and data sources in Tomcat. Please refer to
`http://docs.codehaus.org/display/BTM/Tomcat13` for doing so.

The `resources.properties` file in Tomcat's `conf` directory should contain:

```
resource.ds1.className=bitronix.tm.resource.jdbc.lrc.LrcXADataSource
resource.ds1.uniqueName=jdbc/testDS1
resource.ds1.minPoolSize=0
resource.ds1.maxPoolSize=5
resource.ds1.driverProperties.driverClassName=org.h2.Driver
resource.ds1.driverProperties.url=jdbc:h2:mem:testDS1
resource.ds1.allowLocalTransactions=true
```

Code listing 9: Tomcat's data source configuration (`resources.properties` file).

Note that we're allowing local transactions. This is needed for automatic schema
creation (remember `hibernate.hbm2ddl.auto` was set to `create-drop`).

After this step, the data sources and the transaction manager should be accessible from Tomcat's JNDI tree.

Deployment

The deployment involves copying the contents of the webRoot directory into Tomcat's webapps directory and renaming it to sampleApplication. Then create a new lib directory under webapps/sampleApplication/WEB-INF/ and copy all of the libraries that are on the classpath into this directory (all except those libraries that you've already put into Tomcat's lib directory). All of the other resources on the classpath should go to webapps/sampleApplication/WEB-INF/ classes directory. That is all in terms of deployment. Tomcat can be started and we can access the application with the following URL: http://localhost:8080/ sampleApplication/. The index.jsp welcome page should be displayed.

The deployment can be even easier if you have installed the Eclipse plugin called **WTP (Web Tools Platform)**. You can then create a 'Dynamic Web Project', setup a server (Tomcat), and the WTP plugin will do the deployment for you. Note that the WTP plugin is a standard part of 'Eclipse IDE for Java EE Developers' (http://www.eclipse.org/downloads/).

Repositories

The infrastructure for the persistence layer is almost set up (only the transaction setup is missing). We can implement the repositories that will be responsible for persistence and lookup of the domain objects. Let's start with JPACustomerRepository. JPACustomerRepository uses EntityManager to find a customer by customerUuid or firstName and lastName. It is also used to add a new customer or update an existing one.

```
@Repository
public class JPACustomerRepository implements
    CustomerRepository {

  @PersistenceContext(unitName="entityManagerFactory")
  private EntityManager em;

  public Customer findCustomerByUuid(String customerUuid) {
    return em.find(Customer.class, customerUuid);
  }

  public List<Customer> findCustomerByName(String firstName,
      String lastName) {
    return em
        .createQuery(
```

```
         "from Customer as c where c.firstName = :first" +
         " and c.lastName = :last")
      .setParameter("first", firstName).setParameter("last",
         lastName).getResultList();
}
/**
 * stores new customer
 */
public void addCustomer(Customer customer) {
  em.persist(customer);
}
/**
 * stores existing customer
 */
public Customer updateCustomer(Customer customer) {
  return em.merge(customer);
}
```

Code listing 10: JPA customer repository implementation
(`JPACustomerRepository.java` file).

The first thing to note after looking at code listing 10 is that `JPACustomerRepository` has the `@Repository` annotation. This annotation clarifies the role of this class. Next, the `EntityManager` property is declared with the `@PersistenceContext` annotation. Thanks to this annotation, `EntityManager` will be automatically injected by Spring. We neither have to write a `set` method for this property nor do we have to set `EntityManager` as a required property in `applicationContext.xml` (see last two lines of code listing 6). Note that we explicitly specify the name of the bean by using `unitName="entityManagerFactory"`. This guarantees that the correct entity manager factory will be used even if there are multiple factories defined.

The methods from code listing 10 should be clear; they show a standard usage of the JPA.

Please note that we won't be writing any unit or integration tests in this chapter. Normally, every piece of code should be tested. Refer to the BTM web site on how to configure the transaction manager in a local environment.

Validation

In this section, we'll describe the 'validation slice' of this application (from bottom to top). That includes the definition of validation knowledge base, validation service, and the user interface.

We already have the validation service implementation. We'll now configure it with Spring. The first step is to build the validation knowledge base that will be used by the validation service. It will be managed by Spring like any other bean. The configuration goes into the `applicationContext.xml` file.

Unfortunately, Drools, as of version 5.0, doesn't integrate with Spring out of the box. This means that we'll have to create our own Spring 'factory bean' that knows how to build a knowledge base. The implementation of such a factory bean (`KnowledgeBaseFactoryBean`) will be shown in Chapter 11, *Integration*. Now, the actual validation knowledge base bean definition is as follows:

```
<bean name="validationKnowledge"
      class="droolsbook.integration.spring.KnowledgeBaseFactoryBean">
  <description>validation knowledge base factory bean </description>
  <constructor-arg>
    <map>
      <entry key="classpath:validation.drl" value="DRL" />
    </map>
  </constructor-arg>
</bean>
```

Code listing 11: Extract from the Spring configuration (`applicationContext.xml` file), validation knowledge base configuration.

The validation knowledge base is created by `KnowledgeBaseFactoryBean`. It takes a map of `ResourceType` instances (as map values) and their locations (as map keys). Based on this map, it builds the validation knowledge base. Note that the `validation.drl` file needs to be on the classpath.

Next, we can define the validation service itself. The implementation comes from Chapter 3, *Validation* (for simplicity, we'll use stateless validation service) — `BankingValidationServiceImpl`. The service has two dependencies — `validationKnowledgeBase` and `reportFactory`, which were defined earlier.

```
<bean name="validationService"
      class="droolsbook.bank.service.impl.
      BankingValidationServiceImpl">
  <property name="reportFactory" ref="reportFactory" />
  <property name="knowledgeBase" ref="validationKnowledge"/>
</bean>
```

Code listing 12: Extract from the Spring configuration (`applicationContext.xml` file), `validationService` bean definition.

The `validationService` bean definition is straightforward — one bean with two properties. This service is now ready to be used.

Services

Now that we have defined repositories and `ValidationService`, we can implement the first part of `BankingService` from the sample application design diagram, and more specifically, the methods for adding a new customer and saving an existing customer. These methods will validate the customer with the validation service and if everything goes well, the customer will be persisted with the repository.

```
/**
 * validates and stores a new customer
 */
public void add(Customer customer) {
  validate(customer);
  customerRepository.addCustomer(customer);
}
/**
 * validates and stores an existing customer
 */
public void save(Customer customer) {
  validate(customer);
  customerRepository.updateCustomer(customer);
}
/**
  * validates customer,
  * @throws ValidationException if there are any errors
 */
private void validate(Customer customer) {
  ValidationReport report = validationService.validate(customer);
  if (!report.getMessagesByType(Type.ERROR).isEmpty()) {
    throw new ValidationException(report);
  }
}
```

Code listing 13: Code extract from the `BankingServiceImpl.java`.

As can be seen in code listing 13, both `add` and `save` methods use a `validate` helper method. This method calls `validationService` and if the returned `ValidationReport` contains some messages of type `ERROR`, then `ValidationException` is thrown. Use of exceptions in this case allows us to deal only with the normal flow of execution and worry about the exceptional cases in some exception handler.

If the validation passes, the customer is added/updated with `customerRepository`.

Before being able to use this service in the presentation layer, we have to define it as a Spring bean. `bankingService` will have several dependencies. We already know that we need `customerRepository` and `validationService`. For additional functionality, we'll also need `loanApprovalService` and `cepService`.

```xml
<bean name="bankingService"
      class="droolsbook.bank.service.impl.BankingServiceImpl">
  <property name="customerRepository"
            ref="customerRepository" />
  <property name="validationService"
            ref="validationService" />
  <property name="loanApprovalService"
            ref="loanApprovalService" />
  <property name="cepService" ref="cepService" />
</bean>
```

Code listing 14: Extract from the Spring configuration (`applicationContext.xml` file), `bankingService` bean definition.

Simply add this bean definition to the `applicationContext.xml` file.

Transactions

The persistence of a valid customer is almost complete. The final missing pieces from the service layer perspective are transactions. We have to make sure that the system remains consistent under all circumstances (for example, if the server crashes while saving the customer record to the database, the database might be only partially updated).

Luckily, with Spring this can be implemented very easily and it's just a matter of configuration.

We'll now add the transaction configuration into the `applicationContext.xml` file. It consists of three parts as follows:

1. **Transaction manager**: It manages the transactional resources (in our case, the database).
2. **Aspect-oriented configuration**: It specifies the boundaries of the transaction.
3. **Transaction advice**: It configures various attributes of a transaction.

More information can be found in the Spring documentation.

```xml
<bean id="transactionManager"
      class="org.springframework.transaction.jta.
            JtaTransactionManager" />

<aop:config>
  <aop:pointcut id="bankingServiceMethods"
                expression="execution(*droolsbook.bank.service.
                            BankingService.*(..))" />
  <aop:advisor advice-ref="transactionAdvice"
               pointcut-ref="bankingServiceMethods" />
  </aop:config>

<tx:advice id="transactionAdvice"
           transaction-manager="transactionManager">
  <tx:attributes>
    <tx:method name="*" rollback-for="Exception" />
  </tx:attributes>
</tx:advice>
```

Code listing 15: Extract from the Spring configuration (`applicationContext.xml` file), transaction configuration.

We've chosen `JtaTransactionManager` as our transaction manager implementation. It will simply delegate to the already configured transaction manager in Tomcat. The transactions will automatically begin whenever any method on `BankingService` is executed—`execution(* droolsbook.bank.service.BankingService.*(..))`. Note that we're referring to `BankingService` interface rather than implementation (this is needed for Spring to create a transactional proxy correctly).

By default, the transaction propagation is set to `REQUIRED`. This means that an existing transaction must be running or a new transaction will be created. The configuration specifies that all of the methods will run under a transaction. Whenever an exception is thrown by banking service methods, the transaction will be rolled back automatically.

The following JTA transaction setup diagram shows how it will all work:

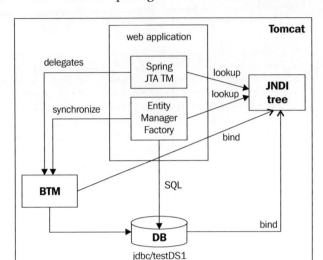

We've already defined the **BTM** transaction manager and the data source in Tomcat. When Tomcat starts, it will register these two resources in its **JNDI tree** (see the two 'bind' arrows). Next, when our application starts, it can lookup these resources (see the two 'lookup' calls). When we execute a method on the banking service, the Spring JTA platform transaction manager detects it and tells **BTM** to start a new transaction. We can then use the **Entity Manager Factory** to insert/update records in the database and when we return from the banking service, Spring will automatically tell **BTM** to commit or rollback the transaction.

Presentation layer

We'll now write a web form for adding new customers into the system. For simplicity, our customers can define just their first name, last name, and a phone number. This form will be stored in a file called `customerSave.jsp` within the `webRoot/WEB-INF/jsp/` folder. This JSP will also be capable of displaying any errors and warnings that occurred while the new customer was saved into the system.

```
<%@ taglib prefix="c" uri="http://java.sun.com/jsp/jstl/core"%>
<%@ taglib prefix="fmt" uri="http://java.sun.com/jsp/jstl/fmt"%>
<%@ taglib prefix="form" uri="http://www.springframework.org/tags/
form"%>
<html>
  <head>
    <title><fmt:message key="title" /></title>
    <style>
      .error {
```

```
            color: red;
        }
      </style>
  </head>
  <body>
    <h1><fmt:message key="customerSave.heading" /></h1>
    <form:form method="post" commandName="customerSave">
      <table width="100%" bgcolor="f8f8ff" border="0"
             cellspacing="0"  cellpadding="5">
          <c:forEach items="${errors}" var="error">
              <span class="error"><c:out value="${error.type}"/>:
              <c:out value="${error.messageKey}"/></span><br/>
          </c:forEach>
          <c:forEach items="${warnings}" var="warning">
            <c:out value="${warning.type}"/>
            <c:out value="${warning.messageKey}"/><br/>
          </c:forEach>
          <tr>
              <td align="right">First name:</td>
              <td><form:input path="firstName" /></td>
          </tr>
          <tr>
              <td align="right">Last name:</td>
              <td><form:input path="lastName" /></td>
          </tr>
          <tr>
              <td align="right">Phone number:</td>
              <td><form:input path="phoneNumber" /></td>
          </tr>
      </table>
      <br>
      <input type="submit" align="center" value="Execute">
    </form:form>
    <a href="<c:url value="index.jsp"/>">Home</a>
  </body>
</html>
```

Code listing 16: Customer save form (`customerSave.jsp` file).

The first few lines of this JSP declare the tag libraries that will be used. It is the standard `core` library, `fmt` library, and the Spring `form` tag library.

Next, `customerSave.jsp` defines the form—`<form:form method="post" comman dName="customerSave">`. Please notice `commandName` as we'll use it when we'll be wiring this form to its controller. Thanks to this attribute, Spring will know which controller is responsible for handling this form. The next two `forEach` elements display `error` and `warning` messages. Next, we can see the three input fields `firstName`, `lastName`, and `phoneNumber`. They contain the form body that will be sent when the form is submitted.

Localized messages

The JSP uses localized messages that are displayed by the standard `<fmt:message key="someKeyName" />` tag. `someKeyName` must be present in a properties file that we'll call `messages.properties`, which must be on the classpath. Our file might look like the following code:

```
title=SampleApplication
customerSave.heading=Save Customer
```

Code listing 17: Localized messages (`messages.properties` file).

We have to tell Spring about this file. This can be done with the following bean configuration. It'll define a `messageSource` bean that will be of type `ResourceBundleMessageSource`. It's `baseName` property will be set to `messages` — the name of our localized messages file.

```
<bean id="messageSource"
      class="org.springframework.context.support.
             ResourceBundleMessageSource">
  <property name="basename" value="messages" />
</bean>
```

Code listing 18: Extract from the Spring configuration (`sampleApplication-servlet.xml` file), `messageSource` bean definition.

Customer save form controller

We'll now write a controller for this form. Lets start with Spring definitions. In this case, the bean name will be set to `/customerSave.htm`. This is also a part of the URL under which this form will be accessible.

```
<bean name="/customerSave.htm"
      class="droolsbook.sampleApplication.
             web.CustomerSaveFormController">
  <property name="sessionForm" value="true" />
  <property name="commandName" value="customerSave" />
  <property name="commandClass"
            value="droolsbook.bank.model.Customer" />
  <property name="formView" value="customerSave" />
  <property name="successView" value="index.jsp" />
</bean>
```

Code listing 19: Extract from the Spring configuration (`sampleApplication-servlet.xml` file), `CustomerSaveFormController` bean definition.

Note that the `sessionForm` is set to `true`, which means this form will be stored in the HTTP session instead of HTTP request. This ensures that a new form is not created every time between validation attempts.

When the user enters the /customerSave.htm URL, Spring will automatically forward the user to formView, which is, in this case, set to customerSave. After the view translation, this becomes webRoot/WEB-INF/jsp/customerSave. jsp. Similarly, successView specifies the name of the view that the user will be forwarded to upon successful form submission. It's set to index.jsp (in this case, it's the full name of a JSP page).

All of the submitted customer forms will be processed by CustomerSaveFormController. This controller will extend the Spring MVC SimpleFormController. It will overwrite an onSubmit method, which will be executed every time a customer form is submitted. It will use the bankingService and bankingFactory beans to create a new customer and add this customer into the system. After a successful request, the user will be redirected to the success view.

```java
public class CustomerSaveFormController extends
    SimpleFormController {
  @Autowired
  private BankingService bankingService;
  @Autowired
  private BankingFactory bankingFactory;
  public ModelAndView onSubmit(Object command,
      BindException errors) throws ServletException {
    Customer customer = (Customer) command;
    try {
      bankingService.add(customer);
      return new ModelAndView(new RedirectView(
          getSuccessView()));
    } catch (ValidationException e) {
      ValidationReport report = e.getValidationReport();
      Map model = errors.getModel();
      model.put("errors", report.getMessagesByType(
          Message.Type.ERROR));
      model.put("warnings", report
          .getMessagesByType(Message.Type.WARNING));
      return new ModelAndView(getFormView(), model);
    }
  }
  protected Object formBackingObject(HttpServletRequest request)
      throws ServletException {
    Customer customer = bankingFactory.createCustomer();
    return customer;
  }
}
```

Code listing 20: Controller for processing the new customer form (CustomerSaveFormController.java file).

Please note that the bankingService and bankingFactory beans are declared with the @Autowired annotations. This means that Spring will automatically set these properties when this controller is created. We also don't have to create set methods for these properties.

If the Customer object is not valid, then ValidationException is thrown by bankingService. CustomerSaveFormController handles this case with a try/catch block. The validation report is extracted from the exception and the 'model' (as in MVC) is updated with ERROR and WARNING messages from the report. The control flow is then forwarded back to the form view using return new ModelAndView(getFormView(), model);.

The formBackingObject method will be called when a user displays the customer save form. In our case, it creates the Customer object itself. This is a shortcut and in a real application, we'd create something like a CustomerForm data transfer object (DTO), which will hold all of the data needed by the view and then, in the controller, we'd create a normal Customer object from this CustomerForm.

We can now deploy the application and access it by the following URL: http://localhost:8080/sampleApplication/customerSave.htm. After entering a **First name**, a **Last name**, and leaving the **Phone number** field blank, we should get the following response:

The **Save Customer** form with validation messages screen is shown in the preceding screenshot. It informs us that the **Phone number** is missing (**ERROR**) and that the address is required (**WARNING**). As we're not dealing with addresses, the warning message is expected. After entering the **Phone number**, the customer will be successfully stored in the database and we'll be redirected to `index.jsp` page.

As you can see from the previous screenshot, the screen doesn't actually display the messages themselves but only the message key names. This key can now be mapped to the real message and the message can even be localized based on the user's preferred language. To do this, we'll now replace the standard output tag—`<c:out value="${error.messageKey}"/>` (in code listing 16) with its localized version: `<fmt:message key="${error.messageKey}"/>`. We can do this for both error and warning messages. Then, it is a matter of defining these messages. Add the following to `messages.properties` file:

```
phoneNumberRequired=Customer phone number is required.
addressRequired=Customer address is required.
```

Code listing 21: Extract from the file—`messages.properties`.

If we now reload the screen, full localized messages should be displayed.

Complex Event Processing service

We'll now integrate the CEP service into the banking service. The CEP service basically needs all kind of events so that it can make complex decisions. One such event is a customer created event or a customer updated event. The CEP service has one notify method that takes an event. The `add` and `save` methods of `bankingService` can be modified to create these events and send them to `cepService`. By adding `cepService.notify(new CustomerCreatedEvent(customer));` at the end of these methods, an event referencing the current customer is created. (This is for the `add` method, the `save` method will create a new instance of `CustomerUpdatedEvent` instead). The CEP service contains a rule session that is maintained throughout the lifetime of this service as we've discussed in Chapter 7, *Complex Event Processing*.

Loan approval

We'll now create screens for the loan approval process (another vertical slice of the application). This consists of loan request form, task list screen, task manipulation (claim a task, start a task, complete a task, and so on), and final supervisor's approval. In this case, we'll follow a top-down approach starting with the presentation layer.

Loan request form

The **Loan Request** form screenshot is as follows:

Let's start with the implementation of `loanRequest.jsp`, which will display the **Loan Request** form. We can copy the `customerSave.jsp` file and just replace the form section with the following:

```
<form:form method="post" commandName="loanRequest">
    <table width="100%" bgcolor="f8f8ff" border="0"
            cellspacing="0" cellpadding="5">
        <tr>
            <td align="right">Amount:</td>
            <td><form:input path="amount" /></td>
        </tr>
        <tr>
            <td align="right">Duration:</td>
            <td><form:input path="durationYears" /> years</td>
        </tr>
    </table>
    <br>
    <input type="submit" align="center" value="Execute">
</form:form>
```

Code listing 22: Extract from the loan request form (`loanRequest.jsp` file).

This form is very similar to our earlier form. In this case, the form body contains loan amount and loan duration.

Upon submission, `LoanRequestFormController` will be responsible for starting the loan approval process. This controller can be defined as follows:

```
<bean name="/loanRequest.htm"
      class="droolsbook.sampleApplication.web.
             LoanRequestFormController">
  <property name="sessionForm" value="true" />
  <property name="commandName" value="loanRequest" />
  <property name="commandClass"
            value="droolsbook.bank.model.Loan" />
  <property name="formView" value="loanRequest" />
  <property name="successView" value="index.jsp" />
</bean>
```

Code listing 23: Extract from the Spring configuration (`sampleApplication-servlet.xml` file), `LoanRequestFormController` bean definition.

`commandClass` is set to the `Loan` class. This mapping is very similar to what we've done for the `customerSave` controller. Again, the form is stored in the session—`sessionForm` is set to `true`.

Similar to `CustomerSaveFormController`, `LoanRequestController` will overwrite the `onSubmit` method and will call `bankingService` as follows:

```
bankingService.requestLoan(loan, customer);
return new ModelAndView(new RedirectView(getSuccessView()));
```

Code listing 24: Extract from the `onSubmit` method of `LoanRequestController`.

The `loan` object shown in code listing 24 is pre-populated with values entered by the user. The `customer` represents the currently logged-in user. We won't go into detail about how to get this user. The user is then redirected to the success view, which is set to `index.jsp`.

The `bankingService.requestLoan` method is shown in code listing 25. It simply delegates to the `loadApprovalService` method.

```
@Override
public void requestLoan(Loan loan, Customer customer) {
  loanApprovalService.requestLoan(loan, customer);
```

Code listing 25: Method for requesting a loan (`BankingServiceImpl.java` file)

Process persistence

As we already know, the loan approval process can take hours, days, or even months to finish. It is, therefore, important to persist the loan approval processes rather than keeping them in memory all the time.

We'll use a special persistable knowledge session implementation called CommandBasedStatefulKnowledgeSession. It acts like a standard StatefulKnowledgeSession. However, with each method call, it persists its state. We just have to remember sessionId and we can recreate the session at any stage.

This implementation comes form drools-persistence-jpa module. If we look under the hood of this session implementation, we'd see that each of its methods creates a command and executes it with a command service called SingleSessionCommandService.

org.drools.persistence.session.SingleSessionCommandService

A command service implementation that uses JPA to persist the session's state. It has two constructors — one that is used to create a new knowledge session and one for loading existing persisted knowledge session by sessionId. It's execute method then takes a command and executes it on the knowledge session.

This command service needs EntityManagerFactory. The name of the JPA persistence unit is org.drools.persistence.jpa.

This service uses JTA to programmatically manage transactions. The two constructors *always* create a new transaction and the execute method can also join existing transactions or create a new one if no transaction is running.

Please note that when using SingleSessionCommandService, the default implementations of processInstanceManagerFactory, workItemManagerFactory, and processSignalManagerFactory need to be overwritten with their 'persistence aware' counterparts (for example, JPAWorkItemManagerFactory). For example, imagine a situation when workItemManager is notified that workItem has been completed. As this workItemManager might be different than the one that created this workItem, workItem may not be in memory and must be loaded first from the persistent storage.

We can now create JPA persistence unit in Spring. The configuration will look exactly the same as our earlier persistence unit except for persistenceUnitName:

```
<bean id="droolsEntityManagerFactory"
      class="org.springframework.orm.jpa.
             LocalContainerEntityManagerFactoryBean">
  <property name="persistenceUnitName"
            value="org.drools.persistence.jpa" />
  <property name="jpaPropertyMap" ref="jpaPropertyMap" />
</bean>
```

Code listing 26: Drools persistence entity manager factory
(`applicationContext.xml` file).

The next step would be to include the loan approval service that we've written in
Chapter 8, *Drools Flow*, unchanged. However, it is unfortunate that the command
service programmatically manages transactions and creates a new transaction
whenever a new instance of `SingleSessionCommandService` is created. As we're
already using Spring to manage our transactions, we'll create a simple workaround.
We'll define a new `JPAKnowledgeSessionLookup` class that will deal only with
creating new persistable sessions. We'll then call this class outside our Spring
transaction. Our transaction will suspend and the persistent session will be able to
create its own transaction. The interface for this `JPAKnowledgeSessionLookup` class
is as follows:

```
/**
 * knows how to create a new or lookup existing knowledge
 * session
 */
public interface KnowledgeSessionLookup {
  /**
   * creates a new session
   */
  StatefulKnowledgeSession newSession();

  /**
   * loads an existing session
   */
  StatefulKnowledgeSession loadSession(int sessionId);
}
```

Code listing 27: `KnowledgeSessionLookup` interface.

We can now modify our transaction setup in `applicationContext.xml`. Simply add
the following code to the `aop:config` section:

```
<aop:pointcut id="knowledgeSessionLookupMethods"
              expression="execution(* droolsbook.org.drools.
                      persistence.KnowledgeSessionLookup.*(..))" />
<aop:advisor pointcut-ref="knowledgeSessionLookupMethods"
             advice-ref="noTransactionAdvice" />
```

Code listing 28: Extract from the `aop:config` section
(`applicationContext.xml` file).

We've declared `pointcut` that captures all of the method executions on the
`KnowledgeSessionLookup` interface.

Note that the order is important. Put `pointcut` after our first `pointcut` and `advisor` after our first `advisor`.

`advice` will then suspend any currently running transaction:

```
<tx:advice id="noTransactionAdvice">
  <tx:attributes>
    <tx:method name="*" propagation="NOT_SUPPORTED"/>
  </tx:attributes>
</tx:advice>
```

Code listing 29: Not supported transaction advice (`applicationContext.xml` file).

After this `aop` configuration, `SingleSessionCommandService` will be able to begin its own programmatic transaction freely.

The implementation of the `JPAKnowledgeSessionLookup` class is as follows:

```
/**
 * works with persistable knowledge sessions
 */
public class JPAKnowledgeSessionLookup implements
    KnowledgeSessionLookup {

  @PersistenceUnit(unitName="droolsEntityManagerFactory")
  private EntityManagerFactory emf;

  private KnowledgeBase knowledgeBase;
  private Environment environment;

  private WorkItemHandler emailHandler;
  private WorkItemHandler transferFundsHandler;
  private WorkItemHandler humanTaskHandler;

  public void init() {
    environment = EnvironmentFactory.newEnvironment();
    environment.set(EnvironmentName.ENTITY_MANAGER_FACTORY,
        emf);
    environment.set(
        EnvironmentName.OBJECT_MARSHALLING_STRATEGIES,
        new ObjectMarshallingStrategy[] { MarshallerFactory
            .newSerializeMarshallingStrategy() });
  }

  public StatefulKnowledgeSession newSession() {
    StatefulKnowledgeSession session = JPAKnowledgeService
        .newStatefulKnowledgeSession(knowledgeBase, null,
            environment);
    registerWorkItemHandlers(session);
```

```
      return session;
   }
   public StatefulKnowledgeSession loadSession(int sessionId) {
      StatefulKnowledgeSession session = JPAKnowledgeService
         .loadStatefulKnowledgeSession(sessionId,
            knowledgeBase, null, environment);
      registerWorkItemHandlers(session);
      return session;
   }
   /**
    * helper method for registering work item handlers
    * (they are not persisted)
    */
   private void registerWorkItemHandlers(
       StatefulKnowledgeSession session) {
      WorkItemManager manager = session.getWorkItemManager();
      manager.registerWorkItemHandler("Human Task",
         humanTaskHandler);
      manager.registerWorkItemHandler("Email", emailHandler);
      manager.registerWorkItemHandler("Transfer Funds",
         transferFundsHandler);
   }
```

Code listing 30: Class for initializing persistent `StatefulKnowledgeSession`
(`JPAKnowledgeSessionLookup.java` file).

The knowledge sessions (`CommandBasedStatefulKnowledgeSession`) are
created through the `JPAKnowledgeService` factory class that has two methods:
`newStatefulKnowledgeSession` and `loadStatefulKnowledgeSession`. They both
take the knowledge base, knowledge session configuration (null in our case), and
`environment`. The latter method also takes `sessionId`.

As we can see, `environment` is initialized in the `init` method with
`droolsEntityManagerFactory` and also a 'serialize' marshalling strategy.
We want to carry out full session serialization.

Please note that both the `newSession` and `loadSession` methods call
`registerWorkItemHandlers` method, which registers all of the work item handlers
used in our process. This is necessary because work item handlers are not persisted.
Hence, we need to set them for each new knowledge session.

This `JPAKnowledgeSessionLookup` class can be defined in Spring as follows:

```
<bean id="knowledgeSessionLookup" init-method="init"
        class="droolsbook.org.drools.persistence.
                JPAKnowledgeSessionLookup" >
    <property name="knowledgeBase"
              ref="loanApprovalKnowledge" />
    <property name="emailHandler" ref="emailWorkItemHandler"/>
    <property name="humanTaskHandler"
              ref="approveLoanWorkItemHandler"/>
    <property name="transferFundsHandler"
              ref="transferFundsWorkItemHandler"/>
</bean>
```

Code listing 31: `knowledgeSessionLookup` Spring bean definition
(`applicationContext.xml` file).

With this setup done, we can now implement the `loanApproval` service, which will be a slightly modified version of what we've done in Chapter 8, *Drools Flow*. We'll use the session lookup to create the knowledge session and `LoanApprovalHolder` to keep a track of current requests. The `holder` class will contain the customer requesting the loan, `sessionId`, and `processInstanceId`. `processInstanceId` will be needed for sending the final loan approval event.

```
public LoanApprovalHolder requestLoan(final Loan loan,
    final Customer customer) {
  LoanApprovalHolder holder = new LoanApprovalHolder();
  StatefulKnowledgeSession session = sessionLookup
      .newSession();
  try {
    Map<String, Object> parameterMap =
      new HashMap<String, Object>();
    parameterMap.put("loanSourceAccount",loanSourceAccount);
    parameterMap.put("customer", customer);
    parameterMap.put("loan", loan);
    session.insert(loan);
    session.insert(customer);
    ProcessInstance processInstance = session.startProcess(
        "loanApproval", parameterMap);

    holder.setCustomer(customer);
    holder.setSessionId(session.getId());
    holder.setProcessInstanceId(processInstance.getId());
    em.persist(holder);

    session.insert(processInstance);
    session.fireAllRules();
```

```
    } finally {
      session.dispose();
    }
    return holder;
  }
```

Code listing 32: Implementation of the `requestLoan` method
(`LoanApprovalServiceImpl.java` file).

A new persistable session is created, `loan` and the `customer` instances are inserted
into the session, the process is started, the `sessionId` and `processInstanceId`
values are set, rules are fired, and that's it for the `requestLoan` method.

> At the time of writing this book, I had to comment out the line where
> `processInstance` is inserted into the session; otherwise, the session
> wouldn't serialize properly. It meant that I could request only loans with
> an amount less than 5,000.

What we've achieved so far is that the loan approval service is transactional. A new
transaction will be started when a user calls `bankingService.requestLoan` method
and the call will be delegated to `loanApprovalService.requestLoan` method. From
this method, we'll call `sessionLookup.newSession` method. Upon entering this
method, the transaction suspends and `SingleSessionCommandService` can begin
its own transaction that creates a new knowledge session and persists it. When the
`newSession` method returns, our transaction will resume. The only disadvantage of
this approach is that when our transaction rolls back at a later stage, the knowledge
session will remain as an orphan record in the database.

> As an alternative to creating `KnowledgeSessionLookup` and
> suspending the running transaction, consider using your own
> implementation of `CommandService`; one that will use declarative
> transactions, as opposed to programmatic transactions. It has lots of other
> benefits that declarative transactions do have (for example, we can avoid
> expensive JTA transactions and use cheap local resource transactions).
>
> If you look under the hood of `JPAKnowledgeService`, you'll notice that
> it is only a convenience implementation that sets up some predefined
> values for `KnowledgeSessionConfiguration`. For example, the
> command service used.

Note that if you want to test this application so far, you have to start the
WS-HumanTask server as we've seen in Chapter 8, *Drools Flow*.

To provide even further reliability, our transactions should span to the WS-HumanTask server. This won't be shown. However, it is a matter of configuration.

Task list

Once the loan is successfully requested, the bank employees can start working on the created task. We'll now create a screen that will list all of the available tasks. The **Task List** screen is shown in the following screenshot:

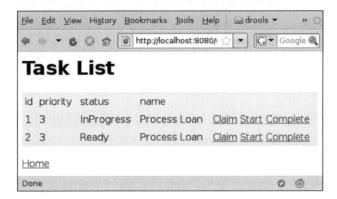

The **Task List** screen displays a table of all the available tasks for a user (bank employee). We can see two tasks in the preceding screenshot. Some important properties of the tasks are displayed, such as the task **id**, its **priority**, **status**, and **name**. One task is **InProgress** and the other task is **Ready**. The user can **Claim**, **Start**, or **Complete** a task.

 Possible improvement: Once the user claims a task, the **Claim** link should be disabled or, ideally, not shown (this won't be implemented).

This **Task List** screen will be implemented in the taskList.jsp file. Code listing 33 shows the core of this page—a task list table. This JSP will operate on collection of TaskSummary objects, which will be accessible under the model.tasks bean. TaskSummary is the description of a task as returned from the WS-HumanTask server. Let's now look at the JSP itself:

```
<table width="100%" bgcolor="f8f8ff" border="0"
        cellspacing="0" cellpadding="5">
  <tr>
    <td>id</td><td>priority</td><td>status</td><td>name</td>
```

```
    </tr>
    <c:forEach items="${model.tasks}" var="task">
    <tr>
      <td><c:out value="${task.id}"/></td>
      <td><c:out value="${task.priority}"/></td>
      <td><c:out value="${task.status}"/> </td>
      <td><c:out value="${task.name}"/></td>
      <td>
        <a href="<c:url value="taskClaim.htm">
            <c:param name="taskId" value="${task.id}"/></c:url>">
            Claim
        </a>
        <a href="<c:url value="taskStart.htm">
            <c:param name="taskId"value="${task.id}"/></c:url>">
            Start
        </a>
        <a href="<c:url value="taskComplete.htm">
            <c:param name="taskId" value="${task.id}"/></c:url>">
            Complete
        </a>
      </td>
    </tr>
    </c:forEach>
  </table>
```

Code listing 33: Extract from the task list JSP (taskList.jsp file).

As we've discussed, taskList.jsp iterates over tasks in the ${model.tasks} collection and displays some important information for a task. It is worth noting that the three commands are using taskId as an argument. The controllers that these commands will map to will need this ID to identify a task.

A controller can be defined as follows:

```
<bean name="/taskList.htm"
      class="droolsbook.sampleApplication.web.TaskListController">
</bean>
```

Code listing 34: Extract from the Spring configuration (sampleApplication-servlet.xml file), TaskListController bean definition.

The task list doesn't involve any web form, so the Spring definition is much more simple.

The controller implementation is as follows:

```
public class TaskListController extends AbstractController {
  @Autowired
  private MinaTaskClient client;
```

```
    @Autowired
    private WebSessionUtils webSessionUtils;
    @Override
    protected ModelAndView handleRequestInternal(
        HttpServletRequest request,HttpServletResponse response)
        throws Exception {
      BlockingTaskSummaryResponseHandler responseHandler =
        new BlockingTaskSummaryResponseHandler();
      User user = webSessionUtils.getUser();
      client.getTasksAssignedAsPotentialOwner(user.getUserId(),
          user.getLanguage(), responseHandler);
      List<TaskSummary> tasks = responseHandler.getResults();

      Map<String, Object> model = new HashMap<String, Object>();
      model.put("tasks", tasks);

      return new ModelAndView("taskList", "model", model);
    }
}
```

Code listing 35: Controller for displaying a task list
(`TaskListController.java` file).

This controller extends `AbstractController`. It requires two
properties — `MinaTaskClient` and `WebSessionUtils`. The first one is a
client that we've already seen in Chapter 8, *Drools Flow*. This is its re-usable version.
This client connects to the WS-HumanTask server at the web server startup time. It
is then shared between various controllers dealing with WS-HumanTasks. The next
property — `webSessionUtils` is a utility class that contains various convenience
methods (for example, method for getting the current authenticated user).
Implementation of this utility class is out of scope of this book. We'll use user's ID
and locale for getting the task list. All of the controller's logic is contained within
the `handleRequestInternal` method. It uses `client` to get all of the available
tasks by calling the `getTasksAssignedAsPotentialOwner` method. As this call is
asynchronous, the controller uses `BlockingTaskSummaryResponseHandler` to wait
for the response. Finally, a model is created that contains these tasks and the user is
forwarded to the `taskList` view.

Working on a task

By clicking on the claim/start/complete link, a user can claim/start/complete a task.
(Please note that we're not implementing other actions such as suspend or skip). Let's
look at the claim action in more detail. Its controller can be defined as follows:

```
<bean name="/taskClaim.htm"
      class="droolsbook.sampleApplication.web.TaskClaimController">
</bean>
```

Code listing 36: Extract from the Spring configuration (`sampleApplication-servlet.xml` file), `TaskClaimController` bean definition.

The `handleRequestInternal` method's implementation of `TaskClaimController` follows. This controller also uses `client` and `webSessionUtils` 'auto wired' Spring beans. This controller will read `taskId` as a parameter from the request and will use the client to claim the task with this ID for the current user — `client.claim(taskId, user.getUserId(), ..)`.

```
/**
 * claims specified task for the current user
 */
@Override
protected ModelAndView handleRequestInternal(
  HttpServletRequest request,HttpServletResponse response)
  throws Exception {
   long taskId = Long.parseLong(request.getParameter("taskId"));
   User user = webSessionUtils.getUser();
   BlockingTaskOperationResponseHandler
     operationResponseHandler =
       new BlockingTaskOperationResponseHandler();
   client.claim(taskId, user.getUserId(),
       operationResponseHandler);
   operationResponseHandler.waitTillDone(5000);

   return new ModelAndView("redirect:taskList.htm");
}
```

Code listing 37: `handleRequestInternal` method of a controller for claiming a task (`TaskClaimController.java` file).

Similar to task list controller, this controller uses `BlockingTaskOperationResponseHandler` to wait for the result.

After we've implemented all of the three controllers (start, claim, and complete), we can deploy and run this application. However, if we do it, as soon as we complete the human task, it will fail with the following exception: `java.lang.IllegalArgumentException: Removing a detached instance org.drools.persistence.processinstance.WorkItemInfo#1`.

Hibernate is informing us that we're deleting an entity outside the transaction (there is no active entity manager). It is because the WS-HumanTask handler listens for completed tasks and if it sees that a task has been completed, it notifies its work item manager, which in turn, cleans up resources that are no longer needed. In this case, the work item manager tried to delete a `WorkItemInfo` entity.

The WS-HumanTask handler is called asynchronously outside our transaction. Remember? Our transaction is only around `BankingService` methods.

In order to fix this, we'll have to modify the WS-HumanTask handler implementation to perform some of its operations in a transaction. This is mainly notifying its manager that a task has been completed or aborted.

Our implementation of the WS-HumanTask handler will also need to know the session ID in order to load the correct persisted session. `sessionId` can be passed in many ways. We could set it as a process parameter and then set it on the human task work item. Or we could maintain a synchronized map of `processInstanceId` to `sessionId` mappings. (You can get the current `processInstanceId` from `workItem` that is accessible within the handler), The `loanApprovalService.requestLoan` method would have to insert this session to this map whenever a new loan is requested. We'll use the latter.

Make a copy of the default `WSHumanTaskHandler` and replace each `manager.completeWorkItem` call with the following:

```
handler.getTransactionTemplate().execute(new TransactionCallback() {
  public Object doInTransaction(TransactionStatus status) {
    Integer sessionId = handler.getProcessIdToSessionIdMap()
                      .get(workItem.getProcessInstanceId());
    StatefulKnowledgeSession session = handler
      .getKnowledgeSessionLookup().loadSession(sessionId);
    try {
      session.getWorkItemManager().completeWorkItem(
          workItemId, results );
    }
    finally {
      session.dispose();
    }
    return null;
  }
});
```

Code listing 38: Completing work item in a human task handler (`JPAWSHumanTaskHandler.java` file).

Note that in this implementation we're using the synchronized `processIdToSessionIdMap` to lookup `sessionId`. Also note that our handler uses the same `KnowledgeSessionLookup` class as the loan approval service. Further, it uses Spring transactional template to execute this code within a transaction. This human task work item handler can be defined in Spring as follows:

```
<bean name="approveLoanWorkItemHandler"
     class="droolsbook.sampleApplication.drools.persistence.
           JPAWSHumanTaskHandler" >
   <property name="transactionTemplate"
             ref="transactionTemplate" />
   <property name="knowledgeSessionLookup"
             ref="knowledgeSessionLookup" />
</bean>
<bean id="transactionTemplate"
     class="org.springframework.transaction.support.
           TransactionTemplate">
   <property name="transactionManager"
             ref="transactionManager" />
</bean>
```

Code listing 39: Human task work item handler Spring bean
(`applicationContext.xml` file).

Loan approval event

For a successful loan approval, a supervisor must send an 'approved' event.
Normally, we'd create a 'loans waiting for approval' screen where the supervisor
would pick the loan for approval. This screen would be driven by the persisted
`LoanApprovalHolder` instances. We won't be creating this screen and instead let's
pretend that the supervisor knows `sessionId` of the process that needs the approval.

Loan approval event will be handled by an ApproveEventController:

```
<bean name="/approveEvent.htm"
     class="droolsbook.sampleApplication.web.ApproveEventController">
</bean>
```

Code listing 40: Extract from the Spring configuration (`sampleApplication-
servlet.xml` file), `ApproveEventController` bean definition.

Our controller will use `sessionId` to send the event to the correct session. First, we'll
search for `LoanApprovalHolder` by `sessionId` (note that it is the *primary key*). Then,
we'll call `bankingService.approveLoan` method.

```
/**
 * sends 'loan approved' event to specific process
*/
@PersistenceContext(unitName="entityManagerFactory")
EntityManager em;

@Override
protected ModelAndView handleRequestInternal(
   HttpServletRequest request,HttpServletResponse response)
```

```
    throws Exception {
  String sessionId = request.getParameter("sessionId");
  LoanApprovalHolder pendingLoanApprovalHolder = em.find(
      LoanApprovalHolder.class, Integer.valueOf(sessionId));
  bankingService.approveLoan(pendingLoanApprovalHolder);
  return new ModelAndView("redirect:index.jsp");
}
```

Code listing 41: `handleRequestInternal` method of a controller for sending an approval event (`ApproveEventController.java` file).

The user is redirected to the `index.jsp` page (note `redirect:index.jsp`).

 As an alternative to `LoanApprovalHolder`, we could use the persisted process data and search for all processes that are waiting for approval. However, in Drools 5.0, the process data is stored as an array of bytes, which makes it impossible to search through the data. This will be improved in future versions of Drools.

`bankingService` delegates to the `approveLoan` method of the `loanApproval` service as follows:

```
public void approveLoan(LoanApprovalHolder holder) {
  StatefulKnowledgeSession session =
    sessionLookup.loadSession(holder.getSessionId());
  try {
    SignalEventCommand command = new SignalEventCommand();
    command.setProcessInstanceId(
      holder.getProcessInstanceId());
    command.setEventType("LoanApprovedEvent");
    command.setEvent(true);
    session.execute(command);
  } finally {
    session.dispose();
  }
}
```

Code listing 42: `approveLoan` method of the loan approval service (`LoanApprovalServiceImpl.java` file).

The method looks up the knowledge session using `sessionId`. A new `SignalEventCommand` is created, `processInstanceId` is set together with the event type and event's value. The command is then executed.

After the bank employee completes the loan task process and the supervisor sends the approve event, the loan approval process will successfully finish, the money will be transferred, and the customer will be informed with an email.

Summary

In this chapter, we've learned how to write a basic web application. The application brought together some of the services we've defined in the previous chapters.

The application has layered architecture. The entire configuration was carried out with Spring Framework (data sources, repositories, transactions, knowledge bases, services, view controllers, and others). Spring makes it easy to change the configuration without recompiling the code.

We've learned how to integrate transactions with our services. For example, all new customers are validated, persisted, and all of this happens within a transaction. Further, the complex event processing service is notified about all of the important events within the application.

The loan approval process shows how to deal with a long running rule session. Sessions have to be persisted during the user's 'think time'; otherwise, they will consume resources that could have been used in a much better way. As this is the first release of `drools-process-task` and `drools-persistence-jpa` modules, the persistence support had minor glitches and we had to do some workarounds. However, this should be fixed in future versions of Drools.

10
Testing

Testing is an important part of the development life cycle. In the earlier chapters, we've learned how to write unit and integration tests. This chapter will provide some additional information about testing and troubleshooting rules. It will focus on how to write good unit tests, integration tests, and acceptance tests. It will look at testing support in Guvnor (the BRMS) including some support for static analysis of rules, and finally some useful advice for rule debugging will be given.

How to write unit tests for rules

By definition a 'unit' in a unit test is the smallest testable part of an application—in our case, a rule. Writing a unit test for every rule is expensive. It effectively doubles the cost of writing a rule. However, it is well worth the effort. To minimize this cost, we should focus on each rule in isolation. For the purpose of isolating all of the external factors such as calls to services, repositories, and so on, any mocking library can be used.

A mocking library can create a dummy implementation (a mock) of a service that we can use for testing the rules. The mock can record methods that have been called and return predefined values. We can verify that the correct method was executed the expected amount of times with the correct set of arguments. In Chapter 8, *Drools Flow*, **jMock** was used, but **easyMock** is another good alternative.

By isolating all of the external factors, our unit tests will work even if they change. For example, the implementation of global objects can change, but as the rules use their mocked version, the changes in rule unit tests will be minimal.

Each condition in a rule should be covered in a unit test. When we change a condition, ideally, one test should break. This will give us confidence when refactoring rules that the functionality hasn't been changed. This also applies when a new functionality is being added or an existing functionality is being removed. The test should account for cases where there is no fact, there is one fact, or many facts present in the knowledge session. However, as with everything, always use your common sense when writing tests. For example, it probably doesn't make sense to test every possible scenario in a decision table.

A ruleflow test can be usually divided into two parts: testing of the ruleflow definition and rules.

> When testing the ruleflow definition, note that the knowledge base can be created just from a `.rf` file.

A ruleflow definition unit test should test every ruleflow node to make sure that every branch of a ruleflow works as expected—especially, ruleflow nodes with some conditions/actions.

Further, unit tests are a sort of living documentation. They are usually updated immediately with the code/rules. Through a unit test, others can understand its API, how this unit works, and how to use it.

Rule integration testing

An integration test is a higher level test for the whole knowledge base. It tests rule interactions. Instead of mock objects, it uses fully setup objects (services, repositories, and so on). A ruleflow integration test should test the whole ruleflow—definition and rules together.

An integration test involving rules is no different from a standard integration test. We'll now look at rule acceptance testing.

Rule acceptance testing

By definition, acceptance testing is a black-box testing performed on a system prior to its delivery. Acceptance testing is often preformed by the user. There are various tools for implementing acceptance testing. FIT is one of them (**FIT** stands for **Framework for Integrated Test**. More information can be found at `http://fit.c2.com/`). The FIT tests consist of initial configuration setup, setup of input data, and setup of expectations. All this is stored in a human readable document (`.doc` or `.rtf`). It can even be a part of the system requirements (for example, a table within a document that contains input data and expectations).

Drools adopted FIT style acceptance testing early on with the **FIT for Rules** project (More information about FIT for Rules can be found at `http://fit-for-rules.sourceforge.net/`). This has been later enhanced in Guvnor.

> Guvnor is a BRMS—a web application for managing rules. It can create, edit, build, and test rules. For more information about Guvnor, please look into Drools documentation. In this book, we'll only cover Guvnor's testing support and static analysis of rules.
>
> Download, install, and start Guvnor. Open your web browser and navigate to `http://localhost:8080/drools-guvnor`. You can login using any credentials.

We'll now look at testing support in Guvnor. It can be considered as kind of rules acceptance testing. Its biggest benefit is that it can be preformed by a more technically skilled business user. We can define expectation and verify that they were met. When the acceptance test runs, it creates facts from the given input data inserts them into the knowledge session, fires all rules, and then verifies expectations. All of the violations are reported.

Guvnor's testing support can be found in the main menu under heading **QA**. It provides support for running tests and static analysis of rules under the following two subsections: **Test Scenarios in packages** and **Analysis**. In this chapter, we'll cover both.

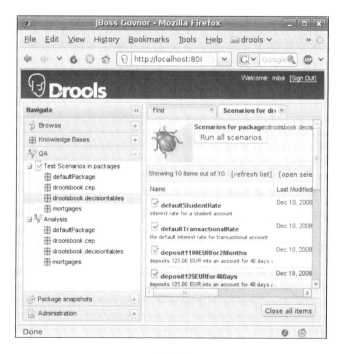

By expanding **Test Scenarios in packages** on the left, we can see all of the configured packages in Guvnor. The already defined tests are listed on the right side of the preceding screenshot. Please ignore them for now.

Let's assume that we've defined rules for calculating interest rates in `droolsbook.` `decisiontables` package in Guvnor (again, please consult the Drools documentation about how to do this. A quick solution would be to use our existing `.xls` file from Chapter 5, *Calculating the interest rate* section, converting this file to `.drl` by using `DecisionTableFactory`, and importing the resulting `.drl` file into Guvnor. Please note that the model and referencing libraries need to be imported as well). After the package in Guvnor successfully builds, we can start with writing some rule acceptance tests.

Creating a test scenario

Before we can run the tests, we have to define them. This is done in the **Knowledge Bases** navigation section. Select **Knowledge Bases** and then **Create New | New Test Scenario**. Give it a name, for example, we can use the same name as we've used for our Java tests—`deposit125EURfor40Days`. A scenario is essentially one JUnit test method. Set the correct package (the one with interest rating calculation—`droolsbook.decisiontables`). Then a new screen for entering the test data should be displayed. Add input data and expectations as shown in the following screenshot:

The **GIVEN** section defines facts that will be inserted into the knowledge session. In the preceding screenshot, we're inserting one fact of type `Account`. This fact is bound under variable name `account`. The five lines shown in this screenshot set the account's properties. `currency` is of type `String`, so the value can be simply set. The other four properties: `balance`, `type`, `startDate`, and `endDate` are more complex objects and must be set as `mvel` expressions. Each value that starts with the 'equal to' (`=`) symbol is considered as a `mvel` expression and properly evaluated.

The `balance` property is of `BigDecimal` type. The full value of `balance` field is `=new java.math.BigDecimal("125.00")`. In this case, we're creating a new instance of an object using `mvel` expression. The `type` field is set to `=droolsbook.bank.model. Account$Type.SAVINGS`. Please note that we're referring to the internal enum type as `Account$Type` instead of `Account.Type` as is the case in `.drl` files. `startDate` is set to `=new org.joda.time.DateMidnight(2008, 1, 1).minusDays(40)` and the `endDate` is set to `=new org.joda.time.DateMidnight(2008, 1, 1)`. The duration of the interval defined by `startDate` and `endDate` is exactly 40 days. By selecting the **GIVEN** button, we can add more facts.

The next section, **EXPECT**, defines expectations. Its first line is used for setting the `SessionClock` (its purpose was described in Chapter 7, *Complex Event Processing*), which is mainly used when working with CEP. The scenario has one expectation on a fact field. It expects that an account's `interestRate` property will be `equal` to `3.00`, which is written as `=new java.math.BigDecimal("3.00")`. We can add as many expectations such as this as we want. Another supported expectation type can verify which rules were fired and how many times.

By clicking on the **More...** button, more input and expectations can be defined. It is something like a round two within this test scenario. The knowledge session will be reused.

A scenario can be further configured to limit the rules that are allowed to fire. This is very useful if we have rules that have side effects and should be omitted from testing (for example, if they are accessing an external service). Further, simple global objects can be defined. It is similar to defining a fact.

Globals

Our rules often interact with external services that are accessible through global variables. Similar to what we did in rule unit tests, in order to test these rules, a mocked version of services could be defined. The test could then verify that the service was called n times with expected parameters.

At the bottom of the preceding screenshot is a description of the test scenario. This helps with understanding the purpose of this test.

Running a test scenario

After defining a test scenario, it can be executed by clicking on the **Run scenario** button in the top left corner of the preceding screenshot. Guvnor then executes this scenario and displays the results in the top part of the screen as shown in the following screenshot:

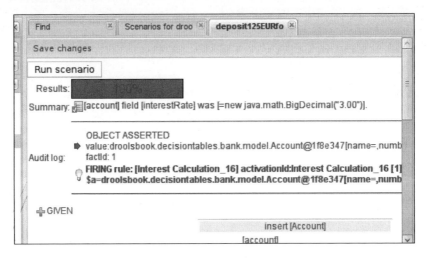

Results consists of a bar graph representing the success rate of this test scenario. In our case, it is **100%**—one test out of one passed. The **Summary** section summarizes which expectations were met (green tick icon) and which were not met (yellow exclamation point). The actual values are also shown. In the following example, account's fact `interestRate` field was set to `3.00`, which was expected. If the expectations aren't met, that is, if the actual value is different from the expected one, both values would be shown and the expected value would be also displayed in the **EXPECT** section with a red rectangle around it as shown in the following screenshot:

The **Audit log** in the preceding screenshot gives us a detailed view of what happened during the test execution. We can see that an `Account` object has been inserted. Its values can be seen (as represented by the `toString` method of `Account`). The next line shows a **FIRING rule** event, which means that a rule has been executed just after the `Account` fact was inserted. The rule name is **Interest Calculation_16**. The facts that activate this rule are shown as well. (Note that these rules come from a `.xls` spreadsheet, the rule names were auto generated, hence, the unusual name **Interest Calculation_16**).

The test can be now saved by clicking on the **Save changes** button in the top part of the screen just below the tabs section. More tests can be defined in the similar manner. We can take all tests that were written for interest rate calculation and rewrite them in Guvnor.

As you can see, this interface is targeted more towards technically skilled business users. They can easily write and maintain these tests. However, for developers, it probably makes more sense to use the IDE and Java for writing these tests as we've done in Chapter 5, *Human-readable Rules*.

Running all test scenarios

After all of the tests are written, they can be run all at once like a JUnit test suite. In the **QA** navigation section, click on the `droolsbook.decisiontables` package. All of the tests within this package can be run by clicking on the **Run all scenarios** button. The results are shown in the following screenshot:

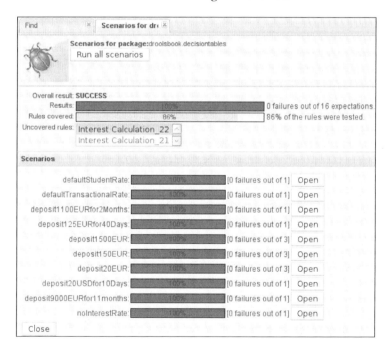

As we can see, the overall result is **SUCCESS**, which means that all of the tests within this package have successfully passed. There were zero failures out of 16 expectations. The next yellow bar shows the test coverage—what percentage of the rules were exercised by the tests. Only **86%** of the rules in this package were tested. The rules that were not tested are shown in the **Uncovered rules** list box. In a real scenario, most of the rules should have at least one to three tests.

The next section displays each executed test scenario in more detail. By clicking on the **Open** button, we can get to the test scenario in question.

These tests can also be called externally through a URL. It is especially useful if we have a continuous integration server that can run these tests every time a package is changed. This URL can be found in the **Knowledge Bases** navigation section. Click on the package you want to test and the URL will be displayed in the bottom of the screen, on the right. For example, **URL for running tests: http://localhost:8080/drools-guvnor/org.drools.guvnor.Guvnor/package/droolsbook.decisiontables/ LATEST/SCENARIOS**.

Static analysis of rules

Testing is useful but it can be very time consuming. We have to write the test and then maintain it. It would be nice if we had an automatic way of testing.

Static analysis is what we're looking for. It is another powerful technique that can be used anytime for achieving high quality rules. The rules are analyzed by a specialized program without actually running them. It can be applied to any rules without any initial investments.

Drools comes with a module called `drools-verifier` that uses rules to analyze rules. This module can be used standalone (through API or as an ant task) or it is also included in Guvnor under the **QA | Analysis** navigation section. Analysis can be started by clicking on the **Run analysis** button. The results are shown in the following screenshot:

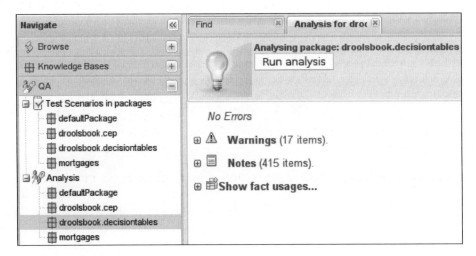

Drools-verifier analyzes rules in a package and creates a report with **Errors**, **Warnings**, and **Notes**. Further, it provides various other information about rules (for example, field usages by fact type and so on). The **Errors** represent significant problems often resulting in the rules not being able to compile. **Warnings** and **Notes** highlight potential problems with rules (for example, a redundant rule—a rule that is already covered by another rule). The `dools-verifier` module is relatively new. New rules for analyzing rules are being constantly added.

Troubleshooting techniques

If we have trouble writing a new rule or fixing a broken rule, we should first isolate this rule from others. This can be done by commenting out other rules or by extracting the rule to a new file and working there.

The Drools Eclipse plugin has a 'Rete Tree' view. The Rete Tree view is accessible as the second tab of the `.drl` editor. It shows the graphical representation of the Rete network (more about it has been discussed in Chapter 12, *Performance*). Behind the scenes, it compiles the `.drl` file and so it can be used to quickly check if the `.drl` file is valid. If not, an error is displayed.

If the rule compiles, but it still isn't doing what we want. We can use a debug event listener to see if the expected facts were inserted into the knowledge session, if the rule was actually activated, and if it fired.

If the rule hasn't been activated, there might be an issue with rule's conditions. In this case, it helps to comment out some conditions and try to make the rule fire without them. This will help us to narrow down the specific rule's condition that is preventing this rule from firing (later in this chapter, we'll also see how to use `mvel` do to some low level debugging of rule conditions).

If the rule fired but it didn't do what was expected, there is probably an issue with the rule's consequence. Rule's consequence is essentially a block of Java code. We can simply put some `System.out` statements, for example, to print out some variables. If this isn't enough, inside the `drl` editor, we can put breakpoints into the rule's consequence. As we already know, Drools, behind the scenes, creates a class from/for each consequence. We can review the source of this class to see any potential problems.

In the following sections, we'll look at some of these techniques in more detail.

Event listeners

Event listeners, or in other words, **callback handlers**, have a large variety of uses. They can be used for audit purposes, debugging, and also for externalizing some functionality from rules. For example, if we look at the validation example in Chapter 3, *Validation*, each rule's consequence is creating a message and adding this message to a report, this can be easily done in an `afterActivationFired` method of `AgendaEventListener`. This way, we're abstracting the reporting aspect from the rules. We can easily change the reporting code without touching every rule. Further, more event listeners can be applied at the same time.

Drools supports four types of event listeners. We'll now look at their interfaces:

1. `org.drools.event.rule.WorkingMemoryEventListener`: Listens to the events on a knowledge session. Fact inserted/updated/retracted events.

2. `org.drools.event.rule.AgendaEventListener`: Listens to the events on the knowledge session's agenda. Activation created/cancelled events, before/after activation fired events, and agenda group popped/pushed events.

3. `org.drools.event.knowledgebase.KnowledgeBaseEventListener`: Listens to the events on the knowledge base. Additions/Removals of packages, rules, and functions. Lock/Unlock events on the knowledge base.

4. `org.drools.event.process.ProcessEventListener`: Listens to events on a process instance. Before/After process started/completed events and process node left/triggered events.

Drools provides various implementations for these listeners. Worth noting is `DebugXXXEventListener` (for example, `org.drools.event.rule.DebugWorkingMemoryEventListener`), which prints everything to the console. Similar to 'debug' type, there is a 'default' type (for example `DefaultWorkingMemoryEventListener`), which is designed for extensibility. All of its methods are empty so that it can be easily extended and only necessary methods are overwritten.

 Use only event listeners from the `drools-api` module. Event listeners from the `drools-code` module won't work with the new Drools API and will be removed in a future version of Drools.

Sample Java code for adding an event listener to a knowledge session is below:

```
session.addEventListener(new DebugWorkingMemoryEventListener());
```

Code listing 1: Setting a debugging knowledge session event listener that prints all events to the console.

By default the `DebugXXXEventListeners` print out very limited information. You'll probably want to extend them and print out more specific information. For example, in case of the `beforeActivationFired` method of `AgendaEventListener`, you could print out the rule name and facts that caused the activation event.

Debugging

Drools Eclipse plugin provides a powerful environment for debugging rules (please refer to the Drools documentation for instructions to install this plugin— `http://www.jboss.org/drools/documentation.html`). Open a `.drl` file in Eclipse and double-click to the left of the line in the rule consequence, where you want to place a breakpoint.

```
rule "addressRequired"
    when
        Customer( address == null )
    then
        warning(drools);
    end
```

The breakpoint will be triggered when the rule fires next. The application needs to be started through a special Drools launcher. The same applies when we want to debug JUnit tests. Right-click on the **Main** class/**JUnit test** class and from the context menu select **Debug As | Drools Application/Drools JUnit Test.** (At the time of writing this book, Drools supported only debugging of JUnit tests version 3.X. We're using JUnit version 4 in this book). As with standard Java debugging, we can see the current stack trace, access global, and local variables or even execute custom expressions.

When debugging the applications that were started with the Drools launcher, various Drools Eclipse **Views** become available. For example, the **Agenda** (can be used to explore activated rules that are placed on the agenda), **Global Data** (used to explore values of global variables), **Working Memory** (used to explore facts in current knowledge session), and **Audit** (can show all events that happened during the rule engine execution, similarly to what we've seen when running test scenarios in Guvnor).

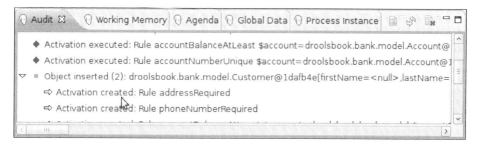

The Audit view only works 'offline'. It can open a pre-recorded knowledge session from a log file. The following code listing shows how to create such log file:

```
KnowledgeRuntimeLogger logger = KnowledgeRuntimeLoggerFactory.
               newFileLogger(session, "log_file_name");
...
logger.close();
```

Code listing 2: Audit logger for logging all events in a knowledge session.

Please note that the `newFileLogger` method takes a knowledge session as an argument. The `logger` should be created right after the `session` and before any objects are inserted into the session or any rules are fired. The output file (in this case called `log_file_name.log`) will be stored in the current JVM working directory. This log file can then be stored for future analysis. After we finish working with the session, the `logger` should be closed by calling `logger.close()`.

Ruleflow

The Eclipse plugin provides additional views for debugging ruleflows. These views are: **Process Instances** (show all of the currently running process instances; each process instance is shown in a tree-like structure and its properties can be examined) and **Process Instance** (shows a graphical representation of a process instance with the currently active nodes highlighted).

In order to activate these views, a breakpoint can be inserted into the `beforeNodeTriggered` method of `ProcessEventListener` or rule consequence as we've done before. When this breakpoint is triggered, the **Process Instances** view will be populated with the current process instance. After double-clicking on this process instance, we can switch to the **Process Instance** view to see the graphical representation of this process with currently active nodes highlighted.

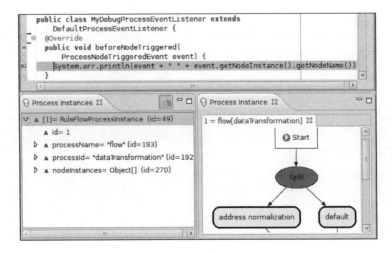

The preceding screenshot shows a breakpoint that has been triggered in a process event listener's `beforeNodeTriggered` method. The **Process Instances** view shows currently running process and **Process Instance** view shows currently active ruleflow groups.

Source of generated classes

When the Drools compiler compiles a rule file, it also generates various Java classes to represent rule consequences and semantic blocks of code (for example, 'evals', 'inline evals', and 'return values'). For performance reasons, these classes are kept only in the memory; they are never stored on disk. However, we can force Drools to dump the source code of these classes to some folder on the disk. There are two ways how to accomplish this:

1. From the command line, we can start the application as normal, just add the following:

   ```
   -Ddrools.dump.dir="target/dumpDir"
   ```

   Code listing 3: Specifying the dump directory from the command line.

2. Through the API:

   ```
   KnowledgeBuilderConfiguration configuration =
      KnowledgeBuilderFactory.newKnowledgeBuilderConfiguration();
   configuration.setOption(DumpDirOption.get(
         new File("target/dumpDir")));
   ```

   Code listing 4: Specifying the dump directory through the API.

   `KnowledgeBuilderConfiguration` can then be used to create the `KnowledgeBuilder` that is used in the knowledge session creation process.

Please note that in both cases, the target directory (in our case `target/dumpDir`) must exist.

This can be useful for understanding the Drools internals in depth and it can also help while troubleshooting to find out exactly what code is being executed.

mvel tricks

As `mvel` is an expression language, it allows us to do more work where just one statement is expected. This can be especially useful for low-level debugging. For example, instead of writing:

```
dialect "mvel"
when
   Account( balance > 1 )
```

Code listing 5: Some rule condition.

It is allowed to write:

```
dialect "mvel"
when
    Account ( eval(System.out.println("matched"); balance > 1) )
```

Code listing 6: Rule condition with multiple expressions inside single inline eval.

We've inserted a `System.out.println("matched");` statement into the inline eval. Every time the rule engine evaluates this inline eval, **matched** message is printed on the console.

Use this with caution; it is only meant for debugging.

Summary

We've learned some principles on how to write rule unit tests, integration tests, and acceptance tests. Unit tests should test each rule in isolation while mocking all of the other components. Integration tests should test a knowledge base as a whole. The acceptance tests are geared towards more technically skilled business users. With a nice web interface provided by Guvnor, a user can test the rules by setting up input data with expectations. Guvnor then executes these tests and reports the results back.

Static Analysis of rules was shown as a very cheap way of testing rules. Currently it provides very limited value but as the Drools-verifies module evolves, it may be a powerful tool in the future.

We've seen some techniques for rule troubleshooting. Starting with listeners that have a lot of other uses, debugging in Eclipse, and to get deeper understanding of the inner workings of a rule engine, we've learned how to view the source of generated classes and how to get advantage of powerful expression language—`mvel`.

11
Integration

The focus of this chapter is on various integration points of the Drools engine with other systems.

We'll start with discussion of having Drools artifacts (rules and processes) change on their own life cycle that is independent from the application. We'll see how to build and dynamically load Drools artifacts.

We'll look at how to run rules remotely from a lightweight client. A simple client that can talk to a Drools execution server will be written in Ruby.

Finally, we'll cover integration with the Spring Framework and some rule standards will be discussed.

Dynamic KnowledgeBase loading

In almost all examples in this book, the Drools artifacts were packaged together with the application. However, rules, processes, and other Drools artifacts often have different life cycles than the applications that use them. These artifacts tend to change more often than the rest of the application. It would be more beneficial if we could build, release, and deploy them separately. In order to achieve this:

- We need to build `KnowledgeBase` independently from the application
- The application should be able to dynamically (re)load this `KnowledgeBase` at runtime

Guvnor (the Business Rules Management Server) meets our first requirement. It can build, release `KnowledgePackage`, and make it available through a URL. Later on in this chapter, we'll also show how we can use a general build tool such as Ant for this task.

For the second requirement, we'll now look at `KnowledgeAgent`.

KnowledgeAgent

KnowledgeAgent allows us to load Drools artifacts dynamically as they change. It is designed to support both poll and push models. However, only the polling model is implemented in Drools.

 In future, the Drools team plans to add implementation for the push model as well. As a result, the interfaces are subject to change.

It periodically scans if a resource has been changed. The following diagram shows how it works in more detail:

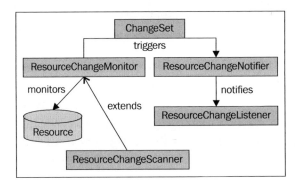

A resource can represent a single .drl file (see org.drools.builder.ResourceType enum for all supported resources) or a directory (it can contain multiple resources). ResourceChangeMonitor monitors these resources for changes. When a change is detected, ChangeSet is created that holds all of the information about this change. ChangeSet holds resources that were added, modified, and removed. ResourceChangeScanner extends ResourceChangeMonitor to provide 'poll type' monitoring. It can be configured to scan for changes in pre-defined intervals.

When the monitor detects a change, it triggers ResourceChangeNotifier, which is responsible for sending notifications to listeners. All of the listeners must implement the ResourceChangeListener interface.

KnowledgeAgent is a type of listener that caches one knowledge base. The knowledge base can be accessed through the getKnowledgeBase method. The agent keeps this knowledge base up-to-date as the resources change (currently it can only create a new KnowledgeBase instance. In future, it will be able to update existing KnowledgeBase as well). The following code listing shows how to use it:

```
ResourceFactory.getResourceChangeScannerService().start();
ResourceFactory.getResourceChangeNotifierService().start();
```

```
KnowledgeAgentConfiguration conf = KnowledgeAgentFactory
  .newKnowledgeAgentConfiguration();
conf.setProperty("drools.agent.scanDirectories", "true");

final KnowledgeAgent agent = KnowledgeAgentFactory
  .newKnowledgeAgent("validation agent", knowledgeBase, conf);
```

Code listing 1: `KnowledgeAgent` usage.

The first two lines start the monitor and notifier services. They must be started explicitly.

Next, `KnowledgeAgentConfiguration` is created that provides some configuration options for the knowledge agent. It can specify whether the agent should scan resources or directories, or whether this agent should listen for `ChangeSet` events. Code listing 1 shows how to enable the `scanDirectories` setting—`conf.setProperty("drools.agent.scanDirectories", "true");`.

`KnowledgeAgentFactory` is then used to create an instance of `KnowledgeAgent` using our configuration `conf`. The factory method also takes `knowledgeBase` as an argument. We can create this knowledge base as we normally do.

> The knowledge base retains the locations of its resources. This is possible only when it is created from a file, URL, or a resource on the classpath (as can be seen in the following example). The location information is lost when the knowledge base is created from a byte array, `InpuStream`, or `Reader` resource.

The agent subscribes for notifications to all of the resources that this knowledge base contains. When a resource is changed, the agent recreates the knowledge base. In our application, we have to get this knowledge base by calling `KnowledgeAgent.getKnowledgeBase()` before every stateless/stateful session creation.

In the previous chapter, we've mentioned that Drools Guvnor can also build artifacts. Artifacts are grouped into packages. Packages can be built and then accessed through a URL. Our application can then use this URL for creating `KnowledgeBase`. If we'd like to load the validation `KnowledgeBase` from Guvnor, we could add it to `KnowledgeBuilder` as follows:

```
kbuilder.add(ResourceFactory.newUrlResource(
"http://localhost:8080/"+
"drools-guvnor/package/droolsbook.validation/LATEST"),
ResourceType.PKG);
```

Code listing 2: Adding a validation package built by Guvnor.

We're specifying the URL where the package is accessible. The package name is droolsbook.validation and we're using the LATEST snapshot of this package. With this configuration change, we don't need the drools-compiler library on the classpath because the package is already compiled. KnowledgeAgent will periodically poll this URL for changes and will update its locally cached KnowledgeBase.

External artifact building

We already know that we can use Guvnor to build packages externally. In this section, we'll look at how to do it with a build tool called Ant. We can then easily add artifact compilation steps into our existing build process.

Building with Ant

Apache **Ant** is a general purpose building tool. More information about Ant can be found at http://ant.apache.org/. Module drools-ant, from the standard Drools binary distribution, contains an Ant task for building Drools artifacts. We'll build validation knowledge base from Chapter 3, *Validation*, using this Ant task.

All of the information required by Ant will be stored in a file called build.xml. We'll now go through this file step-by-step. It starts with a project definition as follows:

```
<project default="compileArtifacts">
  <property name="projectPath" value="" />
  <property name="droolsPath" value="drools_lib" />
```

Code listing 3: build.xml file—project definition—part 1/4.

As it is usual with Ant build files, the project definition contains a default Ant target that will be called when no target is specified. This default target is called compileArtifacts. The next two lines define two properties: projectPath and droolsPath. The first property is a path to the current project and the second is a path to Drools libraries.

The following code listing defines Drools libraries that will be needed:

```
<path id="drools.classpath">
  <pathelement location="${droolsPath}/drools-ant.jar" />
  <pathelement location="${droolsPath}/drools-api.jar" />
  <pathelement location="${droolsPath}/drools-core.jar" />
  <pathelement location="${droolsPath}/drools-compiler.jar" />
  <pathelement location="${droolsPath}/antlr-runtime.jar" />
  <pathelement location="${droolsPath}/mvel2.jar" />
```

```
        <pathelement location="${droolsPath}/org.eclipse.jdt.core_3.4.2.v_
                          883_R34x.jar" />
    </path>
```

Code listing 4: `build.xml` file—Drools classpath definition—part 2/4.

Note that the libraries in code listing 4 don't have versions. It has been removed to make this code listing more concise. For example, if you're using version 5.0.1 of Drools, `drools -ant.jar` will be `drools-ant-5.0.1.jar`.

`drools.classpath` references Drools artifacts that are required by validation rules (including their dependencies). You can add more Drools artifacts to this list depending on the features you're using (for example, if you use decision tables, add `drools-decisiontables.jar` and so on). Please note the use of `droolsPath` variable to locate all of the Drools libraries.

`drools-ant.jar` contains the Drools Ant task. We'll now use `drools.classpath` to tell Ant about the Ant task.

```
    <taskdef name="compiler" classpathref="drools.classpath"
            classname="org.drools.contrib.DroolsCompilerAntTask" />
```

Code listing 5: `build.xml` file—Drools compiler definition—part 3/4.

The `taskdef` element defines a `compiler` Ant task. It is implemented by the `DroolsCompilerAntTask` class.

Now, we can use this Ant task to compile the validation rules.

```
    <path id="model.classpath">
      <pathelement location="${projectPath}lib/banking-model.jar" />
      <pathelement location="${projectPath}lib/joda-time.jar" />
    </path>

    <target name="compileArtifacts">
      <compiler srcdir="${projectPath}src/main/resources"
        tofile="${projectPath}target/validation.pkg"
        binformat="package" bintype="knowledge"
        classpathref="model.classpath">
        <include name="validation.drl" />
      </compiler>
    </target>
</project>
```

Code listing 6: `build.xml` file—Target for building validation rules—part 4/4.

First, another classpath called `model.classpath` is defined. It contains all of the model libraries. In our case, they are: `banking-model.jar` file and `joda-time.jar` library. The first JAR file contains all of the classes used in the model. The second JAR file is a library that our model references.

Finally, the `compileArtifacts` target gathers all of the information together in order to compile the validation rules. Target's body consists of a `compiler` target. It defines:

- `srcdir`: It points to the directory with our validation rules.
- `tofile`: It specifies the destination file. In our case, it is `validation.pkg`.
- `binformat`: It specifies that we want to build only a package. If we didn't specify this, the whole knowledge base would be built.
- `bintype`: It is here just for compatibility purposes. It should always be set to `knowledge`.
- `classpathref`: It is a reference to our model classpath.

The body of the `compiler` element is a collection of files that should be compiled. In our case, it is only one file called `validation.drl`. Other valid options are artifacts ending with `.brl`, `.xml`, `.dslr`, or `.xls`. More files can be imported at once using wild cards (for example, all of the rule files with `*.drl`).

You can try this 'build file' from a command line. Just navigate to the directory where it resides and type `ant`. Ant will execute the default target, which is set to `compileArtifacts` in our case. After a few seconds, you should see a **BUILD SUCCESSFUL** message and the `validation.pkg` file should exist. This package can now be used to create a knowledge base.

 Drools doesn't support Maven by default. As a workaround, it is possible to call an Ant task from within a Maven build.

Drools execution server

The Drools execution server is a web application that allows us to execute rules remotely. The server is accessible through a REST-like interface (**REST** stands for **Representational State Transfer**—`http://en.wikipedia.org/wiki/Representational_State_Transfer`). Thanks to REST, we can build very lightweight clients that don't need any Drools libraries for rule execution (not even a JVM). To demonstrate this, we'll build a client using Ruby language.

Drools server can be found in the standard Drools binary distribution within the web application module `drools-server.war`. The Drools web server application needs to be deployed to an application server and started. It uses multiple knowledge agents to cache `KnowledgeBase` instances. Configuration for these knowledge agents is provided during startup through property files.

After the startup, the server waits for requests from clients. When it receives a request, it creates `StatelessKnowledgeSession` for rule execution (the Drools team might add stateful support in the future). After creating the session, it sets global variables, inserts facts, and executes rules. When rules finish firing, the results are returned back to the client.

The server can communicate with the client using XML or JSON formats. JSON is a lightweight data-interchange format—`http://www.json.org/`.

The client can access the server through the following URL: `http://localhost:8080/drools-server/knowledgebase/interestcalculation`. The last part—`interestcalculation`—identifies the knowledge agent configuration that should be used. In this case, the server will search for the file called `interestcalculation.properties` on the classpath.

Interest rate calculation example

To see how all of this works, we'll:

- Deploy a Drools server with interest rate calculation knowledge base that we've defined in Chapter 5, *Human-Readable Rules*
- Create a client that will issue a request using JSON protocol to this server and display a response

The server

We have to modify `drools-server.war` to know about our interest rate calculation knowledge base. Create a file named `interestcalculation.properties` with the following contents:

```
newInstance=true
file="/some/absolute/filesystem/path/interest calculation.xls"
```

Code listing 7: Agent configuration file—`interestcalculation.properties`.

It specifies that we want to create a knowledge base from a decision table—`interest calculation.xls`—that contains our rules. The `newInstance=true` part specifies that we want to create a new knowledge base whenever the decision table changes (this setting needs to be set to `true`). Please change the path to the decision table appropriately.

Add the properties file to the `WEB-INF/classes` directory of `drools-server. war`. Next, add libraries to the `WEB-INF/lib` folder. The following ones are needed: `drools-decisiontables.jar`, `drools-templates.jar`, `jxl.jar`, `commons-lang. jar`, and `joda-time.jar`. These libraries come with the standard Drools binary distribution. Most importantly, add the domain model classes that are also packaged in a JAR file—`interest_calculation.jar`.

`drools-server.war` can be deployed and started. We can verify that everything is running correctly by going to `http://localhost:8080/drools-server/` (note that the port number varies depending on the application server used). We should see a page with the title, **Execution server is running**, with some usage information as shown in the following screenshot:

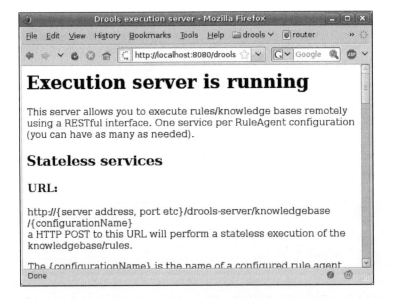

 The server implementation is very lightweight. It consists of a single servlet and a few additional value holder classes. It is easily embeddable in the existing web applications.

The client

Our client will query for an interest rate on a student account with balance 1,000 EUR. Since this client will be very lightweight, a dynamic and interpreted language such as Ruby is ideal for this kind of a task. For more information about Ruby, please refer to http://www.ruby-lang.org/en/. Please consult Ruby's manual about how to install this interpreter. We'll also require an additional library for Ruby called json, which will allow us to communicate using JSON protocol.

The full client source code is displayed as follows:

```ruby
require 'net/http'
require 'json'
http = Net::HTTP.new('localhost', 8080)
path = "/drools-server/knowledgebase/interestcalculation"
headers = {
  "Content-Type" => "application/json"
}
post_data = {"knowledgebase-request" => {
 :inOutFacts => {
   "named-fact" => [ { :id => "account", :fact => {
     "@class"=>"droolsbook.decisiontables.bank.model.Account",
     "type" => "STUDENT", "balance" => "1000",
     "currency" => "EUR" } } ]
 }
}}
resp, data = http.post(path, post_data.to_json, headers)
answer = JSON.parse(data)
puts answer["knowledgebase-response"]["inOutFacts"]\
         ["named-fact"][0]["fact"]["interestRate"]
```

Code listing 8: Ruby client (interest_request.rb file).

The first few lines until post_data ... are straightforward. We'll be connecting to the server with a specified URL and sending data using the JSON format. The post_data hash data structure holds all information we'll be sending. It is one fact named as account of the droolsbook.decisiontables.bank.model.Account class. It's type property is set to STUDENT, balance to 1000, and currency to EUR. Please note that Account.currency is of type String. The type property is enum and balance is BigDecimal.

The next line with `.. http.post ..` sends this request to the server and waits for the response. Note that the data within the `post_data` variable is converted to JSON format by calling `post_data.to_json`. The response is stored within the `data` variable. Since it is in a JSON format, we have to convert it into a Ruby structure by using `JSON.parse(data)`. Finally, the client displays calculated `interestRate` by using: `puts answer["knowledgebase-response"]["inOutFacts"]["named-fact"][0]["fact"]["interestRate"]`. The response has exactly the same structure as the request because our request contains only `inOutFacts`, which means that all of the facts it contains will be a part of both, the input and the output message.

The request can have four parts. In our example, we've used only one — `inOutFacts`. The client can send a list of global objects, input facts, input/output facts, and a list of queries that should be executed. The response can have three parts — global objects, input/output facts, and output facts. Further, we can name these facts for easier accessibility. Please refer to the Drools documentation for more information.

We can run this client with the following command: `ruby -rubygems interest_request.rb`. The output should be **1.00**, which is the correct interest rate for this account. (Note that you may need to install `rubygems`, which manages third party libraries for Ruby — http://rubygems.org/read/chapter/3, and also install `json` library by running `gem install json`).

When the server receives the request, it must create facts/global objects from it that can be inserted into the knowledge session. After the rules are executed, it needs to convert these facts/global objects into JSON/XML format. The Drools server uses `XStream` library to perform this marshaling/un-marshaling. As we've seen, it has no problem with types such as `String`, `enum`, or `BigDecimal`. This library can even deal with much more complex custom data structures. Please consult its manual for more information — http://xstream.codehaus.org/. For example, if we'd like to set `startDate` and `endDate` that are of type `DateMidnight` for our `account` fact, we'd have to map them as complex objects together and specify their type. I've found XStream's ability to convert ordinary objects to JSON or XML and print the result out to be quite useful. It'll give you an idea about how to represent even more complex objects.

Spring Framework integration

Drools, as of version 5.0 doesn't provide out of the box integration with the Spring Framework. It is planned to be included in version 5.1+.

In this section, we'll perform our own integration.

KnowledgeBaseFactoryBean

We'll define the Spring `FactoryBean` for creating `KnowledgeBase`. The bean will be called `KnowledgeBaseFactoryBean`. It will take a list of Spring resources and will build a knowledge base out of them. We've already seen the usage of this bean in Chapter 9, *Sample Application* where we created the validation knowledge base. To refresh our memory, here is another example that creates a loan approval knowledge base:

```
<bean name="loanApprovalKnowledge"
        class="droolsbook.integration.spring.KnowledgeBaseFactoryBean">
    <description>loan approval knowledge base factory bean
    </description>
    <constructor-arg>
      <map>
        <entry key="classpath:loanApproval.drl" value="DRL" />
        <entry key="classpath:loanApproval.rf" value="DRF" />
        <entry key="classpath:ratingCalculation.drl"
              value="DRL" />
        <entry key="classpath:ratingCalculation.rf"
              value="DRF" />
      </map>
    </constructor-arg>
</bean>
```

Code listing 9: `loanApprovalKnowledge` Spring bean declaration (`applicationContext.xml` file).

As we can see, the constructor of `KnowledgeBaseFactoryBean` takes a map. The keys of this map are resource locations and the values are actual resource types. `KnowledgeBase` is created out of four files—two `.drl` files and two `.rf` files. All of the files are on the classpath.

Now, let's look at the implementation of `KnowledgeBaseFactoryBean`. The implementation will take advantage of Spring's property editors. The keys that we saw in code listing 9 will be automatically converted to Spring's `org.springframework.core.io.Resource` type and the values will be automatically converted to `org.drools.builder.ResourceType` as required by `KnowledgeBuilder`. Our implementation will then simply iterate over the Spring resources and will build them with `KnowledgeBuilder`.

```
public class KnowledgeBaseFactoryBean implements FactoryBean {

  private KnowledgeBase knowledgeBase;

  /**
    * builds the knowledge base and caches it
```

```
 * @param resourceMap source resources (DRL, RF files ...)
 * @throws IOException in case of problems while reading
 * resources
 */
public KnowledgeBaseFactoryBean(
    Map<Resource, ResourceType> resourceMap)
    throws IOException {
  KnowledgeBuilder builder = KnowledgeBuilderFactory
      .newKnowledgeBuilder();
  for (Entry<Resource, ResourceType> entry : resourceMap
      .entrySet()) {
    builder.add(ResourceFactory.newInputStreamResource(entry
        .getKey().getInputStream()), entry.getValue());
  }
  if (builder.hasErrors()) {
    throw new RuntimeException(builder.getErrors()
        .toString());
  }
  knowledgeBase = KnowledgeBaseFactory.newKnowledgeBase();
  knowledgeBase.addKnowledgePackages(builder
      .getKnowledgePackages());
}
/**
 * returns cached knowledge base
 */
@Override
public Object getObject() throws Exception {
  return this.knowledgeBase;
}
/**
 * returns the KnowledgeBase class
 */
@Override
public Class<KnowledgeBase> getObjectType() {
  return KnowledgeBase.class;
}
/**
 * returns true since the knowledge base is a singleton
 */
@Override
public boolean isSingleton() {
  return true;
}
}
```

Code listing 10: Spring `FactoryBean` for building `KnowledgeBase`
(`KnowledgeBaseFactoryBean.java` file).

Note that the factory bean doesn't support some resources such as decision tables that require an advanced configuration. The factory uses the default knowledge builder configuration and knowledge base configuration. This can be easily extended.

Similarly, Spring factory bean can be defined for `KnowledgeAgent`.

Standards

The idea behind standards is to provide better interoperability between rule engines and to reduce the time required to learn how to use a new rule engine. We should be able to change the rule engine provider without modifying the application.

JSR94 (Java Rule Engine API) provides guidelines for rule engine administration and runtime. It is supported by Drools and we'll look at it in the following section. Standards for unifying the rule language are, for example, **RuleML** (the **Rule Markup Language** is a markup language developed to express rules in XML) or **RIF** (**Rule Interchange Format**). They are not supported by Drools, so we won't cover them.

JSR94 Java Rule Engine API

This API is for accessing a rule engine from the Java platform. It defines APIs to parse rules, register and unregister rules, inspect rule meta data, execute rules, and retrieve and filter results. However, it doesn't standardize the language used to describe rules, the rule engine itself, nor the execution flow or deployment mechanism. This means it has quite limited value, especially since Drools version 5, when Drools not only became rule orientated, but also process orientated. Rules and processes are treated equally. However, this API covers only rules, which means that we have to use Drools native API for process interactions anyway.

Drools supports this API through the `drools-jsr94` module. For more examples, please see the Drools documentation or `drools-jsr94` module's source code.

Summary

In this chapter, we've learned about various integration points available in Drools. The Drools server allows us to build very lightweight, platform agnostic, and quick to write clients that can execute rules remotely. It can be provided as a service for our customers who require more fine grained integration with our rules; for example, to provide the service with a different UI or add their own services on top of it. Another use case might be that we don't want to share our rules with our customers; we just want to give them the ability to execute them.

We've learned that it is better to give the rules/processes a different life cycle than the rest of the application. Rules and processes tend to change more often. We know how to build KnowledgeBase externally and how to (re)load it dynamically while the application is running.

We've seen some standardization efforts to make rule engines more interchangeable. The 'rule' side of Drools supports the JSR94; however, to work with the 'process' side, we still have to work with Drools native API.

12
Performance

Performance is an important requirement in most of the applications. To get the best out of any technology, we need to understand how it works. We can then make better decisions about how to use it, and what and where to optimize.

However, performance shouldn't be the most important factor when considering a rule engine. After all, a rule engine is a general purpose `if-then` statement executor. It will never achieve the performance of a custom built system. You may also find that with a custom build system, its performance is excellent at the start but it degrades as the system grows with complexity. If we don't rewrite it over and over, we'll eventually end up with the so-called *spaghetti code*. The performance of a rule engine is relatively constant and it has the benefits of declarative programming: maintainability, flexibility, and code readability that comes with **reasonable performance**.

In this chapter, we'll look at the *Rete algorithm* that is behind Drools in more detail. We'll also get a better understanding of what is possible with Drools and what is not. For example, we'll learn that it doesn't make sense to measure the execution time of a single rule but only the execution time of all rules as a whole. It may clear some questions about rules execution; for example, why are rules evaluated during the insert stage and not `fireAllRules` stage.

Rete algorithm

If you had to implement a rule engine, you'd probably start with a simple iteration over all of the rules and checking one by one if their conditions are true. The Rete algorithm improves this by several orders of magnitude.

From Wikipedia:

The *Rete algorithm* is an efficient pattern matching algorithm for implementing productions systems. The Rete algorithm was designed by *Dr Charles L. Forgy* of *Carnegie Mellon University*, first published in a working paper in 1974.

Pattern matching is the act of checking rules against known facts to determine which rules can be executed.

The advantage that this algorithm brings is efficiency; however, it comes at cost of higher memory usage. The algorithm uses a lot of caching to avoid evaluating conditions multiple times.

The word 'Rete' is taken from Latin where it represents a 'net'. It is generally pronounced as *ri ti* or *ree-tee*. This algorithm generates a network from rule conditions. Each single rule condition is a node in the Rete network. For example:

```
Customer( name != null )
```

Code listing 1: Single rule condition that maps to one node in the Rete network.

The Rete network is a rooted, acyclic, and directed graph. You can think of it as a tree that has some branches joined. In Drools, it is represented by the `KnowledgeBase` class. The network is created when we add knowledge packages into the knowledge base. Rules, from a package, are sequentially added to the network, and the network is updated as needed. A sample Rete network is shown in the following diagram:

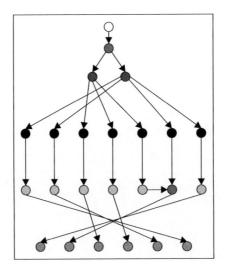

The preceding figure shows a sample Rete network generated by the Drools Eclipse plugin for rules in the `validation.drl` file in Chapter 2, *Basic Rules*. The network consists of various node types. Each node type has a different color. Please note that for real life `.drl` files with hundreds of rules, the network is much bigger. It is usually very wide with the shape of a 'flying saucer'. Don't be surprised if you see it—it is normal.

The performance of the Rete algorithm is theoretically independent of the number of rules in the knowledge base. If you are curious and want to see some benchmarks, you can find them in the `drools-examples` module that is downloadable from the Drools web site. There are also some web sites that regularly publish benchmarks of various rule engines solving well-known mathematical problems (usually 'Miss Manners' test and the 'Waltz'), for example, `http://illation.com.au/benchmarks/`. Performance of Drools is comparable to other open source or even commercial engines.

 Drools uses an enhanced version or the Rete algorithm called **ReteOO**.

Node types

We'll now describe each node within the Rete network in more detail. Each node can have one or many input connections depending on its type and many output connections. Let's imagine that we have the following simple rule:

```
rule "accountBalanceAtLeast"
    when
        $account : Account( balance < 100 )
    then
        warning(drools, $account);
end
```

Code listing 2: Rule that has constraint on one fact.

This rule alone translates into the following Rete network. You can see this network from within the Drools Eclipse `.drl` file editor. Just switch the tab to **Rete Tree** in the bottom left corner of the editor's screen.

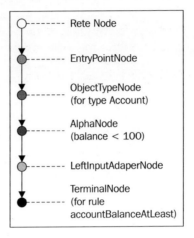

The figure above shows a Rete network for the `accountBalanceAtLeast` rule from code listing 2. At the top is the Rete node.

Rete node

This node is the default entry point into the network. When we insert a fact into the knowledge session (by calling the `session.insert(fact)` method), it enters the Rete network through this node.

 In Eclipse, if you open the **Properties** view and then click on a node in the Rete network, you'll see some useful information about a node; for example, its name, type, and depending on node type, various other information.

EntryPointNode

Next node that follows is the `EntryPointNode`. This node corresponds to an entry point. As we've seen in Chapter 7, *Complex Event Processing*, we can have many named entry points. In this chapter, we'll be dealing only with the default `EntryPointNode` (our diagrams will start at this node).

ObjectTypeNode

The inserted fact then continues to a node called `ObjectTypeNode` (the next node). This node acts as a fact type filter. It passes only through the facts with matching type. In our case, only objects of type `Account` are allowed to continue. All of the nodes that descend from this node will deal with constraints on `Account` type. It is also the case with the next node shown in the previous figure.

Each branch descending from the `EntryPointNode` must start with one `ObjectTypeNode`.

AlphaNode

Alpha nodes represent the first level of matching. `AlphaNode` is responsible for evaluating constraints on single facts. Examples of such tests/constraints are literal (for example, `property1=="someValue"`), variable (for example, `property1 == property2`), inline eval (for example, `eval(someList.isEmpty())`), return value (for example, `property1 == (property2 + 2)`), and or. In our case, this constraint is `balance < 100`. If we'd have multiple constraints on the same fact, they will be handled by one `AlphaNode` each. For example, this constraint: `balance < 100`, `currency == "EUR"` would create two `AlphaNode` nodes one after the other.

> The order of constraints in a condition is important. In the given example, the first `AlphaNode` will check `balance < 100` and the second `AlphaNode` will check `currency == "EUR"`. This affects the re-usability of the Rete network as we'll see later on.
>
> Moreover, we should put most restrictive constraints first. Which constraints are the most restrictive, depends on our data. The sooner the fact propagation stops, the less work the engine needs to do.

The flow in the preceding figure continues to the next node.

LeftInputAdapterNode

This node acts as an entry point to the second level of matching—beta nodes. It simply creates a tuple out of a single fact. In our case, it will be a tuple of size 1 that will contain the `Account` fact. The tuple then propagates to the next node in the preceding figure. This is the `TerminalNode`.

TerminalNode

As the name suggests, this is the leaf node of the network. It represents the actual rule consequence that should be placed on the Agenda. (Remember? All of the rules with satisfied conditions are placed on the agenda for later execution). Every rule has at least one `TerminalNode`.

Example 1—inserting a fact

At this point, we've described all of the nodes that are required to represent our rule from code listing 2. To summarize, if we insert an `Account` fact that has `balance` of `50` into the knowledge session, it would enter the Rete network at the Rete node and immediately propagate to `EntryPointNode`. It will then continue through all outgoing connections to `ObjectTypeNode` nodes (in our case only one). `ObjectTypeNode` will check that the propagated fact is of type `Account` and our fact will continue to the next node. `AlphaNode` will evaluate its constraint. As our fact doesn't satisfy the constraint, the execution will stop at this point (the `session. insert(..)` method would return). However, if we insert an `Account` fact with `balance` of `150`, it will successfully satisfy the constraint of the `AlphaNode` and it will continue to the next node. `LeftInputAdapterNode` will wrap our fact into a tuple and it will pass it on to the next node. `TerminalNode` will place a rule that it represents—`accountBalanceAtLeast`—on the agenda.

> As we can see, most of the work that a rule engine has to do happens during `session.insert` time instead of `session.fireAllRules` time. The latter only executes consequences of rules that were previously activated and 'placed on the agenda'. This is important to keep in mind because it is not something that you'd normally expect.

Another node type that is very common in the Rete network is `BetaNode`.

BetaNode

It's a node that evaluates constrains on two or more facts. This node has two inputs: left and right. The left input is for tuples and the right input is for facts. Each input has an associated memory where it stores partial matches.

Let's add another rule to our `accountBalanceAtLeast` rule:

```
rule studentWithLowAccountBalance
    when
        $account : Account( balance < 100,
            type == Account.Type.STUDENT )
        $customer : Customer( accounts contains $account )
```

```
    then
        System.out.println("Customer " + $customer +
        " has student account with low balance");
    end
```

Code listing 3: Rule that has a constraint on one/multiple facts.

The modified Rete network will look like the following figure:

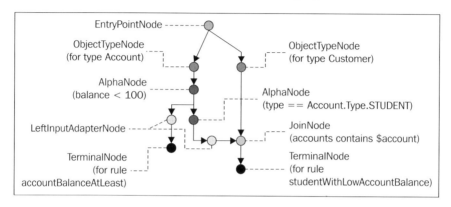

The figure above shows a Rete network for the studentAccountCustomerAgeLessThan rule from code listing 3. We can see that our first network (the Rete network for the accountBalanceAtLeast rule) is still there (the leftmost line from top to bottom). New nodes were added and some of the existing nodes were reused. ObjectTypeNode for type Account and AlphaNode that check the balance property were reused. You can try to change the order of Account constraints by executing, $account : Account(balance < 100, type == Account. Type.STUDENT) and you'll see that only ObjectTypeNode will be reused. We'll look at node sharing later.

The new node (green node) in the preceding figure is a special type of BetaNode called JoinNode. As the name suggests, the purpose of this node is to join the tuple with the fact. The result is then tested if it satisfies constraints of this node. In our case, accounts contains $account. $account comes from the left input and represents the tuple, and $customer is the fact that comes from the right input. If all of the constraints are satisfied, a new tuple is created from the input tuple and input fact. In our case, that will be a tuple of size two that contains the $account and $customer facts.

Example—inserting a fact

To see how this works, we'll go step-by-step through inserting an `Account` fact followed by a `Cutomer` fact. The `Account` fact will enter the network through `EntryPointNode`. It will then propagate through `ObjectTypeNode` for type `Account` to `AlphaNode` that tests the `balance` property. Let's say the test is successful. As we already know, this is the last node that both rules share. The fact then propagates down to two branches, `LeftInputAdapterNode` (where it ends up activating our first rule) and to another `AlphaNode`. This second `AlphaNode` contains the following constraint: `type == Account.Type.STUDENT`. If our fact satisfies this constraint, it continues to another `LeftInputAdapterNode` where it is wrapped into a tuple. This tuple then enters `JoinNode`. The tuple is added to the left memory of `JoinNode`. `JoinNode` then looks into its right memory if it can create a match. As the right memory is empty, no match is created and the propagation finishes.

We'll now insert a `Customer` fact into the knowledge session. The fact enters the network and continues through `ObjectTypeNode` for type `Customer`. It then propagates to `JoinNode`. The customer fact is added to the right memory. `JoinNode` then looks into its left memory if it can create a match. It finds the `Account` fact that has been added previously. `JoinNode` then evaluates its constraint over this possible match—`accounts contains $account`. If this constraint is satisfied, the `JoinNode` creates a tuple of size two that contains both the `Account` fact and `Customer` fact. This tuple is then propagated to the next node, which is `TerminalNode`. The `studentWithLowAccountBalance` rule is activated.

There are various types of `BetaNodes`. We've already seen the `JoinNode`. Others include: `NotNode`, `AccumulateNode`, `CollectNode`, and `ExistsNode`. Their names are self explanatory. Each node represents one rule construct, for example, the `NotNode` represents the `not` construct.

More complex example

For some more complex rules, we also need a node that takes two tuples on its input. For example, imagine we have the following single rule in our knowledge base. This rule will fire if there is no customer with low account balance living at a particular address. To implement this rule, we'll need `not` with nested `and` because we need to test the non-existence of customers with specific accounts. The rule is as follows:

```
rule noCustomerWithLowAccountBalance
    when
        $address : Address( addressLine1 == "Rossa Avenue" )
        not (
            $account : Account( balance < 100 ) and
            Customer( accounts contains $account )
        )
```

```
then
    System.out.println("No customers with low balance in "+
    "their accounts live at Rossa Avenue");
end
```

Code listing 4: Rule with a complex 'not' constraint.

Please note that both `Account` and `Customer` facts are inside one single `not` construct. If we look at the resulting Rete network of this single rule, we'll see the following figure:

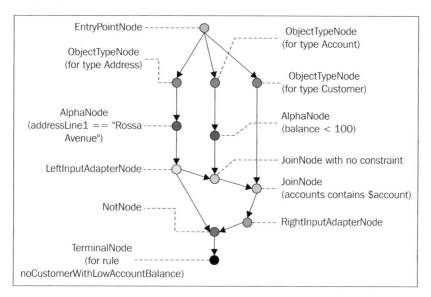

The figure above shows a Rete network for the `noCustomerWithLowAccountBalance` rule from code listing 4. Note that `NotNode`, in this case, takes two tuples on both of its inputs. One comes from `LeftInputAdapterNode`, which contains the `Address` fact. The other tuple consists of the `Customer` and `Account` facts. As we already know, `NotNode` expects a simple fact on its right input. To make this work, `RightInputAdapterNode` is added to the network.

 `RightInputAdapterNode` makes the tuple behave like a single fact. This allows us to build more complex networks.

EvalNode and FromNode

Similar to `TerminalNode`, these nodes have only one tuple input. `EvalNode` implements the `eval` construct (not the inline eval). It evaluates its constraints using the propagated tuple as the context. `FromNode` implements the `from` construct. This node takes facts outside of the Rete network and adds them into the tuple.

Retracting or modifying a fact

We've already seen two examples of what happens when we insert a new fact into the knowledge session. It enters the network through the entry node and propagates down the network to the terminal node. We'll now look at what happens when we retract or modify/update a fact. Because modify/update is implemented as half-way retract and then insert, we can focus only on the retract step.

When we insert a fact into the network and it propagates down. It maintains a linked list of tuples it is a part of. Each tuple knows which node created it. When we retract this fact, the list of tuples is iterated and the tuple is retracted from the nodes that created it.

This is called *asymmetrical* Rete because insert is different from retract. In *symmetrical* Rete (pre Drools 5.0,) retract would behave exactly similar as insert. It was done in this manner because retract needs to go through the same propagation path as insert did. However, instead of creating new tuples and adding them into node memories, they would be removed. (For this to work, the facts couldn't change. In order to follow the same propagation path, the state of the fact had to stay unchanged. This wasn't always possible and so various attempts such as shadow facts were implemented. They didn't solve this problem fully and so version 5.0 of Drools uses asymmetrical Rete that has none of these problems.)

 Performance tip: Facts that are modified often should go at the end of rule condition section. For example, in the rule from code listing 3, if we modify an `Account` fact, both `AlphaNode` and `JoinNode` need to be re-evaluated. However, if we modify a `Customer` fact, then only `JoinNode` needs to be re-evaluated.

Initial fact

Imagine we have a rule that checks if there are no customers in the knowledge session. The rule might look like this:

```
rule noCustomer
    when
```

```
        not Customer()
    then
        System.out.println("No customers");
    end
```

Code listing 5: A Rule with a not constraint as its first condition.

As we already know, a not construct is implemented by NotNode. This node is a type of BetaNode, which means it needs two inputs: right fact input and left tuple input. The right input is, in our case, a Customer fact. However, as the not Customer() condition is the first in our rule (and also the only one), there is no tuple source to connect the left input to. Let's look at the resulting network:

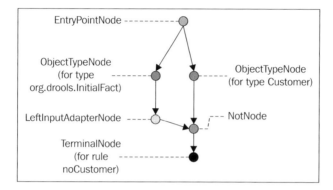

The figure above shows a Rete network for the noCustomer rule from code listing 5. As we can see, there is another ObjectType node for a mysterious fact called InitialFact. Its purpose is just for these situations where there is no tuple source to connect with. InitialFact is automatically inserted into the session as the first fact.

Similar to NotNode, the other nodes that sometimes need this InitialFact are ExistsNode, AccumulateNode, CollectNode, and EvalNode (please note that EvalNode needs only one tuple input).

Node sharing

We've already touched upon node sharing when we've gone through the rule from code listing 3. Node sharing is one of the techniques used to minimize the size of the Rete network. The more nodes two rules share the better. We already know that the order of conditions within a rule and even order of constraints within a single condition affects the order of nodes within the Rete network and hence, affects the sharing of nodes.

The node sharing takes place when the network is built, that is, when we're creating a knowledge base out of knowledge packages. The node sharing is implemented very simply by using the `equals` method of the standard `Object`. When a new rule is added into an existing network, new nodes are created as if the network was empty. These nodes are then inserted into the existing network. When this happens, the algorithm checks if such a node already exists by using the `equals` method. Only the appropriate nodes are being examined at the current 'level' within the network. If a node is found that is equal to the new node, the found node is used instead and the new node is simply discarded.

Example

This may be best shown with the help of an example. We'll build on examples we've seen so far. Let's say that our knowledge base already has the `accountBalanceAtLeast` rule from code listing 2 and we want to add the `studentWithLowAccountBalance` rule from code listing 3. We should end up with a network as depicted in previous figure of the Rete network for the `studentAccountCustomerAgeLessThan` rule.

The `studentWithLowAccountBalance` rule contains two conditions that are joined by an implicit `and`. The first condition is on a single fact—`Account`. It can be handled by two `AlphaNodes`. First, we need to create an `EntryPointNode`; however, as the network already has such `EntryPointNode`, the existing node is reused instead. Next node that is needed is `ObjectTypeNode` for the `Account` type. Continuing from `EntryPointNode`, such `ObjectTypeNode` already exists and so it is reused. Next, we continue from this `ObjectTypeNode`. We create an `AlphaNode` with constraint: `balance < 100`. As there is already such a node, we can reuse it.

Sharing of nodes with the `accountBalanceAtLeast` rule ends here. We create an `AlphaNode` with constraint: `type == Account.Type.STUDENT`. From our current position in the Rete network, we can see that the current node has only one child—`LeftInputAdapterNode`. We cannot reuse this node; instead, we'll add our `AlphaNode` to the current node's list of children nodes. As this is the last `AlphaNode`, we'll add `LeftInputAdapterNode`. At this stage, we have a tuple that contains the `Account` fact. The first condition of our rule is implemented. We'll now remember our current position in the network.

The process continues with the second condition of the
studentWithLowAccountBalance rule. This condition is on the Customer fact. The
Customer fact must similarly go through EntryPointNode that can be reused. It
then continues to ObjectTypeNode for the Customer type, which must be added
because there is none present. Next, we need JoinNode because we already have
a tuple that we have to join with and we also have to implement the constraint:
accounts contains $account. JoinNode is created that takes the tuple on its left
input and the Customer fact on its right input. As before, a check is made if an
equal node, descending from the remembered position, already exists. There is no
such node. Hence, our new JoinNode is simply added to the network. Again, we'll
remember the current position in the network. This is the last condition for this rule,
so TerminalNode is added and the process finishes.

Node indexing

As the facts propagate through the Rete network, another optimization technique is
to index fact values. We can then evaluate each test more quickly.

AlphaNode indexing

When a fact meets the constraints specified by a node, it is propagated to all of its
descending child nodes. This usually means iterating over all of the child nodes
and propagating the fact. This takes some time, especially if there are many child
nodes. Luckily, we can index AlphaNode—AlphaNode with 'equals' constraints
(literal constraints) to be more specific. By default, Drools creates an index (a hash
table) if we are testing a property for more than three different values. The object is
propagated only to nodes, where it makes sense (the test will succeed). This means
that we don't have to iterate over those nodes.

Imagine we have the following types of rules that fire for specific currencies:

```
rule accountEUR
    when
        $account : Account( currency == "EUR" )
    then
        //..
end
```

Code listing 6: A Rule with one literal constraint.

Let's say there is one rule for different currencies (EUR, USD, GBP, and AUD). Then we may also have one rule that checks if the currency is different from EUR: `currency != "EUR"` and one that checks some different property of `Account`, for example, `type == Account.Type.SAVINGS`. These rules will generate the following network (only a part of it is shown):

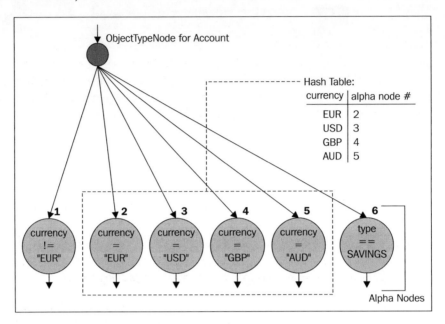

The figure above shows `AlphaNode` indexing. When a fact propagates through `ObjectTypeNode` from above. Let's say that this account has `currency` set to `"USD"`, this fact will propagate to nodes **1**, **3**, and **6** completely avoiding nodes **2**, **4**, and **5**.

Computation complexity

We are going to compare this with imperative style programming. Let's say we have the following code:

```
if (account.getCurrency().equals("EUR")) {}
else if (account.getCurrency().equals("USD")) {}
else if (account.getCurrency().equals("GBP")) {}
...
```

Code listing 7: Imperative style implementation.

If we have an `Account` fact where `currency` was set to `"GPB"`, the program would have to evaluate all of the three conditions until it finds the correct branch. The complexity is **O(n)**, where **n** is the number of `if` branches.

However, if we use index this effectively translates to a lookup in a hash table: `hashtable.get(account.getCurrency())`, which returns correct 'branch'/node. This includes calculating the hash code of `account.getCurrency()` (hash code of string `"GBP"`) and a lookup in the hash table (a quick operation). The complexity is O(1).

BetaNode indexing

As was the case with `AlphaNode`, only 'equal' constraints are indexed. `BetaNode` has 2 types of input. Left input for tuples and right input for the ordinary facts. By default, `BetaNode` has a left and right memory. Each memory can be indexed. Drools can index up to three constraints (with 'equals' tests).

As we already know:

1. When a tuple enters a `BetaNode`, it is added to the left memory of `BetaNode`. Then a match is attempted. Without an index we have to iterate over all of the facts in the right memory and if they match then a new tuple is propagated.

2. This is similar to when a fact enters `BetaNode`. It is added to the right memory of `BetaNode`. Then we iterate over all of the tuples in the left memory, and if a match is found, a new tuple is propagated.

By using an index, we don't have to iterate over all of the facts/tuples in the opposite memory. We will be iterating only over facts/tuples that meet the indexed constraints. For each object found, we have to test the rest of the constraints (the ones that weren't indexed).

Example

Let's consider the following single rule that matches a customer with his/her account:

```
rule accountWithCustomerLastName
    when
        Customer( $lastName : lastName )
        $account : Account( name == $lastName )
    then
        //..
    end
```

Code listing 8: A Rule that matches on two facts that are joined on `Account.name ==` `Customer.lastName`.

This rule will be represented by a network of one Rete node, one `EntryPointNode`, two `ObjectTypeNode` instances, one `LeftInputAdapterNode` (for `Customer`), one `JoinNode`, and finally one `TerminalNode`.

Next, we'll insert the following objects:

1. `new Customer(..)` with `lastName` set to `Edwards`. This fact will be added to left memory (as a tuple of size 1).

2. `new Customer(..)` with `lastName` set to `Parker`. This fact will be added to left memory (as a tuple of size 1).

3. `new Customer(..)` with `lastName` set to `Douglas`. This fact will be added to left memory (as a tuple of size 1).

4. `new Customer(..)` with `lastName` set again to `Douglas`. This fact will be added to left memory (as a tuple of size 1).

5. `new Account(..)` with `name` set to `Morris`. This fact will be added to the right memory and a match will be attempted. As `leftMemory.get("Morris") == null`, it won't succeed. No tuple will be propagated.

6. `new Account(..)` with `name` set to `Parker`. This fact will be added to the right memory and a match will be attempted. However, this time `leftMemory.get("Parker")` returns one object (id=2). As our `BetaNode` has only one constraint, there is no need to do further tests. The new tuple that will be propagated will be of size 2, consisting of objects 2 and 6.

This result is illustrated in the following figure. Please note the contents of the two indexes/hash tables.

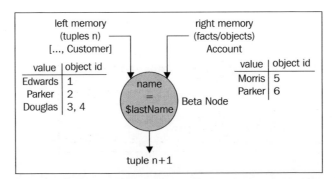

The figure above shows `JoinNode` with its memories. Many of the options described in this section are configurable through `KnowledgeBaseConfiguration` or in the `drools.default.rulebase.conf` file, which can be found in the `drools-core.jar/META-INF` directory.

KnowledgeBase partitioning

Drools supports parallel execution mode. One session can be executed by multiple threads.

The Rete network is split into multiple partitions. Each partition is handled by `PartitionTaskManager`. It manages a list of suspended propagations and makes sure that only one of them is being executed at a time over this partition. When a fact is propagated through the network, it may go through one or more partitions. Once a propagation reaches the boundary between two partitions, the other partition's `PartitionTaskManager` is notified and the current propagation is transferred to its list of propagations. The suspended propagation then waits in this list until the other partition manager is ready to take it further.

> Each knowledge session has a unique set of its own `PartitionTaskManager` instances.

How are partitions formed? When we have an empty network and we want to add a new rule, first we have to add the Rete node, `EntryPoinNode`, and an `ObjectTypeNode`. These types of nodes are always within the partition called **MAIN**. The other nodes that are added for our rule form a new partition called **0**. We now have a network representing one rule that has two partitions. If this rule was the `accountBalanceAtLeast` rule from code listing 2, the partitions would look as follows:

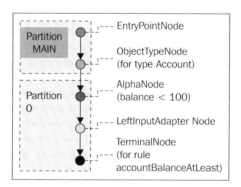

The figure above shows the Rete network for the `accountBalanceAtLeast` rule from code listing 2 with partitions. If we now continue to add more rules into this network, they may reuse the existing nodes as we've learned in the section about node sharing. If a node is reused, its partition is reused as well. If not, a new partition is created and all of the remaining nodes for this rule are added to this new partition.

After adding the `noCustomerWithLowAccountBalance` rule from code listing 3, the partitions will look as follows:

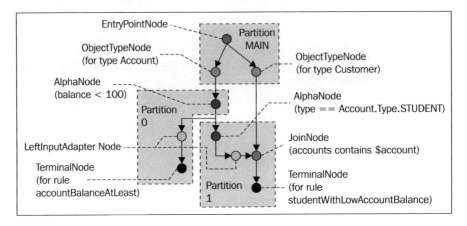

The figure above shows a Rete network for the `studentAccountCustomerAgeLessThan` rule from code listing 3 with partitions. If we want to add more rules this process repeats until we've added all of the rules.

> Only the fact propagations are executed in parallel. Rule consequences are still executed sequentially when you call `fireAllRules`.
>
> If you start the session in the `fireUntilHalt` mode, the rule consequences will be executed immediately (as soon as the rule becomes activated).

Parallel execution

The following code snippet shows how to configure Drools for parallel execution. It is done through `KnowledgeBaseConfiguration`. It provides two options—`MultithreadEvaluationOption` that simply turns this feature on (it is disabled by default), and `MaxThreadsOption` that sets the maximum number of threads across all of the partitions.

```
KnowledgeBaseConfiguration configuration = KnowledgeBaseFactory
    .newKnowledgeBaseConfiguration();
configuration.setOption( MultithreadEvaluationOption.YES );
configuration.setOption( MaxThreadsOption.get(2) );
KnowledgeBase kbase = KnowledgeBaseFactory
    .newKnowledgeBase(configuration);
```

Code listing 9: Enabling multi-thread evaluation.

This knowledge base can be then used as normal. If we don't specify the maximum number of threads, it will be defaulted to the number of partitions we have.

Summary

In this chapter, we've learned about the Rete algorithm, how it works, and that it uses the Rete network to represent our rules. We've explored various types of nodes that are within the Rete network: Alpha nodes (that can apply a constraint on a single fact) and Beta nodes (that can apply a constraint on multiple facts). We've seen various rules and their corresponding Rete networks.

We've learned about various optimizations used within Drools. One of them was node sharing. By sharing the nodes, we can greatly reduce the amount of work a computer must do in order to execute our rules. After all, there is no point in evaluating the same conditions multiple times.

We've seen that the order of the conditions within a rule and even the order of the constraints within a condition are crucial when it comes to node sharing. Drools currently doesn't implement any node rearranging strategy to achieve the best node sharing possible. When designing your rules, try to put the most restrictive conditions and constraints first. Try to keep the same order for them. By doing this, the advantage that you can get from node sharing will be maximized.

The Rete node indexing section described how the alpha and beta node indexing works. Keep in mind that it applies only to constraints with equal operator. However, there are also plans to extend this support for relational operators (greater than, less than, and so on).

Finally, we've learned about knowledge base partitioning, that allows us to execute our rules in multiple threads.

This chapter showed the power of declarative programming. We just declared what had to be done and the engine could then decide how to do it, as effectively as possible depending on the runtime conditions.

A
Development Environment Setup

This section describes the setup of the local development environment needed for working with Drools.

Environment setup

Java version 1.5 and higher is required to run the examples in this book. Drools can be downloaded from `http://www.jboss.org/drools/downloads.html`. You'll need the **Binaries** and **IDE** downloads. The latter is the Drools Eclipse plugin. It helps with writing rules. The Drools 'new project' wizard in Eclipse can create a simple Drools project that is ready to run. When setting up a new project, you need to tell it the location of the 'Drools Runtime' (where you extracted the Drools binaries).

If for some reason the Eclipse plugin is not an option, Drools can be set up by maven or manually. When using maven add the following dependencies to your project's `pom.xml` file:

```
<dependencies>
  <dependency>
    <groupId>org.drools</groupId>
    <artifactId>drools-api</artifactId>
    <version>${drools.version}</version>
  </dependency>
  <dependency>
    <groupId>org.drools</groupId>
    <artifactId>drools-core</artifactId>
    <version>${drools.version}</version>
  </dependency>
  <dependency>
```

```
      <groupId>org.drools</groupId>
      <artifactId>drools-compiler</artifactId>
      <version>${drools.version}</version>
   </dependency>
 </dependencies>
 <properties>
   <drools.version>5.0.1</drools.version>
 </properties>
```

Code listing 1: Drools dependencies in a maven's pom.xml file.

By adding these dependencies into your project's pom file, we're declaring that our project depends on three libraries: drools-api, drools-code, and drools-compiler. Depending on the features used, we may need to add or remove some Drools libraries. Please note the drools.version property, which is set to version 5.0.1. You may need to change it depending on the latest available release.

We also have to tell maven where to get these libraries. They can be downloaded from the official JBoss maven repository which is located at http://repository.jboss.com/maven2/. The following code snippet does the trick:

```
<repositories>
  <repository>
    <id>JBoss Repository</id>
    <url>http://repository.jboss.com/maven2/</url>
    <snapshots>
      <enabled>false</enabled>
    </snapshots>
    <releases>
      <enabled>true</enabled>
    </releases>
  </repository>
</repositories>
```

Code listing 2: JBoss maven repository in a maven's pom.xml file.

Note that the latest snapshot releases can be downloaded from http://snapshots.jboss.org/maven2/.

Let's now look at the libraries that are needed in more detail.

Dependencies and their licenses

JBoss Rules/Drools is licensed under Apache License, Version 2.0 (ASL is a free software license that allows us to develop free, open source as well as proprietary software. Its contents can be found at `http://www.apache.org/licenses/LICENSE-2.0.html`). In order to run the examples in this book, at least the following libraries will be needed on the Java classpath:

- `antlr-runtime-3.1.1.jar`: A parser generator — helps with parsing rule files (licensed under ANTLR 3 License, which is based on The BSD License).

- `core-3.4.2v_883_R34x.jar`: Generic Eclipse Java compiler — it's a part of Eclipse Java Development Tools (licensed under the Eclipse Public License v1.0).

- `drools-api-5.0.1.jar`: Drools user API or also known as the public API — most of the classes we'll be dealing with are located here (licensed under ASL).

- `drools-compiler-5.0.1.jar`: Knowledge compiler — understands rule syntax and compiles rules into Java classes (licensed under ASL).

- `mvel-2.0.10.jar`: mvel is the property extraction and expression language for Java. Some core Drools features are implemented using mvel and it is also used as a dialect in the rule language (licensed under ASL).

- `drools-core-5.0.1.jar`: The Drools engine itself (licensed under ASL).

These libraries are valid for Drools version 5.0.1. Please note that you may need different versions of these libraries depending on your version of Drools. After downloading the binary distribution of Drools (for example, `drools-5.0-bin.zip` file) and extracting it, the file `README_DEPENDENCIES.txt` provides more details on what libraries are actually needed for specific features. Note that all third party libraries are stored under the `lib` folder.

B
Custom Operator

We've already seen various operators that can be used within rule conditions. These include, for example, `==`, `!=`, relational operators such as `>`, `<`, `>=` , temporal operators such as `after`, `during`, `finishes`, or others such as `matches`, which perform regular expression matching. In this section, we'll define our own custom operator.

The `==` operator uses `Object.equals/hashCode` methods for comparing objects. However, sometimes we need to test if two objects are actually referring to the same instance. This is slightly faster than `Object.equals/hashCode` comparison (only slightly faster because the hash code is calculated once for object and then it is cached).

Imagine that we have a rule which matches on an `Account` fact and a `Customer` fact. We want to test if the `Account` `owner` property contains the same instance of `Customer` fact as the `Customer` fact that was matched. The rule is as follows:

```
rule accountHasCustomer
    when
        $customer : Customer( )
        Account( owner instanceEquals $customer )
    then
        //
end
```

Code listing 1: Rule with `instanceEquals` custom operator in `custom_operator.drl` file.

From the rule in code listing 1, we can see the use of the `instanceEquals` custom operator . Most, if not all Drools operators support a negated version with `not`:

```
Account( owner not instanceEquals $customer )
```

Code listing 2: Condition that uses the negated version of the custom operator.

This condition will match `Account` fact, whose `owner` property is of different instance than the fact bound under `$customer` binding.

Some operators support parameters. They can be passed within the angle brackets as we've already seen in Chapter 7, *Complex Event Processing* when we were discussing temporal operators (for example, `this after[0, 3m] $event2`).

Based on our requirements, we can now write this following unit test for our new `instanceEquals` operator:

```
@Test
public void instancesEqualsBeta() throws Exception {
    Customer customer = new Customer();
    Account account = new Account();

    session.execute(Arrays.asList(customer, account));
    assertNotFired("accountHasCustomer");

    account.setOwner(new Customer());
    session.execute(Arrays.asList(customer, account));
    assertNotFired("accountHasCustomer");

    account.setOwner(customer);
    session.execute(Arrays.asList(customer, account));
    assertFired("accountHasCustomer");
}
```

Code listing 3: Unit test for the `accountHasCustomer` rule.

It tests three use cases. The first one is an account with no customer. The test verifies that the rule didn't fire. In the second use case, `Account owner` is set to a different customer than what is in the rule session. The rule isn't fired, either. Finally, in the last use case, `Account owner` is set to the right `Customer` object and the rule fires.

Before we can successfully execute this test, we have to implement our operator and tell Drools about it. We can tell Drools through `KnowledgeBuilderConfiguration`. This configuration is fed into the familiar `KnowledgeBuilder`. The following code listing, which is in fact the unit test setup method shows how to do it:

```
@BeforeClass
public static void setUpClass() throws Exception {
    KnowledgeBuilderConfiguration builderConf =
     KnowledgeBuilderFactory.newKnowledgeBuilderConfiguration();
    builderConf.setOption(EvaluatorOption.get("instanceEquals",
        new InstanceEqualsEvaluatorDefinition()));
    knowledgeBase = DroolsHelper.createKnowledgeBase(null,builderConf,
                    "custom_operator.drl");
}
```

Code listing 4: Unit test setup for custom operator test.

A new instance of the `KnowledgeBuilderConfiguration` is created and a new evaluator definition is added. It represents our new `instanceEquals` operator—`InstanceEqualsEvaluatorDefinition`. This configuration is then used to create a `KnowledgeBase`.

We can now implement our operator. This will be done it two steps:

1. Create `EvaluatorDefinition`, which will be responsible for creating evaluators based on actual rules.

2. Create the actual `Evaluator` (please note that the implementation should be stateless).

The evaluator definition will be used at rule compile time and the evaluator at rule runtime.

All evaluator definitions must implement the `org.drools.base.evaluators.EvaluatorDefinition` interface. It contains all methods that Drools needs in order to work with our operator. We'll now look at `InstanceEqualsEvaluatorDefinition`. The contents of this class are as follows:

```
public class InstanceEqualsEvaluatorDefinition implements
    EvaluatorDefinition {
  public static final Operator INSTANCE_EQUALS = Operator
      .addOperatorToRegistry("instanceEquals", false);
  public static final Operator NOT_INSTANCE_EQUALS = Operator
      .addOperatorToRegistry("instanceEquals", true);

  private static final String[] SUPPORTED_IDS = {
      INSTANCE_EQUALS.getOperatorString() };

  private Evaluator[] evaluator;

  @Override
  public Evaluator getEvaluator(ValueType type,
      Operator operator) {
    return this.getEvaluator(type, operator
        .getOperatorString(), operator.isNegated(), null);
  }

  @Override
  public Evaluator getEvaluator(ValueType type,
      Operator operator, String parameterText) {
    return this.getEvaluator(type, operator
        .getOperatorString(), operator.isNegated(),
        parameterText);
  }

  @Override
```

```java
    public Evaluator getEvaluator(ValueType type,
        String operatorId, boolean isNegated,
        String parameterText) {
      return getEvaluator(type, operatorId, isNegated,
          parameterText, Target.FACT, Target.FACT);
    }

    @Override
    public Evaluator getEvaluator(ValueType type,
        String operatorId, boolean isNegated,
        String parameterText, Target leftTarget,
        Target rightTarget) {
      if (evaluator == null) {
        evaluator = new Evaluator[2];
      }
      int index = isNegated ? 0 : 1;
      if (evaluator[index] == null) {
        evaluator[index] = new InstanceEqualsEvaluator(type,
            isNegated);
      }
      return evaluator[index];
    }

    @Override
    public String[] getEvaluatorIds() {
      return SUPPORTED_IDS;
    }

    @Override
    public boolean isNegatable() {
      return true;
    }

    @Override
    public Target getTarget() {
      return Target.FACT;
    }

    @Override
    public boolean supportsType(ValueType type) {
      return true;
    }

    @Override
    public void readExternal(ObjectInput in)
        throws IOException, ClassNotFoundException {
```

```
    evaluator = (Evaluator[]) in.readObject();
}
@Override
public void writeExternal(ObjectOutput out)
    throws IOException {
  out.writeObject(evaluator);
}
```

Code listing 5: Implementation of custom `EvaluatorDefinition`.

The `InstanceEqualsEvaluatorDefinition` class contains various information that Drools requires—the operator's ID, whether this operator can be negated and what types it supports.

At the beginning, two operators are registered using the `Operator. addOperatorToRegistry` static method. This method takes two arguments: `operatorId` and a flag indicating whether this operator can be negated.

Then there are few `getEvaluator` methods. Drools will call these methods during the rule compilation step. The last `getEvaluator` method gets passed in the following arguments:

- `type`: It is the type of operator's operands.
- `operatorId`: It is the identifier of the operator (one evaluator definition can handle multiple IDs).
- `isNegated`: It is specified if this operator can be used with `not`.
- `parameterText`: It is essentially the text in angle brackets. The evaluator definition is responsible for parsing this text. In our case, it is simply ignored.
- `leftTarget` and `rightTarget`: It specifies if this operator operates on facts, fact handles, or both.

Then the method lazily initializes two implementations of the operator itself—`InstanceEqualsEvaluator`. As our operator will operate only on facts and we don't care about the parameter text, we need to cater to only two cases—for non-negated operations and for negated operations. These evaluators are then cached for another use.

It is worth noting that the `supportsType` method always returns `true`, as we want to compare any facts regardless of their type.

All Drools evaluators must extend the `org.drools.spi.Evaluator` interface (Note that this is the old API that will be replaced with `org.drools.runtime.rule.Evaluator` interface in the future). Drools provides an abstract `BaseEvaluator` that we can extend in order to simplify our implementation. Now, we have to implement a few `evaluate` methods for executing the operator under various circumstances — using the operator with a literal (for example, `Account ( owner instanceEquals "some literal value" )`) or a variable (for example, `Account ( owner instanceEquals $customer )`). The `InstanceEqualsEvaluator` operator's implementation is as follows (please note that it is implemented as a static inner class):

```
public static class InstanceEqualsEvaluator extends
    BaseEvaluator {
  public InstanceEqualsEvaluator(final ValueType type,
      final boolean isNegated) {
    super(type, isNegated ? NOT_INSTANCE_EQUALS
        : INSTANCE_EQUALS);
  }

  @Override
  public boolean evaluate(
      InternalWorkingMemory workingMemory,
      InternalReadAccessor extractor, Object object,
      FieldValue value) {
    final Object objectValue = extractor.getValue(
        workingMemory, object);
    return this.getOperator().isNegated()
        ^ (objectValue == value.getValue());
  }

  @Override
  public boolean evaluate(
      InternalWorkingMemory workingMemory,
      InternalReadAccessor leftExtractor, Object left,
      InternalReadAccessor rightExtractor, Object right) {
    final Object value1 = leftExtractor.getValue(
        workingMemory, left);
    final Object value2 = rightExtractor.getValue(
        workingMemory, right);
    return this.getOperator().isNegated()
        ^ (value1 == value2);
  }

  @Override
  public boolean evaluateCachedLeft(
      InternalWorkingMemory workingMemory,
      VariableContextEntry context, Object right) {
    return this.getOperator().isNegated()
```

```
         ^ (right == ((ObjectVariableContextEntry)
           context).left);
    }
    @Override
    public boolean evaluateCachedRight(
        InternalWorkingMemory workingMemory,
        VariableContextEntry context, Object left) {
      return this.getOperator().isNegated()
           ^ (left == ((ObjectVariableContextEntry)
             context).right);
    }
    @Override
    public String toString() {
      return "InstanceEquals instanceEquals";
    }
  }
}
```

Code listing 6: Implementation of custom `Evaluator`.

Operator's implementation just defines various versions of the `evaluate` method. The first one is executed when evaluating alpha nodes with literal constraints. `extractor` is used to extract the field from a fact and the `value` represents the actual literal. ^ is a standard 'bitwise exclusive or' Java operator.

The second `evaluate` method is used when evaluating alpha nodes with variable bindings. In this case, the input parameters include `left`/`rightExtractor` and `left`/`right` fact (please note that the left and right facts represent the same fact instance).

The third method (`evaluateCachedLeft`) and fourth method (`evaluateCachedRight`) will be executed when evaluating beta node constraints.

For more information, please refer to the API and parent class—`org.drools.base.BaseEvaluator`.

Both the evaluator definition and the evaluator should be serializable.

Summary

This shows us the power of Drools expressiveness. Custom operators can be useful in various situations. For example, if we find ourselves repeating same conditions over and over again or if we want to get rid of some ugly looking inline `eval`—it can be done by writing a custom domain specific operator. The rule then becomes much easier to read and write.

C
Dependencies of Sample Application

The following is a listing of dependencies and their versions as needed by the sample application, which was implemented in Chapter 9, *Sample Application*. The dependencies are given in a maven POM format (Maven is a build tool. For more information, please visit http://maven.apache.org/).

```xml
<dependency>
  <groupId>commons-lang</groupId>
  <artifactId>commons-lang</artifactId>
</dependency>
<dependency>
  <groupId>org.drools</groupId>
  <artifactId>drools-process-task</artifactId>
  <version>5.0.1</version>
  <exclusions>
    <exclusion>
      <groupId>javax.el</groupId>
      <artifactId>el-api</artifactId>
    </exclusion>
  </exclusions>
</dependency>
<dependency>
  <groupId>org.drools</groupId>
  <artifactId>drools-persistence-jpa</artifactId>
  <version>5.0.1</version>
</dependency>
<dependency>
  <groupId>org.apache.mina</groupId>
  <artifactId>mina-core</artifactId>
```

```xml
    <version>2.0.0-M3</version>
</dependency>

<dependency>
  <groupId>org.slf4j</groupId>
  <artifactId>slf4j-jdk14</artifactId>
  <version>1.5.2</version>
</dependency>
<dependency>
  <groupId>org.slf4j</groupId>
  <artifactId>slf4j-api</artifactId>
  <version>1.5.2</version>
</dependency>

<!-- Spring (everything)-->
<dependency>
  <groupId>org.springframework</groupId>
  <artifactId>spring</artifactId>
  <version>2.5.6</version>
</dependency>
<dependency>
  <groupId>org.springframework</groupId>
  <artifactId>spring-webmvc</artifactId>
  <version>2.5.6</version>
</dependency>
<dependency>
  <groupId>aspectj</groupId>
  <artifactId>aspectjrt</artifactId>
  <version>1.5.4</version>
</dependency>
<dependency>
  <groupId>aspectj</groupId>
  <artifactId>aspectjweaver</artifactId>
  <version>1.5.4</version>
</dependency>
<dependency>
  <groupId>org.springframework</groupId>
  <artifactId>spring-test</artifactId>
  <version>2.5.6</version>
  <scope>test</scope>
</dependency>

<!-- Hibernate -->
<dependency>
  <groupId>org.hibernate</groupId>
  <artifactId>hibernate-entitymanager</artifactId>
```

```
    <version>3.4.0.GA</version>
  </dependency>
  <dependency>
    <groupId>org.hibernate</groupId>
    <artifactId>hibernate-annotations</artifactId>
    <version>3.4.0.GA</version>
  </dependency>
  <dependency>
    <groupId>org.hibernate</groupId>
    <artifactId>hibernate-commons-annotations</artifactId>
    <version>3.1.0.GA</version>
  </dependency>
  <dependency>
    <groupId>org.hibernate</groupId>
    <artifactId>hibernate-core</artifactId>
    <version>3.3.0.SP1</version>
  </dependency>

  <!-- Transaction manager -->
  <dependency>
    <groupId>org.codehaus.btm</groupId>
    <artifactId>btm</artifactId>
    <version>1.3.2</version>
  </dependency>

  <!-- HSQLDB -->
  <dependency>
    <groupId>com.h2database</groupId>
    <artifactId>h2</artifactId>
    <version>1.0.77</version>
  </dependency>

  <dependency>
    <groupId>javax.persistence</groupId>
    <artifactId>persistence-api</artifactId>
    <version>1.0</version>
  </dependency>

  <!-- Web -->
  <dependency>
    <groupId>javax.servlet</groupId>
    <artifactId>servlet-api</artifactId>
    <version>2.5</version>
  </dependency>
  <dependency>
    <groupId>javax.servlet</groupId>
    <artifactId>jstl</artifactId>
```

```
      <version>1.2</version>
  </dependency>
  <dependency>
    <groupId>taglibs</groupId>
    <artifactId>standard</artifactId>
    <version>1.1.2</version>
  </dependency>
```

Code listing 1: Extract from the sample application `pom.xml` file.

Please note the exclusion defined for the `drools-process-task` dependency. It is necessary in order to deploy to Tomcat.

Index

H

header, event 133
helper method, data transformation rules 65
high activity rule, fraud detection system
  about 158, 159
  testing 159
human task, loan approval ruleflow
  about 181, 182
  client setup 185
  server setup 183
  testing 183-185

J

Java Persistence API (JPA) 184
JBoss Rules
  stateful session 111
  stateless session 111
JBoss Rules/Drools. *See* Drools
jMock 229
Joda-Time library 50
JSR94 (Java Rule Engine API), standards
  255

K

KISS (Keep it Short and Simple) principle
  111
knowledgeBase loading
  about 243
  KnowledgeAgent 244-246
  KnowledgeAgent, accessing 244
  KnowledgeAgent, working 244
KnowledgeBase partitioning
  about 273, 274
  parallel execution 274, 275

L

layers, configuring
  deployment 200
  JPA annotations, for domain objects
    193, 194
  JPA provider configuration, working with
    194, 195
  persistence layer 193
  Spring, configuring 195-197

Tomcat, setting up 199
web application, setting up 197, 198
web application, tag library 199
LegacyBankService interface
  about 60, 63
  methods, defining 61
loan approval
  about 161
  approved event 225, 226
  loan request form 212, 213
  model 162
  process, persisting 213-219
  ruleflow 162
  tasks, listing 220-222
  tasks, working on 222-225
loan approval ruleflow
  Approve Event node 186
  Approve Event node, parameters 186
  Approve Event node, testing 186
  approveLoan service, implementing 187,
    188
  diagramatic representation 163
  disadvantages 188
  fault node 165
  human task 181, 182
  human task, client setup 185
  human task, server setup 183
  human task, testing 183-185
  invalid loan application form 163
  loans' size, determining 168
  Rating? node 174
  Rating Calculation node 170
  Rating node?, testing 175
  small loan, testing 169
  Transfer Funds node 175
LostCardEvent 136

M

Maven 289
Message interface
  defining 40
  implementation 53, 54
monitoring rule, fraud detection system
  accumulate 143
  averageBalanceQuery 143
  averageBalanceQuery, testing 144

U

UUID (Universally Unique Identifier)
property 38

V

validation
  about 202
  Aspect-oriented configuration 204
  BankingService, implementing 203, 204
  complex event processing service (CEP),
    integrating 211
  configuring, with Spring 202
  JTA transaction setup diagram 206
  knowledge base definition 202
  presentation layer 206
   stateful session, using 112
  transaction advice 204
  transaction configuration, adding 204, 205,
    206
  transaction manager 204
  validationservice, defining 202
ValidationReport interface
  defining 40, 41
  implementation 54, 56
validation rules, writing
  account balance rule 49

addressRequired test method 47
assertReportContains method 48, 49
compareTo method 50
createCustomerBasic method 47
error method, implementing 43
executing, ways 48
global objects 41
KnowledgeHelper, using 44
object required type rules 44
setGlobal method 47
setupClass method 47
students account rule 50, 52
Test Driven Development (TDD), starting
  with 49
unique account number rule 52
unit testing 45, 46
validationReport, using 42

W

warning message 39
Web Services Human Task (WS-Human
  Task) 181

X

XOR-GROUP column type, decision table
  94

**Thank you for buying
Drools JBoss Rules 5.0
Developer's Guide**

Packt Open Source Project Royalties

When we sell a book written on an Open Source project, we pay a royalty directly to that project. Therefore by purchasing Drupal 6 Site Builder Solutions, Packt will have given some of the money received to the Drools project.

In the long term, we see ourselves and you—customers and readers of our books—as part of the Open Source ecosystem, providing sustainable revenue for the projects we publish on. Our aim at Packt is to establish publishing royalties as an essential part of the service and support a business model that sustains Open Source.

If you're working with an Open Source project that you would like us to publish on, and subsequently pay royalties to, please get in touch with us.

Writing for Packt

We welcome all inquiries from people who are interested in authoring. Book proposals should be sent to author@packtpub.com. If your book idea is still at an early stage and you would like to discuss it first before writing a formal book proposal, contact us; one of our commissioning editors will get in touch with you.

We're not just looking for published authors; if you have strong technical skills but no writing experience, our experienced editors can help you develop a writing career, or simply get some additional reward for your expertise.

About Packt Publishing

Packt, pronounced 'packed', published its first book "Mastering phpMyAdmin for Effective MySQL Management" in April 2004 and subsequently continued to specialize in publishing highly focused books on specific technologies and solutions.

Our books and publications share the experiences of your fellow IT professionals in adapting and customizing today's systems, applications, and frameworks. Our solution-based books give you the knowledge and power to customize the software and technologies you're using to get the job done. Packt books are more specific and less general than the IT books you have seen in the past. Our unique business model allows us to bring you more focused information, giving you more of what you need to know, and less of what you don't.

Packt is a modern, yet unique publishing company, which focuses on producing quality, cutting-edge books for communities of developers, administrators, and newbies alike. For more information, please visit our website: www.PacktPub.com.

JBoss Drools Business Rules

ISBN: 978-1-847196-06-4   Paperback: 304 pages

Capture, automate, and reuse your business processes in a clear English language that your computer can understand

1. An easy-to-understand JBoss Drools business rules tutorial for non-programmers

2. Automate your business processes such as order processing, supply management, staff activity, and more

3. Prototype, test, and implement workflows by themselves using business rules that are simple statements written in an English-like language

JBoss Tools 3 Developer's Guide

ISBN: 978-1-847196-14-9   Paperback: 408 pages

Develop JSF, Struts, Seam, Hibernate, jBPM, ESB, web services, and portal applications faster than ever using JBoss Tools for Eclipse and the JBoss Application Server

1. Develop complete JSF, Struts, Seam, Hibernate, jBPM, ESB, web service, and portlet applications using JBoss Tools

2. Tools covered in separate chapters so you can dive into the one you want to learn

3. Manage JBoss Application Server through JBoss AS Tools

4. Explore Hibernate Tools including reverse engineering and code generation techniques

Please check **www.PacktPub.com** for information on our titles

1142671R0

Printed in Great Britain by
Amazon.co.uk, Ltd.,
Marston Gate.